Neither Voice nor Heart Alone

Joyce L. Irwin

Neither Voice nor Heart Alone

German Lutheran Theology of Music in the Age of the Baroque

WIPF & STOCK · Eugene, Oregon

Wipf and Stock Publishers
199 W 8th Ave, Suite 3
Eugene, OR 97401

Neither Voice nor Heart Alone
German Lutheran Theology of Music in the Age of the Baroque
By Irwin, Joyce L.
Copyright©1993 by Irwin, Joyce L.
ISBN 13: 978-1-5326-4136-7
Publication date 9/26/2017
Previously published by Peter Lang Publishing, Inc., 1993

For the pastors, choir members and other musical colleagues with whom I have worked

St. Paul's Methodist Church, Joplin, Missouri
First Baptist Church, Joplin
St. Jakobskirche, Frankfurt am Main
Westville Methodist Church, New Haven, Connecticut
Emmanuel Episcopal Church, Athens, Georgia
First Baptist Church, Hamilton, New York
St. Mary's Catholic Church, Hamilton
St. Thomas' Episcopal Church, Hamilton
Bellevue Heights United Methodist Church, Syracuse
First Presbyterian Church, Oneida, New York

CONTENTS

Prelude: Luther and his Interpreters ... 1

THE FORMULATION OF THE LUTHERAN ORTHODOX THEOLOGY OF MUSIC

1. Between Freedom and Obligation ... 11
2. Between Psychology and Spirituality ... 23
3. Between Sacred and Secular ... 35
4. From Tension to Harmony ... 43

SYNTHESIS AND ANTITHESIS

5. Johann Conrad Dannhauer ... 59
6. The Rostock Pre-Pietists
   A. Joachim Lütkemann and Heinrich Müller ... 67
7. The Rostock Pre-Pietists
   B. Theophilus Großgebauer ... 79
8. Hector Mithobius: Culmination of Orthodoxy ... 89

FROM PIETISM TO THE ENLIGHTENMENT

9. Worship as Edification ... 101
10. The Regeneration of Musicians ... 109
11. Music and Adiaphora ... 117
12. The Cantata Debate ... 127

Finale: Johann Sebastian Bach—A Musician, not a Theologian ... 141

Notes ... 153
Bibliography ... 187
Index ... 205

PREFACE

This scholarly study arose from a personal quest for a theological justification for the centrality of music in my own religious orientation. Phenomenological evidence from the world's religions demonstrated that the association of music and religion is nearly universal; whether in the form of simple chants or complex polyphony, music is present in all but a very small portion of the world's cultic forms, including those of Christianity. But its theoretical grounding has often been omitted or slighted in theological systems, and historical studies of church music have more to do with the evolution of musical forms than with the theological context in which the music was written and performed.

In the English-speaking world a few short books have been published on music and religion in the last forty years,[1] but no serious academic journal and no scholarly society is directed toward exploring this connection.[2] In German-speaking lands, on the other hand, the scholarly tradition of thoroughness has combined with a musical tradition of greatness to produce some lengthy systematic treatments. Winfried Kurzschenkel has brought together a wealth of thought on music from the different Christian traditions in *Die theologische Bestimmung der Musik* (Trier, 1971), but as a theological contribution Oskar Söhngen's *Theologie der Musik* (Kassel, 1967) is unsurpassed. Söhngen was the most systematic thinker of a generation of writers concerned with church music reform, from which the journal *Musik und Kirche* emanated and continues to provide an outlet for scholarly articles on church music, whether from a theological or a musicological perspective.

As a lover of German language and culture, I was happy to locate this arena for addressing my concerns; but as a non-Lutheran American Protestant I also found that these German Lutherans, such as Walter Blankenburg, Oskar Söhngen, Christhard Mahrenholz, and Friedrich Blume, worked within a religious and cultural context which I did not share. Their views of German church music history were indelibly influenced by the liturgical reform movement of the first half of the twentieth century, which aimed at a restoration of the role of music as it had been in the period between Luther and Bach.

One does not have to be a German Lutheran to be imbued with the idea that Luther and Bach represent the pinnacle of good church music: most American

Protestants have been taught that Luther introduced congregational singing into worship and that Bach created an ideal combination of congregational singing and choral artistry in his cantatas. Those who learn a bit more are told that the intervening period—the era of Schütz, Schein, and Scheidt—was the Golden Era of German church music. Some further reading about this period, however, led me to see some tarnish on the gold: evidence indicated that congregational singing was not as legendary as I had been taught and choral singing was not uniformly appreciated. There had been disputes about the proper form and style of church music during this period which revealed much about the reasons for the end of this Golden Age.

My purpose in studying this age of German Baroque music is not to examine the music itself or the actual practice of music but to explore the discussions about its purpose and function in Christian worship. Primarily it was the pastors and theologians who reflected on these questions, but as musicians felt themselves under attack they also took up their pens in defense. The result is that a wide range of perspectives on the theology of music were expressed during this century and a half. Tracing these perspectives allows us insights into the history of Lutheran theology in Germany during this period; to this extent I hope to make a contribution to the field of church history. By exploring the intellectual and theological context in which composers wrote and musicians performed their music, I hope also to further our understanding of music history. Finally, even though I do not seek to formulate a theology of music but rather to examine a church searching for an acceptable formulation, I hope to contribute to serious reflection on the role of music in religion.

On the music history side, the chronological limits of this study need no special defense. Musicologists demarcate the Baroque era as beginning in 1580 or 1600 and extending to 1730 or 1750, the earlier dates applying to Italy, the later to northern countries. In the history of theology, on the other hand, there is no uniform designation of the period. A case can be made for using the periodization 1500–1650 as the age of Reformation, but this demarcation has its basis more in political history than in intellectual history. The end of the Thirty Years' War closes the age of territorial struggles which began with the emergence of Protestantism. Theologically speaking, however, the year 1580 is a watershed in Lutheranism because the Formula of Concord brought an end to major doctrinal debates within Lutheranism. Whether the succeeding period is labelled the age of Orthodoxy or of Confessionalism, it is the era in which academic theologians produced lengthy systematic commentaries on the doctrines formulated in 1580. The ending date of the age of Orthodoxy is less clear, and the label "Pietism" is often combined with that of Orthodoxy to designate a single age where two approaches existed side by side. Enlightenment ideas also overlap toward the end of this period, so that for different purposes differing endpoints can be defended. For this study, the cut-off date 1730 allows the inclusion of the debate concerning cantatas, where the values of the new age of Enlightenment are pitted against those of the outgoing era.

Much has already been written about Martin Luther's views on music and the effect of those views on the development of Protestant church music. I do not intend to add another restatement of Luther's comments on music. Luther is already a figure of past history when this study begins. The age of Confessionalism has taken over from the age of Reformation. Before learning how Luther was interpreted a few decades after his death, however, it is useful to become acquainted with major twentieth-century interpretations.

Following this introduction three chapters drawing primarily on the writings of academic theologians between 1580 and 1630 depict the formulation of an orthodox theology of music. The focus of the chapters moves, roughly speaking, from doctrine to ethics to worship. In the fourth chapter we witness a new approach deriving from natural theology. With these four chapters virtually all the components will have been encountered which reappear in different combinations and relationships later in the century. The theologians who come to prominence later in the book were not selected for their overall importance in Lutheran history but for their contribution to the continuing debate on music from the last half of the seventeenth into the early eighteenth century. The selection criteria are waived when we come to the final chapter. Although J. S. Bach did not contribute to this debate, the Lutheran musical legend demands that the story conclude with him.

Research for this book was supported by fellowships from Colgate University, Alexander-von-Humboldt Stiftung, Herzog August Bibliothek, and the International Research and Exchanges Board, which is funded by the National Endowment for the Humanities, the United States Information Agency, and the US Department of State. I am grateful also for the assistance of librarians at the Herzog August Bibliothek in Wolfenbüttel, the Musikbibliothek der Stadt Leipzig, the Deutsche Bücherei in Leipzig, the Franckesche Stiftung in Halle, and the British Library in London. Other participants in the Aston Magna Academy of 1985 on "J. S. Bach and his World" provided valuable stimulation. The Institute for Ecumenical and Cultural Research in Collegeville, Minnesota, offered the working conditions and the encouragement necessary to bring the project near completion, and the Coolidge Colloquium at Episcopal Divinity School enabled me to complete the final chapter. To recall all these settings is to evoke fond memories of many individuals whose insights, support and friendship were essential to the continuation of my work. I trust they will recognize themselves in these sentences even if they remain unnamed here. Three persons deserve special mention, however: Timothy Socha, my research assistant in the early stages, Louise Grindrod, computer consultant at Colgate University who spent many hours struggling with me to produce a camera-ready copy, and my husband Robert V. Smith, who supported and encouraged me at all stages.

Frontispiece from Hector Mithobius' *Psalmodia Christiana* (1665)
Photograph from British Library, London

PRELUDE

LUTHER AND HIS INTERPRETERS

The problem of discussing Martin Luther is similar to the problem of discussing Jesus Christ. Not that any have ever consciously claimed divinity for Luther, who so readily admitted his own sinfulness. But for members of the Lutheran church and for many other Protestants who have found their way to the gospel through the teachings of Luther, those teachings have attained a kind of sanctity unaffected by the frailties of their author and the turbulent setting in which he lived and wrote. For such persons, Luther's own approach to Christ can provide guidance for an approach to Luther: Jesus as a historical figure was of less importance than the enduring meaning of his message. Similarly, Luther's hermeneutical principle, which drew upon the parts of the Bible where the gospel of salvation by faith alone came clear and minimized those which emphasized works, provides a model for selecting those writings of Luther where the gospel is preached clearly and explaining away the rest. Other approaches result in less uniform and coherent depictions of Luther's theology, just as scriptural exegesis without a guiding hermeneutic may lack unity and consistency.

For those, on the other hand, who desire a picture of either the historical Jesus or the historical Luther in the context of their complex social and political circumstances, a hermeneutical principle serves to oversimplify the picture. Luther spoke against widely differing opponents during the course of several decades, with the result that his standpoint seemed to change, depending on the audience and the situation.

As the present study is not of Luther but of the Lutheran tradition, our concern is not to identify the "historical Luther" but to recognize through the variety of his remarks concerning music how several approaches to the theology of music in the period 1580 to 1730 could all credibly appeal to the authority of Luther.

The twentieth century, to be sure, is no freer from preconceived notions and hidden agendas than was the seventeenth century. Particularly in the area of music, it seems, those who approach Luther come to praise him, not to criticize.[3] Rare are such works as Karl Honemeyer's *Thomas Müntzer und Martin Luther: Ihr Ringen um die Musik des Gottesdienstes* (Berlin, 1974) in which Müntzer is favored over Luther in musical-liturgical matters. The time has not yet come when a writer, even a non-Lutheran, could present a truly detached study of Luther and music. It is my hope that by understanding more about the development of musical thought in the Lutheran tradition after Luther, we may move closer to a historical understanding of Luther in his own time. For the time being, rather than attempt another study of Luther's theology of music, we will do better to understand twentieth-century thinking on the topic.

The most influential treatment of Martin Luther's theology of music in recent years has been that of Oskar Söhngen, whose outstanding work, *Theologie der Musik*, contains an unsurpassed wealth of insight into the field. Yet like any other human creation, it is a product of a specific era and setting. Söhngen was a prominent leader in the renewal of liturgical music in the German Lutheran church of the twentieth century. For this movement the recovery of liturgical richness centered in the revival of historical forms based on a rediscovery of Reformation theology. Thoroughly grounded as this movement was in historical scholarship, the impetus for studying the past was the felt need to revitalize the present. Söhngen's treatment of Luther does not therefore stand on its own but as one element in the *Theologische Grundlagen der Kirchenmusik*, as the earlier version of his work was entitled.[4] It must be understood in the context of a larger effort to reintroduce high quality music into a church which had allowed artistic religious music to be removed to the concert hall. Söhngen's great accomplishment is to have integrated music into systematic theology, thus demonstrating its intrinsic value and purpose in congregational worship.

For such an undertaking Luther was indeed a valuable—perhaps the most valuable—resource. What could have greater potential for a theology of music than Luther's claim that "next to the Word of God, music deserves the highest praise" (*LW* 53, 323)? Although, in proportion to the large number of pages written by Luther in his lifetime, the number of those devoted to music is quite small, nevertheless those short writings on music are extravagant in their appreciation of music. It is from three such writings that Söhngen derives the essential elements of Luther's theology of music: his 1530 sketch *Peri tēs musikēs*, which may have been an outline for a longer treatise never written, his 1538 preface to Georg Rhaw's *Symphoniae jucundae*, and his 1543 "Preface for All Good Hymnals" with its poetic tribute to "Lady Music."

The first statement on which Söhngen draws comes, however, not from these writings on music but from the lectures on Genesis: "Ocularia miracula longe minora sunt quam auricularia" ("The miraculous things we see are of far less importance than those we hear") (*WA* 35, 483f.). This, as Söhngen concedes, does not refer primarily to music, but it includes music as one of the marvelous means by which the gospel is brought to human ears. As Jesus spoke but did not write, so the gospel, for Luther, must be spoken and heard, not just written. The fact that music belongs to this same realm of the auditory shows its natural affinity to theology as well as its potential for communicating the gospel. Söhngen agrees with Dedo Müller in seeing here in Luther's expressions on music "a kind of natural form of the gospel"[5] in the sense that gospel and music always point to one another: "The gospel is an advanced school for singing, just as music for its part leads quite close to the gospel, indeed knows more of the mystery of the gospel than many a highly learned theologian."[6]

The next point is closely related: music is not primarily either art or science but creature. The majority of evidence for this strand in Luther's thought comes from his preface to Rhaw's *Symphoniae jucundae*: "Looking at music itself, you will find that from the beginning of the world it has been instilled and implanted in all creatures, individually and collectively" (*LW* 53, 322); it is a "noble, wholesome, and cheerful creation of God" (324), "the [most] excellent gift of God" (321). Luther hopes that his reader "may by this creation accustom yourself to recognize and praise the Creator" (324). The significance of this theme for Söhngen is that music has a legitimacy in itself, for its own sake, and not merely a legitimacy but a purpose, a mission, which is to be fulfilled through humans. Humans must therefore not first approach music as something to be used for their own purposes, but as something which works through them.

> From the recognition of music's worth as creature of God must come the readiness to let it work within. Before a person takes music for his disposal—as one who pursues and practices music—he must approach it with humble openness, wishing to be nothing more than its object.[7]

Consequently, music in worship is not to be evaluated merely from a utilitarian or a psychological standpoint. Though a means of commmunicating the Word, it should not be regarded as a function of words, by comparison with which the sound is tangential; nor should the sound be regarded as a sensual distraction from the meaning of the words. Rather, the sound is integral to music in its liturgical role as in its broader role within creation. Through such an affirmation Luther distinguished himself from Karlstadt, who favored unison chant as both a sign of unity and a denial of worldly sensuality, and Zwingli, who with the aim of more spiritual worship kept music out of the church. With regard to Luther's position on music in worship, Söhngen writes:

> Because the mature Luther is fully serious in viewing music as a creature of God, he no longer reflects on its appropriateness for worship; to him it is self-evident that we may and must put music, which is a gift from God, into the service of God in the form of unison song as well as of figural and organ music.[8]

What, then, Söhngen asks, is the special mission given to music by God? To answer this, he points to the reasons Luther gives in *Peri tēs musikēs* for loving music: because "it is a gift of God and not of men, because it makes souls happy, because it drives away the devil, because it awakens innocent joy... because it rules in time of peace" (*WA* 30/2, 696). In these points one sees a continuation of the long tradition from ancient through medieval times into the Renaissance in which music was valued for its ethical effects. While this approach is far from original with Luther, Söhngen finds it to be integrated into his theology in a very significant way. Relying on a comment in the Table Talk (Nr. 1096) that grammar and music are "conservatores rerum," Söhngen develops from Luther's thought a concept of natural order in which music serves as one of the means of preserving creation over against the forces of dissolution: "Music also stands for Luther in the service of preserving creation, furthering good and controlling evil."[9] Thus Luther's praise of music, says Söhngen, applies to music in general, not just that which is used in direct service of God.[10]

Yet music serves the gospel as well as the natural order. The kerygma itself inclines to music as expressed in the equation of "new covenant" with "new song." Faith inclines toward singing, which then becomes evidence of the existence of faith. Music in turn can awaken faith when it is accompanied or, one might more appropriately say, led by the Holy Spirit. When in the service of the gospel, as contrasted with the service of the natural order, music and word are integrally related, with the music bestowing on the words a much greater power than they would have by themselves. "Here it comes to a unique marriage of language with music in which the latter can prove its special gift for intensifying the word and thereby making it more forceful."[11]

In this last respect, Söhngen notes, Luther and Calvin have much in common. They both recognize in music a power to refresh and enliven, to lift the soul. Luther often experienced that music made him feel like preaching (*WA TR* 4, 313, no. 4441). He also shared the insight of others that a text that is sung is remembered longer. In the sung word, both intellect and affections work together to heighten the effect either would produce separately. Music also serves to interpret the text by melodic, rhythmic, and harmonic means of intensifying and expressing the meaning. Through such exegesis music becomes more than the product of a skilled artist: it is, like the sermon, the **viva vox evangelii**, the living voice of the gospel. "The same Holy Spirit which according to Augustana V changes the words of the sermon into God's own words and thereby awakens faith when and where God wills is also at work in music, where he touches the consciences of the listeners, calling, transforming, and renewing them."[12]

Beyond the realm where words can heighten the relationship with God, there is a realm of unspeakable joy. Here only a textless **jubilus** can express the overflowing fullness of the heart in God. Augustine had written of this, and Luther also recognizes that "**jubilus** can be defined as a sound resulting from the elevation of the mind to God which can be expressed neither by words nor by letters" (*WA* 3, 267).

On the strength of all these ways in which music is seen to be an integral part of Luther's theology, Söhngen concludes his treatment of Luther with an affirmation of the enduring value of music in Christian worship:

> The public praise of God may never grow silent; it belongs to the seven marks of the church as formulated by Martin Luther in his *Das Schöne Confitemini* of 1539 [sic]: "I call singing...every sermon or public confession by which God's work, counsel, grace, help, consolation, victory and salvation are freely praised before the world" (*WA* 31/1, 141). Thus singing must also always be testimony and confession, and therefore singing will not cease in the church of Jesus Christ as long as his name is recognized.[13]

Söhngen hereby takes exception to Karl Honemeyer's interpretation of Luther's position on church music.[14] On the basis of Luther's three forms of worship as described in the *Deutsche Messe* of 1526, Honemeyer regards church music for Luther as a concession to human weakness. This is based on two comments in the preface to the *Deutsche Messe*: first, for those who "are still becoming Christians or need to be strengthened," Luther would "if it would help matters along...have all the bells pealing and all the organs playing and have everything ring that can make a sound" (*LW* 53, 62). Those "who want to be Christians in earnest," on the other hand, have "no need of much and elaborate singing" (64).

In the attempt to explain such comments, Söhngen distinguishes between Luther as liturgist or educator of the congregation and Luther as theologian. In the passages from the *Deutsche Messe*, we hear Luther the liturgist, who sees music as a means to an end. For those who need more spectacle in worship to stimulate them toward faith, music is a very attractive tool; for those who are already advanced in faith, there is no need for music as a psychological stimulus. Luther, as Söhngen reads him, does not endeavor to coordinate this liturgical view of music with his theological view. The latter approach is beyond all devotional and psychological as well as liturgical considerations; here the determining thesis is that "all music is a creature of God."[15]

It is into this latter context that Söhngen puts Luther's lack of sympathy for Augustine's scruples concerning the sensual attractiveness of the music itself in the singing of psalms. Because Luther does not try to reconcile the psychological with the theological, he disregards such scruples in favor of affirming music as inherently pleasing to God. Söhngen quotes here the statement from Luther's preface to all good hymnals ("Vorrede auf alle gute Gesangbücher") in praise of Lady Music:

> Auch ist ein jeder des wol frey,
> > Das solche freud kein sünde sey,
>
> Sondern auch Gott viel bas gefelt
> > Denn all freud der gantzen welt. (*WA* 35, 483)[16]

Beyond the unresolved tension between the liturgical-pedagogical and the theological approaches in Luther, Söhngen also notes the chronological variation in Luther's thinking. In the early Luther he sees a much more hesitant affirmation of music. The early lectures on the Psalms (1513–16), still under strong Neoplatonic-Augustinian influence, treat music within the devotional, psychological framework. The fourth psalm, Luther writes, was intended "to urge, to provoke, to arouse" (*LW* 10, 42) sluggish spirits; but there is a danger that too much noise might stifle devotion rather than stimulate it. Söhngen finds this psychological approach characteristic only of Luther's youth: "Where the young Luther spoke psychologically, the mature Luther speaks **theologically** concerning music. But that is more than another fashion of speaking: it is another view and another level of music itself."[17]

Whereas Söhngen keeps his gaze on this "other level," Honemeyer looks backward to the Middle Ages to search out the foundation of Luther's musical views. Accordingly, he devotes the greatest attention to Luther's early writings. In the early lectures on the Psalms, he finds Luther continuing in the tradition of medieval exegesis in his understanding of **jubilus** and in his allegorical interpretation of musical instruments. The references in the Psalms to trumpets, harps, cymbals, etc., had long been discussed not in relation to any audible music but to spiritual states.[18] Honemeyer agrees with Söhngen that the mature Luther rejects the allegorical approach but does not see therein a shift in Luther's view of music. "Yet this process is to be evaluated more from the standpoint of the development of Reformation exegesis than as a direct stance in relation to medieval musical symbolism."[19] To say this is not to detract from Luther's high regard for music but it is to credit medieval thinkers in many cases with equally high regard. Luther was by no means unusual in adopting Augustine's definition of **jubilus** as an expression of overflowing joy and of faith rejoicing. The "strongly religious motivation" underlying Augustine's view of music is seen by Honemeyer as influencing the entire Middle Ages.[20]

In the broader area of the philosophy of music, Honemeyer finds Luther dismissing the purely speculative symbolism characteristic of Neoplatonism, but in this he is not an innovator. The shift to a more realistic approach to music had taken place in the Late Middle Ages and is evident in Tinctoris. Honemeyer rejects the view of Hermann Abert that Luther marks the break between medieval and modern views of music. In his belief that music drives away the devil, for instance, Luther stands in the same medieval tradition as Tinctoris and Trithemius.[21]

In other respects, Luther reflects the medieval mystical tradition on music, which criticizes a merely external practice of music. The heart must be in accord with the song if music is to have value. This position is reflected in some statements of Luther in which he appears even to reject music as external ceremony. Significantly, one such statement presented by Honemeyer is precisely the one used by Söhngen as support for the necessity of church music. With the ellipsis filled in, the weight of the sentence falls onto the proclamation of the gospel, leaving singing to be a non-essential, even offensive, outward form. The resulting passage appears to be less an affirmation of the importance of singing than a metaphorical use of singing to represent God's working in the heart to evoke spontaneous praise of him: "I call singing **here not only the ringing or loud crying but also** every sermon or public confession...." Honemeyer agrees with Söhngen, however, in regarding any negative, mystically influenced statements on music as atypical for Luther and limited to his early years.[22]

This chapter cannot attempt an exhaustive analysis of Luther's references to music nor of Söhngen's and Honemeyer's evaluation of them.[23] In succeeding chapters other passages from Luther will appear as a backdrop for debates and analyses from the years 1580 to 1730. It should be evident from this chapter, however, that Luther's ideas on music could lead in different directions depending on the perspective of the interpreter. Given that music was most likely to become a focus of debate in the context of practical, liturgical problems, Söhngen's admission that Luther did not attempt to integrate his liturgical with his theological view of music is crucial. On the basis of the passages we have seen, Luther could lend himself to several different approaches to music: mystical, psychological, evangelical. In fact, all approaches were taken in the two centuries following his death by those who called themselves Lutherans and appealed to his authority.

The danger for modern interpreters, as for 17th-century followers, has been the desire to focus, for the sake of clarity and simplicity, on one saying of Luther as the key to the whole Luther. To do so is to ignore the tensions with which Luther lived and the paradoxical perspective from which he combined apparent opposites. In the next three chapters we will see how Luther's musical tensions moved toward resolution in the cadences of Lutheran Orthodoxy.

THE FORMULATION
OF THE
LUTHERAN ORTHODOX THEOLOGY OF MUSIC

CHAPTER ONE

BETWEEN FREEDOM AND OBLIGATION*

The theology of music in late sixteenth and early seventeenth century German Lutheranism was developed within different theological genres: polemical tracts, doctrinal commentary, biblical exegesis, and sermons or meditations. Not surprisingly, the perspectives of these approaches brought out different points of view regarding music. By the mid-seventeenth century, the systematizers and collectors of theological loci managed to organize all previous comments on music into a grand but bland outline.[24] To understand the conflicts which erupted in the late seventeenth century, however, it is necessary to look not at a finished system but at a process of historical development. Of enormous importance in this process is the fact that whereas the doctrinal status of music in Lutheranism had been determined by the opposition to Catholicism, the discussions of the doctrine in the late sixteenth century were shaped by fear of Calvinism more than of Catholicism.

Music is not explicitly mentioned in any Lutheran confessional statement, but when discussed in dogmatic theology, it came under the rubric "church ordinances" or article 15 of the Augsburg Confession of 1530. This article instructs the retention of humanly devised church orders "which may be observed without sin and which contribute to peace and good order in the church, among them being certain holy days, festivals, and the like."[25] It was to be understood, however, that such things were neither necessary nor contributory to salvation. They were variously labelled "indifferent matters," "middle things," or *adiaphora*. This term had been introduced by Melanchthon in his negotiations at the Diet of Augsburg, much to the dismay of Luther, who thought that calling any religious matter indifferent could easily lead to calling all of them indifferent.[26]

---

*The material in this chapter first appeared under the title "Music and the Doctrine of Adiaphora in Orthodox Lutheran Theology" in *Sixteenth Century Journal*, XIV/2 (Summer, 1982), pp. 157–172.

For Luther, external ceremonies were to be regarded as matters of Christian freedom, the principle which was at the heart of the gospel as he understood it. Reacting against the legalism and ceremonialism of the church as he had known it, Luther stressed that Christian faith was not displayed in outward forms. Yet it was equally legalistic to insist, as had Karlstadt, that the outward forms of the Mass be abandoned.[27] Christian freedom is best expressed in love of others, which may entail retaining religious practices which are helpful to those less advanced in the faith. In the preface to his *Deutsche Messe*, Luther distinguished between those who "are still becoming Christians or need to be strengthened" and those "who want to be Christians in earnest." For the former, if it would help, he would "have all the bells pealing and all the organs playing and have everything ring that can make a sound." The latter, on the other hand, have "no need of much and elaborate singing." (*LW* 53, 62–64)

Because different worship practices were appropriate for different kinds of people, Luther did not ask that his followers be bound by his liturgical reforms. His first instruction in that same preface was, "Do not make [this order of service] a rigid law to bind or entangle anyone's conscience, but use it in Christian liberty as long, when, where, and how you find it to be practical and useful" (*LW* 53, 61). The judgment on whether it is "practical and useful" is to be made in relation to the common people, who are most likely to be confused or offended by rapid changes and profusion of new rites. Luther had heard enough of the confusion which occurred when Karlstadt introduced radical changes into worship in Wittenberg while Luther was at the Wartburg. From that point he exhibited a horror of social disorder which made him a political conservative and, in effect, brought him closer to the ruling authorities and further from the common people. As a result, the value of ceremonies in reinforcing decorum overshadowed the freedom to abandon them. Writing to the Livonians, who had experienced an iconoclastic outbreak after the arrival of Melchior Hoffmann,[28] Luther appealed to the stabilizing power of a common order: "Since the ceremonies or rites are not needed for the conscience or for salvation and yet are useful and necessary to govern the people externally, one must not enforce or have them accepted for any other reason except to maintain peace and unity between men" ("A Christian Exhortation to the Livonians," *LW* 53, 48).

Whether peace and unity ranked higher than Protestant principle became an issue of serious consequence shortly after Luther's death. During the time of the Leipzig Interim (1548), when some Lutheran theologians submitted to the liturgical compromises imposed by the temporarily victorious Catholics, other Lutherans warned against submitting too readily to supposedly neutral ceremonies. Matthias Flacius Illyricus led the resistance by asserting that governmental compulsion to adopt or omit otherwise neutral ceremonies in effect nullified their neutrality; in such circumstances there were no adiaphora.[29] This position was incorporated into article 10 of the Formula of Concord (1580), according to which ceremonies are no longer adiaphora if the persecutor considers them essential and are to be resisted as obscuring the difference between true faith and superstition. For peaceful times the Formula provided less guidance in that it avoided specifying which particular aspects of ceremony were to be thought of as "middle things." Only a general definition was given: "ceremonies or church usages which are neither commanded nor forbidden in the Word of God but have been introduced into the church in the interest of good order and the general welfare."[30] That church music fell into this category was generally assumed, and indeed the dogmatic theologians of the period of Lutheran orthodoxy almost always mentioned music in this context. In debates with Calvinists, who had in some places violently destroyed organs in churches, the Flacian principle began to take effect: it was no longer an indifferent element if others sought to eliminate it by force.

In the process of defending music in church, it became clear that music was more than a liturgical ornament and in reality played a central role in the fostering and expression of faith. Indeed, at a later point in his life, after his reform movement had become well established, Luther had emphasized the God-given character of music and had elevated it to a place next to theology. Quite apart from its liturgical usage, it belongs to the wonder of creation through which God's goodness may be recognized. Writing in the preface to Georg Rhaw's *Symphoniae jucundae*, Luther called music "the [most] excellent gift of God" and "a noble, wholesome, and cheerful creation of God" (*LW* 53, 321,324). From the beginning of time, "it has been instilled and implanted in all creatures, individually and collectively" (322). Accordingly, it is a fitting means of paying tribute to God as Creator; Luther hopes that those who use Rhaw's compositions "may by this creation accustom yourself to recognize and praise the Creator" (324). Music is not only to be used by creatures for praise of the Creator but is a means by which the Word, as through the sermon, can communicate the gospel and move the soul of the listener. In one of his most cited statements, Luther claimed that "next to the Word of God, music deserves the highest praise" (323). The third person of the Trinity also utilizes music to work within the heart: "The Holy Ghost himself honors her as an instrument for his proper work when in his Holy Scriptures he asserts that through her his gifts were instilled in the prophets, namely, the inclination to all virtues, as can be seen in Elisha [II Kings 3:15]. On the other hand, she serves to cast out Satan, the instigator of all sins, as is shown in Saul, the king of Israel [I Sam. 16:23]." (323) In these respects music is an instrument of God and not a "human invention" such as would qualify it for inclusion in the category of adiaphora.

Within the Lutheran tradition, therefore, two approaches to music existed side by side, yet the regard for music as a divine gift was more decisive than the adiaphoristic perspective, even in discussions of outward forms of worship. This was the situation in 1586 at the colloquy of Montbéliard (Mümpelgard), where Calvinist and Lutheran theologians met in an attempt to determine the religious fate of this territory, which was then under the duchy of Württemberg. Although the colloquy had no practical consequences, it became a fundamental source for subsequent commentaries on music by Lutheran writers.

Jakob Andreae, the Lutheran spokesman at Montbéliard, came with certain preconceptions about the Reformed position, which were not all fulfilled by his Reformed counterpart, Theodore Beza. Having heard of incidents in which horses were brought into Reformed churches to tear out the organs, Andreae interpreted such incidents as reflecting a belief that organs were forbidden by God. Such a belief would of course take organs out of the realm of adiaphora. Hence Andreae was apparently caught off guard when Beza agreed with him in condemning such destructive incidents and in defending the adiaphoric nature of organs. Music, Beza noted, indeed had been abused under the papacy, as when it served only to delight the ears, but, used for the praise of God, it has a special power for moving the human spirit to devotion and true worship. In itself, therefore, music is neither good nor evil, neither commanded nor forbidden, but depends for its value on being used in such a way as to promote true worship.[31]

Having been prepared to confront a negative view of organs and church music, Andreae noted briefly, in agreement with Beza, that organs were neither commanded nor forbidden[32] and proceeded on to a defense of music where its adiaphoric nature was virtually denied. Noting that music was not mere sound nor source of aural pleasure but a hidden power of God, capable of driving away the evil spirit, Andreae denied that a sung text was necessary for making music beneficial. While understanding of the text was Beza's criterion for distinguishing between useful and harmful music, Andreae, by disagreeing with such a criterion, was leaning toward affirmation of music as a positive good rather than as neutral. In the course of his response, he in fact urged Beza to admit as much:

> So indeed it is apparent to everyone, also on the basis of your confession, that they [adiaphora] are neither commanded nor forbidden by God and thus in themselves are not only permitted but also a gracious ornament of the church if only they are used for the praise and glory of the name of God. In this manner they are not only not forbidden but rather expressly commanded in order that one praise God therewith, as is written in Psalm 150.[33]

Beza was alert to Andreae's inconsistency here. Not only could Beza himself not agree that such Old Testament ceremonial music was binding on the Christian church; surely Andreae didn't really mean that either:

> If the other external things [in addition to Word and Sacrament] are used for building up the church, so be it. But that such is prescribed as if it were commanded in the law of God, we think is not even your opinion.[34]

Andreae agreed that there was no specific command regarding instrumental music even for the Old Testament kings but argued that there was a general command to do everything one can to praise God. Because the human voice is one of the most glorious gifts of God, there is an obligation to make use of that gift by singing God's praise. God is also pleased (noticeably a weaker formulation) when instruments are used for the purpose of praising him. Gradually scaling down his argument, Andreae ends with a mere affirmation of the adiaphoristic position: "But we are herein in agreement with one another that organs and instrumental music are a free matter which one may have or not and for which each church has power and authority."[35] One is left wondering whether Andreae wanted to designate instrumental music as adiaphora and vocal music as obligatory, but such a distinction, though occasionally implicit, is not formulated.

Beza, who cautioned against the abuse of music's sensual power, nevertheless consistently maintained an adiaphorist position:

> I do not consider such to have been so strictly commanded that any should be scolded who do not have such music in their churches nor hold it for useful. In sum, I do not believe that we are bound to install organs in the churches again. Where they still exist, one may use them if one wishes. But that it is necessary from the instruction and commandment of God to play on the organ and in the church, I do not hold.[36]

Beza's tone at the council of Montbéliard had been more irenic than his Lutheran counterpart had expected. Ten years later the issue came to the fore again in a much less polite controversy. The Reformed theologians of Zerbst-Anhalt published an attack on ceremonies which would have met Andreae's expectations of Calvinist fury had he been alive to read it. Although the Reformed influence is unmistakable, the Anhalters base their case on Luther's writings, thereby misrepresenting his position. Much more straightforwardly than Beza at Montbéliard, these German Calvinists reject the authority of the Old Testament in ceremonial matters: "It is not valid here to appeal to the Old Testament. For we are not Jews; otherwise circumcision would have to be instituted again. The shadows are lifted because the body itself has come (Colossians 2:17)."[37] The writers claim the Hebrews were always able to understand the sung words above the instrumental accompaniment, contrasting this with the incomprehensible singing of their own day. Nevertheless, the outward musical forms of the Old Testament are only "a typos or image of the joyful sermon of the gospel which in the New Testament would sound quite loudly through the whole world."[38]

Although the Psalms are of value and should be retained in the Christian church, the Anhalters continue, other elements of Old Testament worship have at best allegorical value and at worst impede true worship. Organs and Latin singing are human inventions, which leaves them no place in sacred worship. *Adiaphora* is not a meaningful concept for the Anhalters. Those things which were not commanded by God are of no use toward pleasing God. "For he neither commanded them nor himself held them with his apostles, but rather they are purely vain human ordinances with which one does God no favors."[39] Such a statement could conceivably fit with an advocacy of the concept of adiaphora, but other, stronger statements exclude the possibility. Any singing which cannot be understood conflicts with I Corinthians 14 and cannot therefore be a neutral activity. Anything, in fact, which is added to the "pure preached word of God and the true use of the holy sacrament according to the Lord's institution...is nothing other than a deceiving hypocrisy and an abomination before God and all the angels in heaven."[40]

The Anhalt appeal for purification of church ceremonies evoked numerous outraged responses from Lutheran theologians, several of whom charged the Anhalters with reviving the spirit of Karlstadt. The most influential response was that of the theological faculty at Wittenberg in 1597.[41] As its title, *Notwendige Antwort*, suggests, it is an answer to the assertions of the Anhalters rather than a full theological statement. Hence for the most part the Wittenbergers content themselves with pointing out the falsifications and fallacies of the Anhalters. But in the process of pointing up errors in the Anhalters' presentation of Luther, the Wittenbergers reaffirm much of Luther's theology of music.

The Anhalt misinterpretation of Luther, according to the Wittenberg theologians, consisted partially in misconstruing a list of ceremonial items which Luther had designated as opposed to the faith only if they were thought to represent special service. Otherwise they were merely beyond what was necessary.[42] This is equivalent to calling them adiaphora, as indeed seems to have been Luther's intention. But the mention of adiaphora enters the Wittenbergers' counter-attack only when organs are grouped together with such things as bells, holy water, vestments, pictures, candles, etc. When attention is paid solely to music, no further mention is made of adiaphora.

Although the Wittenbergers stop short of labelling music a command of God, they are certain of the value of both vocal and instrumental music. "Instrumental music is in itself such a gift of God as to move the hearts of men with power even when no human voice sings along."[43] Regarding the requirement of I Corinthians 14 that worship be understandable, the Wittenbergers are satisfied if instrumental music communicates its genus. That is, so long as one perceives that an organist is playing spiritual music, the power of that music can be felt and its effect achieved. Similarly, a call to battle effectively communicates its message without words. Instruments were used on various occasions, particularly festival days, among the ancient Hebrews and had power to arouse the spirit, excite joy, or announce the new year. Further, the Wittenbergers find it unrealistic to suppose that when all kinds of wind and stringed instruments were played in the temple, the listeners were always able to hear and understand the words being sung. As for Luther's alleged purely allegorical interpretation of Old Testament music, the Wittenbergers assert that this never occurred to him. To be deprived of the gift of music was in the Old Testament a punishment of God (Jeremiah 7:16, 34).[44] There is no reason to think it otherwise in the Christian church. The Wittenbergers could hardly think with equanimity of music as dispensable, even though in theory they might label it an adiaphoron.

The two Reformed-Lutheran debates discussed thus far set the tone and provide much of the argumentation for Lutheran musical theology in the first third of the seventeenth century. Writings in which music is discussed vary in the extent to which they are obviously polemical, but few are without some reference to the Calvinists, usually to Beza, sometimes to Peter Martyr Vermigli, sometimes to the Anhalt theologians. In a context in which the opponent was taking either a strongly negative or an adiaphorist position, the Lutherans could not settle for adiaphorism. Thus, this age sees a new Lutheran offensive. As Calvinists pressed further into Germany, Lutherans saw more cause to praise music both in academic theology and in popular sermon.

Only occasionally in these various writings does one find mention of "Christian liberty" or "adiaphora." Philipp Arnoldi, pastor at Tilsit and author of *Caeremoniae Lutheranae...den Calvinischen Ceremoniestürmern entgegengesetzt*, included Christian liberty as one of many reasons for defending Lutheran music. On the question whether musical instruments should be abandoned in the age of the New Testament, Arnoldi finds no warrant for this: "For where is it forbidden? Against which article of faith does it contend?"[45] There is not much evidence in the New Testament to support instrumental music, Arnoldi admits, but still enough upon which to base our right to use instruments. Christ himself sang with his apostles (Matt. 26:30), and the Apostle Paul instructs us to sing in Ephesians 5:19, Colossians 3:16, and I Corinthians 14:26. In the first of these the Apostle even uses the word "play." Hence there is no reason to consider instruments forbidden, but rather "by virtue of Christian freedom conceded and bequeathed."[46] A great benefit is in fact to be received from such delightful music. The same argument holds for the use of foreign languages in singing. If there are those present who understand Latin or Greek and can explain the text to the common people, Christian freedom permits the use of these tongues. After all, at the Cross the Savior's title was given in Hebrew, Greek, and Latin. Arnoldi's conclusion is a clear statement of the adiaphorist position:

> In sum, as far as our figural and instrumental music in German and Latin language is concerned, we have as support the example of our forefathers and Christian freedom. In the Old Testament they necessarily had to perform according to their ceremonial law, but we are not bound to this and do not defend it with such great necessity as the adversaries exert themselves and cry loudly for abolishment.[47]

As clear a statement of the adiaphoric nature of music is not to be found in Balthasar Meisner's *Collegii Adiaphoristici*, in spite of the title. Although this series of treatises on adiaphora begins with a general definition and a statement that "figural and organ music and organs themselves"[48] fit this definition, his discussion of music itself does not treat music as indifferent. This is to some extent a reflection of this general position that Lutherans should not yield to Calvinist pressures merely because they are doctrinally free to do so.[49] It is, however, also a reflection of the fact that Lutheran theology of music was difficult to subsume under the category "adiaphora."

Meisner notes that adiaphora are "middle things" because they are midway between the divinely commanded and the divinely prohibited.[50] Elsewhere he seems to think music was divinely commanded: "The Holy Spirit is not so much opposed to the sweet joy of holy Psalms as that he required and demanded the same from his faithful in both Testaments."[51] To be sure, Meisner finds no specific prescriptions for the kind of music to be used in the church but finds the faithful urged by Paul to "love and pursue the holy harmony of songs."[52]

Not only is there enough positive scriptural warrant for music to bring the activity close to the realm of the "divinely commanded," but it is difficult to reconcile Meisner's other comments with the idea that music as adiaphoron is "in its nature neither good nor bad."[53] We are told that God himself is to be praised for providing man with the principles of music and the voice with which to sing and to praise the Creator who gave him this gift.[54] Of course, music can be abused through levity and licentiousness,[55] but with God as the source it hardly seems to be by nature neutral, much less a humanly devised tradition in the terms of the Augsburg Confession. Furthermore, the description of adiaphora as neither promoting nor impeding the eternal salvation of men[56] hardly seems to apply when Meisner points out how music serves to increase devotion and to drive out the evil spirit.[57] Meisner repeats here some standard examples: music led Augustine to the tears which were the beginning of his conversion; David's playing of the psalter caused the evil spirit to flee from Saul. A refinement of the cause-effect relationship whereby the spiritual power might be said to lie not in the music itself but in the Holy Spirit working through music is not to be found in Meisner's discussion.

Meisner's *Collegii Adiaphoristici*, then, are shaped by their polemical context. As the subtitle indicates, they are "Calvinianis oppositi"—"in opposition to the Calvinists." Free as the Lutherans might be doctrinally to use or not to use music, this freedom was not to be exercised by giving in to pressure, whether that of the Roman church as in the time of the Leipzig Interim, or that of the Calvinists as they gained control of more territory in Germany. Flacius' principle of resistance was being applied more broadly, resulting in an uncompromising defense of Lutheran practice.

This intolerance is seen in academic theologians as well as popular preachers. Those who cannot tolerate figural or instrumental music in churches "sin gravely," according to Meisner's Wittenberg colleague Fridericus Balduinus.[58] As support he refers to Andreae's Montbéliard condemnation of the use of horses to tear organs out of churches; Beza's agreement with Andreae in this point is ignored. Even less objective in his treatment of Calvinist writers is the preacher Hieronymus Theodoricus in his organ sermon *Corona Templi*. In contrast to most Lutheran accounts of abuses in church music, Theodoricus labels as abusers not those who play frivolous music in church but those who criticize church music. This includes some Lutherans and virtually all Turks and Jews; but of greatest concern are the Calvinists, of whom Beza, Peter Martyr, and the Anhalt theologians are mentioned. According to Theodoricus, these Calvinists call organs the "trumpets by which the Antichrist is favored and called to court."[59] The phrase "tubas Antichristi," however, is not to be found in any of the Calvinist sources cited but rather in a Lutheran attack comparing Calvinists to Antitrinitarians.[60] The term apparently stems from the Antitrinitarians rather than the Calvinists.

Just as Beza's actual position at Montbéliard failed to demonstrate the intolerance said to characterize the Calvinist position, so the other Reformed theologian cited here, Peter Martyr Vermigli (1500–1562), fails to live up to Theodoricus' caricature. To be sure, he has no sympathy for organ music, but his position is hardly as narrow-minded as Theodoricus claimed. In fact, whereas Theodoricus views church music as a duty whereby God is pleased, ignoring any possibility that it might be misused among Lutherans, Vermigli concludes the passage Theodoricus cites with a genuinely adiaphorist statement:

> I affirm that faithful and religious singing may be retained in church; but I do not confess that any precept exists on this matter in the New Testament. Wherefore if there be a church which does not use it, for just cause, it may not rightly be condemned, provided that it does not defend this matter illicitly by its nature or by the precept of God nor stigmatize other churches where singing and music are used or exclude them from the fellowship of Christ.[61]

This is not to overlook some unfriendly remarks Vermigli made elsewhere concerning organs. Organs, he asserts, are incapable of communicating spiritual understanding and have accordingly no role in worship "since from their rumbling nothing of the word of God may be understood."[62] But such remarks do not excuse the misrepresentations and false charges of Lutheran writers. At least in the writings cited, the Reformed were far less antagonistic than they were said to be by the Lutherans. Vermigli, for instance, rather than blaming the Roman Antichrist for organs, gave credit to the papacy for never having allowed organs into the papal chapel.[63] Throughout his commentary he showed more willingness to consider both sides of the question, i.e. both the positive and the negative potential of music, than did any of the Lutheran writers involved in the controversy.

Even in the less blatantly polemical Lutheran writings, the firm defense of both instrumental and vocal music was evident and the scorn for their critics never entirely absent. The most respected thinkers sometimes distorted or gave misleading impressions of opposing practices. The Wittenberg theologian Aegidius Hunnius, for example, attached to his putative opponent a Zwinglian position, which was easier to mock than the Calvinist position:

> This is to be observed against those fanatics and gloomy spirits who assert that it is unfitting and disgraceful to ask anything from God in song; and for that reason they rave that songs are to be eliminated from the gatherings of the church.[64]

In this way he implied that the Lutheran position was superior to that of any of its critics, ignoring the fact that the contemporaneous Calvinist critics would have had few objections to his other comments. Hunnius in fact skirted the questions of musical instruments, figural singing, and foreign language singing. Instead, he emphasized music's value for praise and edification and insisted on the harmony of the heart, mouth, and life.[65] Because the monks under the papacy were ignorant of the Latin they were singing, he regarded their singing as fruitless and reprehensible. Yet he avoided the implications of such a principle for Lutheran practice.[66]

The Calvinist-Lutheran differences are more explicit and more precisely stated in Matthias Hoe's *Commentary on the Apocalypse*.[67] Hoe mentions Peter Martyr's disapproval of figural music and quotes verbatim from Beza's criticisms at the colloquy of Montbéliard. Yet in spite of this element of objectivity, he cannot refrain from calling these critics "amusical hypocrites."[68] Confronting their demand for textual understanding, Hoe uses what is by this point a fairly standard Lutheran mode of response:

> For even if the words are not understood by all, nevertheless just as soldiers are enlivened by the sound of a trumpet, so in the meetings of the church and in the spiritual army the very variety of voices and the harmony of the organs excites devout minds greatly to earnest prayers and works of grace.[69]

As to the appropriateness of figural music there can be no doubt, according to Hoe; it, as well as unison choral singing, is a gift of God, and it is his will that this be added to worship of him.[70]

Fair use of evidence is also characteristic of Conrad Dieterich's *Ulm Organ Sermon* of 1624. Dieterich does not content himself with the standard references to Beza, Peter Martyr, and the Anhalt theologians of the previous century; he also provides more up-to-date information from his own century. He is aware, for instance, that in some Calvinist churches, particularly in Holland, organs had been retained and were being used for recreational purposes outside the times of worship.[71] He also credited other Calvinists with recognizing this as an undesirable custom and noted that some Calvinist churches were even installing new organs for worship purposes, as for example in Hessen in 1605. Yet this does not prevent Dieterich from a harsh characterization of the Calvinist position: their charge that instrumental music is a mere clang which delights the ears but distracts from worship is itself "a sheer hollow Calvinist racket."[72] To the contrary, says Dieterich, the Holy Spirit moves the heart through instruments. Nor is it necessary to understand what is being played as long as one knows the genus. The adiaphorist doctrine puts the burden on the Calvinists, as Dieterich sees it. Given the long-standing use of instruments in the Christian church and their demonstrated usefulness for praising God, arousing the mind and ornamenting worship, there is no way of removing them without causing harmful annoyance.[73] While recognizing that they are neither commanded nor forbidden in the New Testament, Dieterich cannot seriously regard them as indifferent.

On the whole, then, the Lutheran theologians and clergy in the early decades of the seventeenth century pushed the adiaphoric question into the background in their discussions of music. Under attack by the Calvinists, whose presence in various parts of Germany was becoming more threatening, Lutheran writers indulged in polemical overstatements. Although the most serious writers might distinguish between an obligation to praise God and an obligation to praise him with choirs and organs, the popularizing preachers obscured the distinction. Johannes Scarlach, for example, in a question and answer book on the Formula of Concord, instructed his readers to respond to the Calvinist attack on organs with "the advice and command of the Holy Spirit" in Psalm 150.[74] Similarly, Christoph Frick, preacher in Burgdorf and later in Bardewick, gave "the command of God" as the first reason for preserving music, supporting the point with standard references from the Psalms, Ephesians, Colossians, etc.[75] Neither in the 1615 *Musica Christiana* nor in the revised and greatly expanded 1631 *Music-Büchlein* does the adiaphoric question receive any mention.[76] There is in fact no room in Frick's theology for opponents of music. Without making distinctions among Karlstadt, Zwinglians, and Calvinists, Frick castigates them all as having scorned music "out of falsely pretended wisdom."[77] In a significant twist, Frick argues not, as had the Wittenberg theologians, that those who offend God are punished by loss of music, but that ignorance and scorn of music is itself just cause of divine punishment.

> It is certain that such people will be at the place where there will be nothing but howling and gnashing of teeth; with the hellish wolves

and all the damned in eternity they will cry out dolefully. May God protect us graciously against this one and all.[78]

Frick's devotional book represents a different genre from most works discussed in this chapter, which explains something of the difference in tone. He was writing for ordinary people, not for other theologians. Perhaps he was not intellectually capable of writing academic theology, but to the extent that we can surmise his world view he seems to belong to a different theological circle, which we will discuss in chapter 4. The Baroque world-view, which was not specific to Lutheranism, emphasized the harmonies of the universe and regarded human music as an imitation of the larger cosmos. Where Lutherans adopted this cosmology, their frame of thought became even less adaptable to a doctrine of musical adiaphora than before.

At no time in the late sixteenth or early seventeenth centuries, we may conclude, were Lutheran theologians content to relegate music entirely to the realm of indifferent matters. The contrary interpretation has been advanced by Friedrich Kalb in his *Theology of Worship in 17th-Century Lutheranism* and taken over by Oskar Söhngen, who on this basis bemoaned the loss of the "deep music-theological perceptions of Martin Luther."[79] To be sure, profound and original thought was not characteristic of the period, but the love of music as a gift and instrument of God was still strongly felt.

Whether the failure to take seriously the adiaphorist doctrine was harmful or beneficial is worth considering, however. As the Calvinist-Lutheran tensions increased, even the **pro forma** acknowledgements of the adiaphoric status of music were omitted and love of music became an article of faith. Having been shaped by the polemical situation, the Lutheran stance became intolerant and uncompromising. The command to praise God with voice and instruments was remembered; the freedom from outward forms of worship was forgotten.

CHAPTER TWO

BETWEEN PSYCHOLOGY AND SPIRITUALITY

Insofar as music was regarded as a religious obligation, it was directed toward the honor and praise of God; but Lutherans were equally aware that music offered many benefits to human beings as well. As theologian and music theorist Cyriacus Schneegass wrote in 1590, "For music, both instrumental and vocal, is an exceptional gift of the Holy Spirit and has great power for stirring and soothing the affections of the mind."[80] What is noteworthy here is the juxtaposition of religious and psychological claims. Neither the claim that music was a gift of God nor that it stirred the affections was original or controversial, but the tendency to claim that the stirring of the affections was connected to the divine source of music separated Lutherans from Calvinists. As the Lutheran position was being developed, there were a variety of positions concerning the relationship of psychological and spiritual forces in music, as we shall observe in the course of this chapter. Over against Reformed thinkers, however, there was a certain unanimity: whereas for Calvinists the psychological perspective remained distinct from the theological, Lutherans integrated the two perspectives into one theological claim.

The lack of distinction between the two levels has its source for Lutherans in one of Luther's oft-cited statements about music. Although reference was made to this passage in the introduction, it is useful for our present purposes to quote it at length:

> We can mention only one point (which experience confirms), namely, that next to the Word of God, music deserves the highest praise. She is a mistress and governess of those human emotions—to pass over the animals—which as masters govern men or more often overwhelm them. No greater commendation than this can be found—at least not by us. For whether you wish to comfort the sad, to terrify the happy, to encourage the despairing, to humble the proud, to calm the passionate, or to appease those full of hate—and who could number

all these masters of the human heart, namely, the emotions, inclinations, and affections that impel men to evil or good?—what more effective means than music could you find? The Holy Spirit himself honors her as an instrument for his proper work when in his Holy Scriptures he asserts that through her his gifts were instilled in the prophets, namely the inclination to all virtues, as can be seen in Elisha [II Kings 3:15]. On the other hand, she serves to cast out Satan, the instigator of all sins, as is shown in Saul, the king of Israel [I Sam. 16:23].[81]

In noting the psychological or emotional effects of music, Luther was hardly original. A long tradition from the early Greeks on had pointed out the beneficial effects of music. The church fathers had adapted them to their purposes, and through Augustine, Chrysostom and others, they were transmitted to the medieval thinkers.[82] At the end of the Middle Ages, Johannes Tinctoris published a book with a list of twenty such effects, many of which reappear in this quote from Luther's preface to Georg Rhaw's *Symphoniae iucundae*, including that music drives away sadness and that it drives away the devil.[83] What is significant is that Luther's list of what we might call psychological benefits is sandwiched between two theological claims about music: it is next in importance to theology, and it is an instrument of the Spirit. The fact that he is writing a preface to a motet book ensures that he will praise music and not linger on any misgivings, but does he really mean to say, as it seems, that music in all these functions is in the service of the Holy Spirit? This is the interpretation of Oskar Söhngen, who says Luther "is indeed firmly convinced that music according to God's will has an important office to execute even without an explicit connection to God's word."[84] Luther's affirmation of music is so total, according to Söhngen, that there are no "bad" modes and thus no harmful music.[85]

Since the time of the Greeks musical modes had been associated with certain moods, and some modes had been criticized as having no ethical value. In Plato's *Republic* the Lydian and Mixolydian were said to be "useless even to women," and certain Ionian and Lydian harmonies were considered too relaxed for warriors.[86] Luther was well trained in music, including modes, and in writing his German mass he consciously chose modes he thought fitting for the Gospel and the Epistle. But there is no evidence that he warned against the use of any modes as unsuitable.

An even greater peril for those of the Platonic tradition was that music might appeal too strongly to the senses rather than the intellect. Vocal music often escaped this suspicion because of the text which accompanies the melody, but instrumental music fell victim among Calvinists to the fear of titillated senses and blurred intellect. Luther's view of life, however, was not as a war between the senses and the intellect but between the old man in bondage to evil and the new man freed to do good. As Luther reveals in the passage quoted, music is part of the liberating force in alliance with the Word. It does not tempt the passions; it conquers them and frees the person being held hostage. Thus, just as humans do not stand in the middle making choices between good and evil but are under the power of one force or the other, neither does one choose between beneficial and harmful music. To the one who uses it in faith, it will be beneficial.

This does not mean that there is no such thing as secular music for Luther or that among carnal people there is no harmful use of music. But it does mean that there is no conflict between the pleasure derived from music and the workings of the Holy Spirit. In Christian tradition this was a radical stance for a theologian. Although medieval and Renaissance church music had become fairly elaborate, the process had occurred without much support from theologians, whose views of church music had been shaped by the Church Fathers. Of these the most influential was St. Augustine, who himself was torn, unable either to endorse church music wholeheartedly or to reject it altogether. Augustine's ambivalence made him a useful authority for both Lutheran and Calvinist writers, and we can learn much about the differences between the two groups by looking at their appeals to Augustine's authority.

Although Augustine wrote six books *De Musica*, which are of interest to music theorists, it was his autobiographical reflections in Book X of his *Confessions* which influenced thinking about church music practices. The passage is long, but to include most of it is important for the subsequent discussion:

> I used to be much more fascinated by the pleasures of sound than the pleasures of smell. I admit that I still find some enjoyment in the music of hymns,... But I do not enjoy it so much that I cannot tear myself away. I can leave it when I wish. But if I am not to turn a deaf ear to music, which is the setting for the words which give it life, I must allow it a position of some honour in my heart,...For sometimes I feel that I treat it with more honour than it deserves. I realize that when they are sung these sacred words stir my mind to greater religious fervour and kindle in me a more ardent flame of piety than they would if they were not sung; and I also know that there are particular modes in song and in the voice, corresponding to my various emotions and able to stimulate them because of some mysterious relationship between the two. But I ought not to allow my mind to be paralysed by the gratification of the senses, which often leads it astray. For the senses are not content to take second place. Simply because I allow them their due, as adjuncts to reason, they attempt to take precedence and forge ahead of it, with the result that I sometimes sin in this way but am not aware of it until later.
>
> Sometimes, too, from over-anxiety to avoid this particular trap I make the mistake of being too strict. But when I remember the

> tears that I shed on hearing the songs of the Church in the early days, soon after I had recovered my faith, and when I realize that nowadays it is not the singing that moves me but the meaning of the words when they are sung in a clear voice to the most appropriate tune, I again acknowledge the great value of this practice. So I waver between the danger that lies in gratifying the senses and the benefits which, as I know from experience, can accrue from singing. Without committing myself to an irrevocable opinion, I am inclined to approve of the custom of singing in church, in order that by indulging the ears weaker spirits may be inspired with feelings of devotion. Yet when I find the singing itself more moving than the truth which it conveys, I confess that this is a grievous sin, and at those times I would prefer not to hear the singer.[87]

The hesitation and fears of sensuality which Augustine expressed here in connection with music rang no sympathetic chords in Luther's mind or heart. Music was for Luther too positive a good, too powerful a weapon *against* the devil to allow him to perceive it as a weapon *of* the devil. In his *Table Talk*, Luther expressed confidence that these scruples of Augustine regarding music were not indicative of a fundamentally different attitude:

> Music is the best gift of God. Quite often it has so aroused me and spurred me on that I gained the desire to preach. But St. Augustine had such scruples that he supposed he had sinned through delighting in music. He was a fine man. If he lived in this century, he would be of our opinion. (*WA TR* IV:313, no. 4441)

Given Luther's confidence of likemindedness with Augustine, there was no reason for his successors to re-examine the Augustinian text. If music was not a spiritual danger for Luther, the less profound representatives of the Lutheran tradition were not likely to wrestle seriously with doubts in this matter. Hence, Lutheran writers tended to state in simple terms what seemed to be the main point of Augustine's reflections on music in his *Confessions*: hearing the singing of Psalms led him to tears early in his conversion. This served as clear evidence of the devotional value of music.

In a commentary on Colossians 3:16, which enjoins the singing of psalms, hymns and spiritual songs, the Wittenberg theologian Fridericus Balduinus points out that music was used in the early church as a means of moving the heart to devotion. He notes that Augustine wept at the sweet sounds of singing in the church, which stirred in him the affections of piety. Balduinus ignores Augustine's qualms and reports not his fears of sensuality but his conviction that he is now moved by the things which were sung rather than by the melody itself. Ignoring also Augustine's advocacy of simple psalmody, Balduinus proceeds to express amazement that, given this background, the Calvinists could consider figural and instrumental music a part of Jewish upbringing to be outgrown.[88] Commenting elsewhere on Paul's musical instructions in Ephesians 5, Balduinus quotes a sentence from the preceding chapter of the *Confessions*: "Those voices surged in my ears, your truth flowed into my heart, and from that feelings of devotion boiled up, so that the tears streamed down, and it was well with me."[89] Here indeed music seems to function as a means of grace, a mode of divine communication. Thus Balduinus chastises that amusical Calvinist Spirit who wants to do away with "the external means of devotion." When he then charges the enthusiasts with leaving room only for their own spirit, it seems clear that he believes the Holy Spirit operates through music.

Similarly, Theodoricus points out that "a special power" entered Augustine's heart as he heard the singing in Milan. This was the "first cause" of his conversion, according to Theodoricus, whereas Augustine himself had said somewhat more vaguely that it had occurred "in the beginning of my recovered faith." From the accompanying discussion of music's ability to arouse devotion, it seems evident that Theodoricus indeed ascribed spiritual force to music itself. Citing Ambrose, he asserts that "through sweet sound and pleasing song God's grace and the Holy Spirit is sent."[90]

Conrad Dieterich, whose influential sermon for the dedication of the new Ulm organ was one of the most sophisticated works on this topic, was an exception among Lutherans in even mentioning Augustine's conflict concerning the charms of music; but to use Augustine's authority to reject instrumental or organ music was to him "nothing but empty Calvinist racket" ("lauter ödes Calvinisches Getöse"). Noteworthy for Dieterich is that Augustine said he had "erred by too great strictness" and that he had finally concluded music should be retained in the Church.[91] Dieterich ignored both the tentative nature of Augustine's approval and his insistence on the prominence of the words.

Greater accuracy and greater empathy characterize the Reformed theologian Peter Martyr Vermigli's discussion of Augustine's view of music. Whereas Lutheran theologians of this period seemed unconcerned about any possible conflict or imbalance between text and melody, the Reformed shared Augustine's fears of music's sensual power. As Peter Martyr expressed it, music has power to "seize all men," but "as a delight it is placed in the middle," between the senses and the reason.[92] Only when it is combined with a noble text does it appeal to the reason. Without a text or with an unworthy text, music draws the listener toward the sensual. This was the reason Augustine knew he had sinned when he paid more attention to the musical elements than to the words. And, Peter Martyr continues in a faithful summary of Augustine's *Confessions*,

> he repented of this guilt to the point that he heartily approved the custom of Alexandria under Athanasius, that is, that the reader be instructed to inflect the voice very little in singing psalms so that it

approached more the manner of reciting than of singing. But, noting on the other hand how much he had been moved by these songs from the beginning of his conversion, to the point that tears flowed from him out of the devotion evoked, he agreed that music should be retained in the Church; nevertheless he declared himself ready to change his mind if a more powerful reason could be brought. And he added that those are under penalty of sin who pay more attention to the music than to the words of God.[93]

For Peter Martyr, as for others of the Reformed tradition, the distrust of organ and instrumental music is a reflection of a humanistic view of the nature of music. He is not interested in crediting God or even the Hebrews with the invention of instrumental music, and only when writing about the poetry which is set to music does he use the term "gift of God."[94] Instrumental music is for him lifeless ("inanima") and communicates nothing intelligible.[95] Because the rational faculties are more noble than the affective faculties, it is essential that music which is to arouse devotion also stimulate the mind through the text which is sung.

Luther had no such hierarchical view of human faculties and had rejected the Aristotelianism from which it was derived. The fact that music could be a means of grace resulted from a more integrated, organic view of creation and of human nature based on Hebraic categories. The inseparability of body and soul is expressed in the Lutheran doctrine of ubiquity whereby Christ may be said to be present both physically and spiritually (though non-spatially) in Holy Communion. Calvinists, on the other hand, believing Christ fully present only in heaven, affirm only his spiritual presence in the sacrament. Similarly in music, Lutherans affirm the ability of the physical world to communicate spiritual meaning, while Calvinists affirm music only insofar as it lifts humans above the physical realm. Thus, for Lutherans, even as pure sound without words, music might convey a certain knowledge of God. As a part of creation, music came from God and may lead back to him, as the world in general points back to the Creator.[96]

Accordingly, we find in seventeenth-century Lutheran writers an argument from nature in defense of vocal and instrumental music, but it is nature as God's realm of activity, not as an inanimate finished product. Although some had taken pains to demonstrate that Jubal invented instrumental music, thereby showing that it belonged to Hebrew tradition,[97] Theodoricus preferred to see it as part of God's general providence available to all people. Whether it was the Greeks or the Hebrews who first used musical instruments, he concludes after examining the claims of various writers, the inventor of all the arts was God, "who also bestows the same laudable artistic gifts—and especially the sweetness of musical consonances and harmonizations—not only on the believers among his people but also through his general presence on those people who remain outside the bosom of the church."[98] Similarly, Philipp Arnoldi, in a work on Lutheran ceremony, found music to be a part of creation: "Nature itself shows that vocal and instrumental music, in whatever way it occurs, is implanted and instilled in humans to refresh them."[99] Support for instrumental music comes from the fact that non-verbal beings such as infants and animals respond to the sound of music, and other non-verbal beings such as birds produce it. As Arnoldi writes,

> Singing quiets small children, refreshes the sad and melancholy, and stimulates irrational animals to work....If both large and small birds get their songs from nature, why not humans also? Is it not so? One bird may sing in chorale style, another in figural style, but to human amazement they know how to hit the intervals accurately. Had there been no music from the beginning, one could have conceived and pondered it better from the lovely singing of birds than from the sound of metal.[100]

Music's natural power to influence human moods is further evidence in favor of instrumental music in worship. Conrad Dieterich noted the ancient use of Greek modes to arouse the appropriate "affection" in the listener: Dorian for moving to chastity, Phrygian for calling to battle, Iastian for appealing to reason and clear-thinking, and Lydian for recreation and enjoyment. Why, he wonders, should not this "special power" of music be put to good use in Christian worship?[101]

For Wolfgang Silber there seems to be a physiological basis for the human response to music, though this is not clearly stated. "The natural spirits of our mind and blood are so related to and fond of the lovely song and sound of music that a person is easily moved thereby, yes even enraptured."[102] Silber notes that children in the cradle look around in wonder with open mouths and eyes when they are moved by pleasant sound. This wonder does not depend on understanding what the music means. It is the heart that is first moved, after which the mind is brought to attention. Thus in church when we respond with wonder to the sound of the organ, the effect is to prepare us for the praise of God which is better expressed through both words and melody.[103]

It is important to stress that, however much Lutheran writers praised instrumental music as a divinely created means of moving the heart in the right direction, the combination of text and melody was considered the more effective instrument of the Spirit. It could appeal to the mind as well as the heart and thus have educational as well as psychological benefits. A good summary of these combined possibilities is found in Nicolaus Selneccer's 1571 psalm commentaries and was repeated by others in the decades following:

> For a good melody and beautiful text refreshes body and soul and is an organ or instrument which the Holy Spirit uses to refresh and

comfort hearts, to instruct youth and bring them up in the teaching of God, and to keep the simple people in fresh remembrance of the good deeds of Christ.[104]

Such a statement, however, does not advance our understanding of the way in which the Spirit utilizes music or of the relative importance of Spirit, sound, song and singer. We cannot expect a philosophically precise analysis of this any more than of Luther's doctrine of the Real Presence. But we are able to identify different points of view by looking at interpretations of the incident mentioned above by Luther and recorded in I Samuel 16:23 ("And whenever the evil spirit from God was upon Saul, David took the lyre and played with his hand; so Saul was refreshed, and was well, and the evil spirit departed from him"—*RSV*). Modern commentators on this passage admit that it is an example of a magical or exorcistic use of music, as has been found in many cultures.[105] Most of our writers avoid a magical interpretation of the passage either by emphasizing the power of the words or by identifying the "evil spirit" as melancholy rather than as Satan personified.

It is well known that Luther took the devil seriously, whether or not he actually threw an ink bottle at him. But he understands the fleeing of the devil in this incident at more than one level. Neither the sound of the harp, the faith of David, nor the words of the Psalms alone healed Saul. The evil spirit is personified but is also called a spirit of sadness; insofar as he is Satan it is the power of God's Word combined with David's faith which drives him away; but insofar as the music conveys cheerfulness it drives away not a person but a state of sadness. Singing is here similar to preaching as an outward means of communicating the Word, and both are inseparable from faith.[106] "The evil spirit is uncomfortable when God's Word is sung or preached in correct faith. He is a spirit of sadness and cannot remain where a heart is happy spiritually (that is, in God and his Word)."[107] In another comment on this passage Luther noted that both words and sounds move the human heart, but, because humans have verbal ability, they should use that as well as instrumental ability.[108]

Luther's colleagues and followers took this passage in different directions. Johannes Bugenhagen, writing in 1524 before Luther had written on the text, considered speculations on music's supposed powers against demons a waste of time; it was the faith of David which produced the effect. For Hieronymus Weller music was the wrong answer, for the devil kept coming back; only the Word of God, prayer and repentance can expel him.[109]

Johannes Brenz, Württemberg reformer, took yet a different approach. "Many think," he wrote, "that the faith and prayers of David, which he played on the harp from faith, expelled Satan from Saul, in the same manner as the Apostles cast out demons from men in the name of Christ."[110] But it is wrong to think of David as working a miracle here, Brenz asserts. All the text indicates is that the physicians attending to Saul recommended a skilled harp player to calm Saul's mind. Whether the player was pious or not was incidental. Music was being used here as a purely natural phenomenon, as a medicine with powers of alleviating suffering. "The doctors counseled Saul not with some kind of religious but with naturalistic reasoning, indeed from the precepts of their medical science, that someone skilled in singing psalms be called...."[111] Furthermore, the music did not cure Saul, for it, as an external medicament, could not eliminate the internal *desperatio* which was the cause of Saul's madness. Thus music, helpful as it was in treating side effects, had no power to produce spiritual changes. Brenz makes a clear distinction between the power of the Holy Spirit to heal insanity and the more limited power of music to move the affections.

Brenz' South German secularization of music's power did not suit the Lutheran Orthodox circle around Wittenberg and particularly not those whose aim was to promote church music. Like Brenz, Conrad Dieterich omitted both the Word of God or the faith of David as factors in the Saul episode, but this resulted from his promotion of instrumental music.

> Instrumental music drives away the restless, raging, peeving and grieving spirit and brings forth the free, happy and good spirit. When the evil spirit made Saul restless and David grasped his harp and opened up with it, Saul was reinvigorated, it went better with him, and the evil spirit departed from him (I Samuel 16:23).[112]

Whether Dieterich regards the evil spirit as a being or a psychological state is not clear; his use of that term is only in direct biblical citation. But the curative power of music is not a merely naturalistic process; the Holy Spirit works through the sounds of music: "For the example of David shows that music in general and thus also organs and instrumental music in particular not only titillate and please the ears but also through them the Holy Spirit moves people's minds."[113]

There is not even a suspicion of a naturalistic perspective with Christoph Frick, a popularizing proponent of music who came close to ascribing magical power to music. He avoids this by focussing on the spiritual powers of the musician, i.e. David. It is therefore neither the music nor the text which is primarily efficacious, but rather the singer. Saul, the hearer, becomes incidental, for it is not a psychological state which is to be altered but the Devil who is to be driven away: "Not that just the sound of the harp drove away the devil, but because David played a spiritual song from the depths of his heart and sang it in fervent devotion to Christ, the devil could not remain."[114]

Superficially, this position appears to coincide with that of Luther, as it combines the interior state of the singer with the exterior sound of the music and the authority of the text. But there is a significant shift. Frick speaks not of the Word of God but of a "spiritual song" and not of faith but of "fervent devotion." Whereas for Luther justification was "extra nos" and faith was not a subjective state, for Frick the degree of devotion determined the extent of an individual's spiritual power. No longer is music an instrument of the Spirit preparing the soul for devotion, but is rather an instrument for use by an individual who has been moved by the Spirit. With the inner Spirit no longer intrinsically linked to the outward form, music becomes not a means of grace in Luther's sense but the external element in a sacrament in the medieval sense. Used devoutly, it carries enormous potential for good; used unworthily, condemnation may ensue. Frick's supporting anecdotes are reminiscent of medieval devotional testimonies regarding the power of the consecrated host. Just as a consecrated host, devoutly regarded, could protect against danger and illness, so for Frick music can fend off enemies and disease. No longer is this a mere matter of psychology; the song does not first need to soothe the mind in order to prepare the hearer for God's blessings. For Frick the effects are unmediated. As examples he presents some anecdotes he has found in other sources:

> There was once a son of a gatekeeper traveling in the midst of a great thunderstorm. As he sat on his horse in this heavy storm, he sang the Easter hymn, "Christ is arisen," with great devotion. Thus it happened that even though this storm threw down the horse underneath him, nothing happened to the boy.[115]

Similarly:

> This is the way it happened in the case of the three trumpeters on the tower which fell down in Brandenburg. They get up at three in the morning and signal the day from the tower with the glorious song of prayer
>
> > Wenn wir in höchsten Nothen seyn/
> > Und wissen nicht wo aus noch ein/
> > Und finden weder Hülf noch Rath/ etc.
>
> After they have thus fervently called upon God the Lord to stand by them in deepest need, they lie down again to rest. At 4 o'clock the tower falls down, the players fall down with it, none of them breaks a bone, and they don't know how they got down.[116]

Frick summarizes the lesson to be learned from such incidents as follows: "And so God lets himself be moved by Christian psalms of prayer to protect his own with the host of heavenly angels."[117] This conviction of the protective power of petitionary prayer again displays a kind of piety which had escaped Luther's influence. Acts of devotion become a kind of meritorious work which will gain an instantaneous response. This applied also to acts of blasphemy, which might elicit a strike of lightning. Music is so sacred that to abuse it is tantamount to taking the name of God in vain. "It is an abuse of music, indeed of God's name, when drunkards who have already gotten themselves soused want to talk and sing of God and his Word."[118] Whereas this passage refers to the blasphemous singing of hymns, the singing of bawdy secular songs may bring an immediate act of revenge from God:

> When that crowd of women sang shameless songs and obscene burlesques on the firewagon, God was moved to great anger thereby and gave the devil the reins to overturn the wagon during such brazen singing. The result was that five persons were completely crushed and most of the others broke arms and legs.[119]

Frick's anecdotes are not typical of the Lutheran writings on music, though some of them do reappear in a massive theological tome in Latin by Josua Stegmann.[120] We cannot therefore explain them away entirely as popular folklore. Whether he would acknowledge all the implications I have drawn is doubtful, but his stress on the devotional state of the musician was no mistake. A new circle of devotional writers was emerging for whom the main criterion for religious music was that it express the pious affections of the soul. While all orthodox Lutherans endorsed the position that the heart and voice should be synchronized, the new internalization of music left behind the external means of grace. The heart, not music, was now the instrument of the Spirit.

CHAPTER THREE

BETWEEN SACRED AND SECULAR

It is evident from preceding chapters not only that the Lutheran view of music was quite different from the Calvinist view, but that the Lutheran theological position on music was developed in explicit opposition to Calvinism. Interestingly, this attempt at dissociation from Calvinism remains alive among Lutheran thinkers of our own day. One of the results has been the propagation of the argument that because Luther placed music so close to theology there is no such thing as secular music for him. As Söhngen asserted, "For Luther all music is 'spiritual,' i.e. theologically relevant. There is for him no secular music in the strict sense, only degenerate music."[121] Where warnings are voiced by Lutherans against **levitas** and **lascivia**, Söhngen finds them strangely un-Lutheran, exhibiting connections with Calvin's views.[122] Most musicologists have even ignored the existence of such warnings or else attributed them only to Pietists, who are then explained away as not truly Lutheran.[123] The result, from a musical standpoint, has been an overly idealized picture of Lutheranism's openness to different musical styles. From a theological standpoint, the explanation for Lutheranism's stylistic openness as rooted in a positive view of creation draws on only one aspect of Luther's paradoxical perspective on the world.

As we saw in the previous chapter, Luther does not maintain either a dualistic or a hierarchical approach to the material world. His division between the carnal and the spiritual cuts across the body/spirit divisions of philosophical traditions in such a way as to affirm God's presence in both the natural and the supernatural realms. But to redraw the lines of division is not to abolish all distinctions: Luther was neither a theocrat nor a monist.

Although he spent most of his energy writing about concerns of the kingdom of God, Luther recognized the existence and the legitimacy of the earthly kingdom. Just as the human body was not in itself a threat to the soul, neither is human society in itself in conflict with God's kingdom. To live honorably and peaceably with one's neighbors is a good thing and in accord with God's will; yet it is a civil or secular activity with no merit toward eternal salvation. The fact that

God ordained human governments for the purpose of maintaining order and stability does not make those governments any less human or any more a part of the heavenly kingdom. Similarly, music used to enhance human activity within the civil order is no less secular just because it is one of the good gifts of creation.

Most of Luther's examples of secular music relate to dancing, particularly at weddings. In a sermon on Genesis 24, Luther acknowledges the marital customs of ancient Hebrews as an unobjectionable part of the worldly regime. One lesson of the story of Abraham sending camels and other choice gifts in exchange for a wife for his son is that "a faithful Christian may also leave the world its rights."[124] It is not required to give such wealth to the poor, nor is it sinful if a bride wears a costly dress for her wedding: "God lets it happen in order to honor the wedding, that she may thus be praised. Therefore one must leave the world its rights, except for excess."[125] Similarly, the dancing which is customary at weddings is a quite acceptable activity in itself, but it is nevertheless a "worldly" or secular custom: "Therefore because dancing is also the custom of the world and of the young people who enter into marriage, it is not to be condemned as long as it occurs only for joy, decently, without shameful ways, words or gestures."[126] In his *Table Talk*, Luther's quoted words are even more positive toward dancing and singing, but this is not to be confused with a sacred activity: "When the young single men and women dance rounds with one another and it proceeds with honorable singing and demeanor, it is a function of humanity which I like very much."[127]

In another item from *Table Talk*, Luther is reported as asking "why in carnal matters we have so many fine poems and so many pretty songs and in spiritual matters we have such tired cold things."[128] In the ensuing elaboration Luther places blame on the corrupting wealth of the medieval church that engendered apathy concerning new sacred songs. In regard to the question of sacred and secular music, we can conclude from this that Luther enjoyed secular songs and perhaps wished that the style of sacred songs would come closer to that of secular songs, but there remained a clear distinction between the two, and his concern was for sacred, not secular, songs.

Whereas in the above passage "carnal" seems to equal "secular" and to be morally neutral, Luther elsewhere appears to place "worldly" songs in opposition to spiritual as unfitting for a person of faith. In his 1524 preface to the Wittenberg hymnbook, Luther expresses his hope that the availability of new hymns will cause the youth to abandon "love ballads and carnal songs" ("Buellieder und fleischliche Gesenge") in favor of something wholesome (*LW* 35, 316). In a 1525 commentary on Colossians 3:12, he states even more explicitly that Paul's instruction to sing "spiritual songs" is meant to prohibit the use of "worldly, carnal and coarse songs."[129]

From the context it appears that he is thinking primarily of the text here; there is not sufficient evidence to determine whether Luther wanted to distinguish sacred from secular styles of music. We do know that he wanted church music to proceed "from free desire and love," not to be dull or awkward but to be "charming, sweet melodies that everyone likes to hear" (*WA* 17/2, 121). Elsewhere *simplicitas* is introduced as a prime quality of the music which is most pleasing (*WA TR* 4, no. 4316). He criticizes composer Lucas Edenberger for using too many fugues and neglecting "pleasantness" ("suavitas"). We also know how highly he esteemed some of the foremost composers of his day, primarily Josquin des Pres, but also Pierre de la Rue, Fink and Ludwig Senfl (*WA TR* 3, no. 3516). The music of many existing Latin hymns is also beautiful, he notes, though the texts are often unacceptable (*WA* 35, 480).

One must be cautious in drawing generalizations from Luther's scattered comments about musical style and secular music. Certainly he appreciated more than one style and did not rigidly exclude any genre or style. But his instructions grew out of practical liturgical concerns and a sensitivity to the manner in which melody and text work together. Any attempt to make connections between views on musical style and worldview must keep in mind the ad hoc nature of Luther's remarks. Those who search for a principle in Luther's borrowings from folk tunes may find the wrong principle. The only theological principle which Luther mentioned in conjunction with compositional style was that of freedom from the law.[130] That later centuries would obscure the common sense distinction between sacred and secular music by overloading it with theological baggage surely did not occur to him.

The same caution which should be applied in moving between Luther's theology and his practical liturgical reform should also be maintained when commenting about 17th-century Lutheran theology on the basis of actual musical practice. When Günther Stiller writes that the new Italian style "was in no way understood to be a phenomenon of secularization in the areas of Germany that were under the control of Lutheranism,"[131] whatever evidence he has apparently comes from musicians and musical theorists, not from preachers and theologians. As a result, he associates Pietist criticism of church music with Calvin's insistence on separating sacred from secular styles, thus depicting Pietists as importing alien elements into Lutheranism. What Stiller and many others have failed to see is that Lutheran preachers had never stopped trying to rid the church of secular music. This was not the issue that separated Calvinists from Lutherans.

When Jacob Andreae defended organs against Theodore Beza at Montbéliard, he admitted Beza's charge that "worldly, unchaste songs" are sometimes played on them. As an abuse of a good thing, however, that was not the fault of the organ but of the organist. Where the Reformed Beza thought it better to avoid an occasion for abuse, the Lutheran Andreae, seeing that any good thing could be abused, chose to deal with the abuser: "Therefore, when organists want to play shameful worldly pieces on the organ, one should forbid them to do this and admonish them earnestly not to do it again but to work diligently that the temple no longer be defiled."[132]

The church ordinances of the time show an ongoing attempt to regulate the repertoire and behavior of church organists. As early as 1542, organists in the territories of Hans Ernst von Schönburg were being instructed not to play "lewd and frivolous tunes but instead refined psalms and German Christian hymns."[133] By 1585 the prohibitions include not only "worldly songs" but also "fantasies" and "improvisations."[134] An indication that pastors sometimes found organists insubordinate is the instruction which follows, that "where the pastor would raise objections and forbid [the organist] to do something, the latter should obey him without grumbling and growling."

The defense of organ music in Lutheran churches depended, in part, on the enforcement of such admonitions to play only "Christian spiritual songs." When the Anhalt Calvinists attacked organ music both because it could not be understood and because a "wanton, frivolous, overly carnal dance or passamezzo" substituted for a spiritual psalm, the Wittenbergers responded both that the sacred genre could be distinguished from the worldly and that there were those whose duty it was to assure that no dance or passamezzo would be played in the service.[135] Such enforcement was apparently never fully successful, however, for subsequent writers reverted to the argument that misuse of a good thing does not constitute grounds for rejecting it. Conrad Dieterich dismissed as invalid the argument that organs should be excluded from churches because of the abuse of playing "frivolous dances, passamezzos, courantes and love ballads which belong not in church but in a tavern." If every component of worship which had been abused were to be removed, he responded, almost nothing would remain.[136]

That the secularization of church music by organists was a concern to Lutheran pastors quite apart from Calvinist attacks is evident from Dieterich's return to the topic at the end of his sermon. Not only do organists and other instrumentalists "profane and desecrate worship" when they play "courantes, passamezzos, dances and other unsuitable melodies"; their behavior in the organ loft is also scandalous. Those who do not like to attend worship and listen to sermons "carry on all sorts of frivolous conversation, shameful talk and dissolute activities at the organ and thereby desecrate the holy place....and also make a disgrace and den of thieves out of it."[137]

In a surprising conclusion to a sermon otherwise so strong in its defense of organ music, Dieterich spends most of his final two pages urging greater restraints on church music. Appealing to Aristotle, Plato, and Cicero, he notes the importance of regulating the music which youth or citizens hear in order to avoid moral corruption. New musical styles are particularly suspect, as shown in the example of the Spartan Timotheus Milesius, who was ordered by decree to cut off the new strings which made his cithara-playing too complex and to return to the customary, more serious manner of playing. This might well serve as an example, Dieterich believes, for those who have authority over a too experimental organist:

> Such a Spartan decree needs to be published and sent to many organists on account of their frivolous playing, so that when they are inclined to create a melodic mish-mash they might remain with the old customary, serious church pieces and not make an entertainment organ out of a church organ.[138]

Warnings against abuse of singing are no less frequent than those against abuse of organ playing, but cantors are seldom singled out for blame either for their music or their behavior. One can only speculate on whether this reflects a difference between organists and cantors in religious attitude, educational level, or musical predilections.[139] Nevertheless, whether the advice is meant for cantors, choir members or ordinary churchgoers, the problem of singing without devotion is raised by virtually every writer we have met. Although the problem is not solved solely by placing limits on acceptable styles of music, these writers were certain that some kinds of music were incompatible with a devout life.

Seldom in the theological writings of the early 17th century do we find clear references to contemporary choral styles. One exception is Wolfgang Silber's criticism of certain imported practices: "Nowadays the abuse in such figural music is fairly widespread in the churches, namely that everything has to proceed in Italian and French manner with hopping and jumping."[140] Such abuses have led some churches to get rid of figural singing, but Silber sees it as a mistake to "throw out the baby with the bath." A somewhat later work by Moevius Volschov, a church official in Western Pomerania, while rejecting Calvinist arguments regarding church music, also finds fault with changes taking place in Lutheran churches. Without regard for the old value of simplicity and for the "old devotional hymns and motets," cantors in many places have sought out "new passamezzos and Italians villanellas and concertos," even when that meant pushing aside the unexcelled works of Orlando.[141] Volschov's solution is to have cantors and "Praefecti Musici" submit to their superiors, who would assemble a list of devotional motets suited to the various days of the church year; through annual repetition of this unvarying repertoire, the congregation might be better able to appreciate the singing and thus join in the praise of God.[142]

Suggestions for practical change in choral music are absent from most of the writings prior to the middle of the seventeenth century. In contrast to the criticisms of organists, there is no sense that the criticisms of worldly vocal music are directed at contemporary practices in Lutheran churches. Arguments for a distinction between sacred and secular styles are derived primarily from patristic and medieval sources. As with other elements of the Lutheran theological defense of music, the use of a common source tradition results in a fairly standardized Orthodox position, varying more in the arrangement of material than in theoretical perspective.

The most frequently introduced source emphasizing the indispensablity of devotion in conjunction with music is the verse from Gratian's *Decretum* which is included in a gloss on Jerome's Ephesians commentary:

Non vox sed votum, non chordula Musica, sed cor,
Non clamans, sed amans cantat in aure Dei.[143]

(Not the voice but the prayer;
not the musical string but the heart;
not the one who shouts but the one who loves,
sings in the ear of God.)

This verse is sometimes used in the context of criticizing a godless use of music in social gatherings. David Lobechius cites Isaiah 5:12 on drunken merry-making involving musical instruments and then proceeds to describe acceptable music before introducing the above verse: "Frivolity and wantonness ought to be absent from sacred music, and a serious, modest, virile melody and the devoted attentiveness of the mind ought to be present."[144] Matthias Hoe, citing more positive scriptural examples, namely those of David playing for Saul and the minstrel playing for Elisha, puts music-making in a more favorable light; yet he makes the same demand that "devout minds" accompany the sound of organ, lyre or any other instrument. This requirement having been met, however, one should have no qualms of conscience about using musical instruments "whether in churches, in private homes, or at honorable social gatherings, at the proper time and in the proper manner."[145] In these two examples we see inseparability for these thinkers of the inward frame of mind and the outward style of music: a serious and devout person cannot play frivolous or lascivious music. Nowhere in the texts under consideration here is there any recognition either of a morally neutral realm of human activity or of an uncorrupted secular arena.

Other writers use the Gratian versicle in the context of advising on appropriate vocal music for use in church. Fridericus Balduinus, in his commentary on Colossians, insisted not only on a textual but also a musical differentiation between spiritual and non-spiritual songs: "Moderation should be so employed that the songs are undoubtedly spiritual, both in respect to the subject matter and in respect to the form or melody."[146] The criterion he presents for such a differentiation is that there should be no "levitas" in sacred worship. Similarly, Balthasar Meisner requires that all "levitas" and "lascivia" be banished from choral music and replaced by "gravitas" and the devout attention of the mind. Choices of appropriate musical pieces will also be affected by the social composition of the congregation; where there is usually a mixture of people, many of whom do not understand complex music, the use of simple melodies should prevail. Otherwise the lack of understanding will prevent the devotion which should accompany the singing.[147]

During the early decades of the century no other citation appears as consistently as does the versicle from Gratian, but Chrysostom and Jerome are mentioned with some frequency as admonishing against abuse of music. Bernard's authority is advanced for the instruction that devotional music should be "gravitätisch," and the Fourth Council of Carthage is sometimes listed among the sources stressing that mind and mouth must move together when singing.[148] Among biblical references, Ephesians 5:19 and Colossians 3:16 are standard, but Amos 5:23 ("Take away from me the noise of your songs") also appears with some frequency, as does I Corinthians 14:26 ("Let all things be done for edification").

If we compare the Lutheran argumentation on this issue with that of Calvinists, we find no significant difference in the sources cited; however, without minimizing the earnestness of the Lutheran commentaries, it can be admitted that Calvinists cite more thoroughly and place greater weight on this strand of the tradition.[149] It is even possible that the Lutherans benefited from Calvinist scholarship on this point and borrowed their references. If this is the case, it is not, as Söhngen implies,[150] because the Lutherans were inclined to endorse Calvin's exclusion of organ and polyphonic music. Rather, it was because the communicative power of such music depended on its identification as a sacred genre. By taking a stand against secular music and devotionless singing, Lutherans could show that the Calvinist charges of the worldliness of organ and choral music did not apply to them. As Philipp Arnoldi wrote, "From this it is obvious that the childish Calvinist proof why organs and choral music are to be eliminated from the church does not apply to us, for we do not permit such love ballads and carnal songs to be sung or played. Rather we forbid them in homes and even more so in churches."[151]

In this point Arnoldi sees himself fully in accord with Luther, citing the hymnbook preface where Luther hopes the youth will change their singing habits. Indeed it is likely that much of the treatment of this point among Lutherans of this period was an adaptation of arguments of the early Reformation. When Arnoldi and others of his period speak out against "love ballads and carnal songs," it seems they are repeating earlier charges rather than expressing dismay at contemporary abuses. In 1571 Nicolaus Selneccer had explained more clearly than those who came after him just what the basis of this criticism was. Under the papacy, Selneccer wrote, "wicked idolatrous texts had been set under the notes, or familiar worldly tenor songs and love ballads were played in the churches."[152]

With the church music reforms of the council of Trent the Catholic Church had expressed its opposition to these late medieval practices and had attempted to purge church music of secular elements. Neither these abuses nor the threat of Catholicism were uppermost in the minds of North German Lutherans. The threat of Calvinism, however, made it essential that Calvinists not be able to demonstrate the existence of the same sort of secular practices within Lutheranism. Consequently, a century after Luther, it was not his appreciation of the secular world and innocent dancing which was most remembered but rather those comments which placed music of the world in opposition to music of the Spirit.

CHAPTER FOUR

FROM TENSION TO HARMONY**

The elements of the Lutheran theology of music discussed in the preceding chapters were shaped, as has been emphasized, in a confessional context dominated by Lutheran and Calvinist rivalries. Those who were most influential in formulating the Lutheran position were academic theologians. Alongside the academic treatments of music, however, there emerged around the turn of the seventeenth century a totally different approach to music: the writers of devotional literature began to regard music as a means of expressing universal harmony—not confessional divisions. Certain elements of this new approach were in keeping with Luther's view of music: as part of God's gift of creation, music is seen as an instrument by which God communicates to his creatures. Yet the Lutherans who gave expression to the new devotion of the new century[153] went a step further: not only was music divinely ordained, but the cosmos as a whole was musically, or harmonically, ordained. Harmony, in other words, became the fundamental element of the cosmos. To pursue harmony in one's voice and soul was to prepare oneself for heavenly existence.

    Whatever differences we may encounter among the thinkers with which this chapter is concerned, they share a form of devotion which expresses the union of God and the individual soul through the imagery associated with heaven. Although they admit that the full experience of heavenly existence must await death, they tend to locate heaven within the soul and thereby to make it present in a mystical way within the present life. Because the traditional conception of the activity of saints and angels is that they sing praise to God unceasingly, music is regarded either literally or metaphorically as indispensable in the preparation of the soul for heaven.

    The first spokesman for this new form of Lutheran spirituality was Philipp Nicolai, whose *Frewdenspiegel des ewigen Lebens* (1599) contained in an

---

    **The material in this chapter first appeared under the title "Celestial Harmony in Baroque Lutheran Writings" in *Lutheran Quarterly* III/2 (Autumn, 1989), pp. 281-297.

appendix the hymns for which he is best known: "Wie schön leuchtet der Morgenstern" and "Wachet auf ruft uns die Stimme." Their popularity—both immediate and long-lasting—attests to the vividness with which Nicolai here evoked the sense of joy to be experienced in the presence of the angelic choirs. Both hymns combine the bridal imagery favored by mystics with the musical imagery of harps and angelic choirs:

> Zwingt die Sayten in Cythara
> Und laßt die süsse Musica
>   Gantz frewdenreich erschallen:
> Daß ich möge mit Jesulein/
> Dem wunderschönen Bräutgam mein/
>   In stäter Liebe wallen.
> Singet/ springet/
> Jubilieret/ triumphieret/
> Danckt dem Herren
> Groß ist der König der Ehren.
>   (Strophe VI of "Wie schön leuchtet der Morgenstern")[154]

> Gloria sey dir gesungen/
> Mit Menschen und Englischen Zungen/
>   Mit Harpffen und mit Cymbaln schön:
> Von zwölff Perlen sind die Pforten
> An deiner Statt/ wir sind Consorten
>   Der Engeln hoch umb deinen Thron/
> Kein Aug hat je gespürt/
> Kein Ohr hat mehr gehört/
>   Solche Frewde
> Deß sind wir fro/ jo/ jo
> Ewig in dulci iubilo.
>   (Strophe III of "Wachet auf ruft uns die Stimme")[155]

Elsewhere in the book Nicolai depicts God as the supreme musician, appealing to the elect through the beauty of his voice:

> God also saturates and fills the ears of his elect, and his voice is the loveliest and sweetest that they hear. For they hear joy and delight as the Lord himself speaks and preaches peace to his people and his saints. And this his lovely voice is the loveliest music of all. No harps, no drums, no trumpets, pipes, lutes, zithers, strings, cymbals or other such pleasant-sounding instruments can delight human ears so marvelously and comfortingly as the most friendly voice of God

speaking like an eternal father, like a heavenly groom, and like a true comforter of souls.[156]

Such an emphasis on heavenly music had disappeared with the Middle Ages. In fact Reinhold Hammerstein locates the end of the Middle Ages at the point where sacred and secular music, heavenly and earthly liturgy are consciously separated.[157] The approach of the next era is represented by the council of Trent, where secular music is excluded from the church and church music is given clear definition. Hammerstein might also have used as evidence Calvin's suggestion that audible music would be overcome in heaven just as the instrumental music of the temple was overcome by the vocal music of the early church.

Among Lutherans, however, the lines were less clearly drawn. Neither instrumental music nor secular melodies had been systematically excluded, and heavenly music was occasionally used as a model for earthly. In 1538 Johann Walther, for instance, had ended his poem "Lob und Preis der löblichen Kunst Musica" with a preview of the music which awaits the elect:

Die Music mit Gott ewig bleibt
Die andern künst sie all vertreibt/
Im Himel nach dem Jüngsten tag/
Wird sie erst gehn jnn rechter wag/
Itzt hat man hülsen nür darvon
Dort wird der kern recht auffgethan
Do werdens all Cantores sein
Gebrauchen dieser kunst allein
. . . .
Solchs singen ewig nicht vorgeht
    Wie jnn Apocalipsi steht
Gott helff uns allen auch dorin
    Das wir bey Gott jnn einem sin/
Und allen auserwehlten gleich
    Singen mit freud jnn Gottes reich
Lob/ ehr/ weisheit/ und grosser danck
    Preis/ und krafft sey von anfangk
Immer und ewiglich gethan
    Drumb last uns auch nu heben an
Und Gott den herrn mit grossem schall
    Und seinen namen loben all
Amen Amen das warheit sey
    Dorzu uns Gott sein gnad verley.[158]

A different twist is given to the theme in 1540 by Georg Frölich, town clerk in Augsburg, who in a similar praise of music introduced the Platonic view of reminiscence as an explanation for Christian appreciation of music. Having heard the glorious harmonies of the heavenly host before descending to earth, the soul which reattains a certain level of virtue and contemplative reason is again capable of perceiving these harmonies, which may be revealed in visions. Such inspiration may then bring joy even to those who are not capable of receiving the visions directly. This joy, though not fully understood, is a remnant or deposit which God leaves with us in this earthly life:

> Thus I take the true, natural origin of ordered singing and find that it is no less than a loan and renewed deposit of the melody and harmony of heaven—also of the firmament—which some skilled people here on earth know how to copy and express.[159]

In spite of similarities with these mid-sixteenth-century examples, Nicolai's approach is strikingly different. Unlike Walther, Nicolai does not view the heavenly music as awaiting those who survive the final day of judgment. Walther's concept of universal history, exemplified by his tracing the history of music from creation to the Day of Judgment, is not shared by Nicolai, who is writing not about the ultimate future of mankind but about the individual soul, which, he believes, enters a non-spatial heaven immediately upon the death of the body. Nor is Nicolai interested, as is Frölich, in explaining how some individuals are capable of composing sublimely beautiful music. His attention is not on the joys of this life, but on suffering, death, and eternal life. His book resulted from the awareness of the transience of life implanted on his mind through the 1597 plague, which claimed nearly half the residents of his town, Unna.

Nicolai's reflections on eternal life, however, captured the spirit of the age. There followed other writers such as Valerius Herberger, Johann Arndt, Johann Valentin Andreae, and Johann Mattheus Meyfart, who shared both the sense of the vanity of this life and a vivid imagination for the delights of the next. The characteristics noted in Nicolai are in fact traits of the Baroque age in general, whether manifested in literature or music, art or religion. Just as Nicolai described God as an object of sight, hearing, taste, smell, and touch, so the Baroque mentality was drawn to sensuality and illusion as well as to otherworldly spirituality.[160] The Baroque age reintegrates the two realms of heaven and earth which had been separated at the end of the Middle Ages. Referring to the transition from Mannerist to Baroque art, Harold B. Segel writes, "The usually clear, sharp division in mannerism between the spheres of earth and spirit faded before the Baroque vision of the indivisibility of man's world and God's."[161] What was peculiarly Baroque about this reintegration, however, was the sensuality of the spiritual expression. The term "Baroque" applied to architecture is likely to evoke thoughts of spacious ceilings decorated with fleshy cherubs pointing up to heavenly scenes in a cloud-dotted sky made to appear real by means of illusion. Naturalism in Baroque art, according to John Rupert Martin, "is inextricably bound up with a metaphysical view of the world....But that transcendent world can in turn only be apprehended through the faithful rendering of things seen."[162]

Although the Baroque is often associated with Catholic territories, it is more useful as a way of identifying a mode of thinking found among adherents of both Protestantism and Catholicism. As Irmgard Otto discovered in her study of seventeenth-century views of music, "It was not the dogmatic opposition between Catholicism and Protestantism which brought views of music to collision but rather the contrasts of life style within one and the same religious community."[163] Although not all musicologists agree that Baroque music should be studied from the perspective of a world view,[164] there is considerable evidence that world view and music theory were intrinsically related. Hermann Zenck identified three major components of a Baroque view of music: the use of instrumental as well as vocal music to communicate the Word and to praise God, the rhetorically based doctrine of affections, and, most importantly, the quadrivial approach to music as related to the mathematical order of the universe.[165] Rolf Dammann sees in this concept of music a key to the Baroque conception of reality:

> The thought matter extending through this [doctrine of music] still has a universalistic format....The human being as an actor on the world stage sees the heavens opened up in front of him....The role which a human plays on the great stage of this world reaps approval or awakens disapproval in the heavenly auditorium.[166]

For the devotional writers who exhibit this Baroque mentality, to place human life in cosmic perspective was to demonstrate the basis for hope beyond the crises of plague and war. The Thirty Years' War provided the impetus for the series of meditations on the heavenly Jerusalem published by Johann Matthaeus Meyfart in 1627. Quoting an unnamed church father in his preface, he expresses the hope that such meditations will prove comforting to those affected by the war: "One who in devotion looks toward the glory of eternity easily endures the misery of temporality."[167] Drawing on Nicolai's book, Meyfart proceeds in similar manner but with greater detail to imagine the sights and sounds of the heavenly city. Demonstrating the interest in rhetoric which would lead to his *Teutsche Rhetorica Oder Redekunst* (1634), he states in the introduction to *Das Himlische Jerusalem* his intention to use rhetorical devices to explain his points more clearly to the reader: "For the one who knows how to praise God seeks through rhetorical charm to win for himself a portion thereof; insofar as he can, he places himself in the city of God."[168] This point is reinforced in the text by qualifying his appeals to the imagination with such phrases as "to speak humanly" or "in an earthly manner." By such means he seeks to ward off a literal acceptance of the details of heavenly existence. One such detail is that in the heavenly choir boys and girls will sing soprano, youths and women alto, with men on tenor and the elderly on bass, all joining in a "Holy, holy, holy" which will far overpower the sound of the "golden bells" of Aaron as he entered the holy of holies (Sirach, ch. 45).[169] The powers of imagination are evoked even more effectively when Meyfart asks the reader to hear the reverberations and echoes of this powerful music:

> If in the heavenly Jerusalem palaces were built in earthly manner, how would this resound in the chambers? If there were mountains, how would it echo in the valleys? If there were cities, how glorious would it sound in the lanes? Chiefly because the new song is continually begun and will nevermore be sung to the end.[170]

With such care taken to distinguish between a literal and a metaphorical picture of heaven, neither Nicolai nor Meyfart intend any commentaries on the music actually sung in churches. Nor do they claim any metaphysical reality uniting the music of earth to that of the world beyond. Nicolai's own hymns are surely strong support for the practice of music, but the point is to draw the reader to meditation rather than to improve the quality of church music. Meyfart and Nicolai thus occupy an ambiguous position among those who incline toward the image of heavenly music.

On the one side are those who take the image literally and conclude that the best preparation for heaven is to learn music while on earth. Such is the advice of Valentinus Trotzendorff as quoted by Valerius Herberger and later by Frick:

> When Mr. Valentin Trotzendorf, schoolmaster in Goldberg, wanted to exhort the young students to music, he said, "Learn to sing, dear sons, learn to sing, so that when you get to heaven the holy angels will let you come into their choir."[171]

Contrasted with this is the conclusion of Johann Arndt that, while the best preparation for heaven is indeed to imitate the angels, the important aspect of their activity is the praise of God, not the singing itself.

> No one will become like the angels on that day unless he becomes like the angels in this world. There is no better way for this to happen than through daily devout praise of God, for that is the office of the angels.[172]

Using many of the references other theologians had used in support of instrumental and vocal music in church, Arndt focusses entirely on the internal devotion expressed by the heart. In his discussion of creation Arndt asserted that the regenerate have nothing to do with the "natural" or astronomical heaven, but only with that higher heaven of God and his angels.[173] Similarly, he argues in his treatment of the praise of God that musical instruments are a piece of outward ceremony which belong to the past. The trumpets, psalteries, harps and cymbals of the Old Testament are to be understood as "our heart, spirit, soul, mind, and mouth."[174] This is not to say that Arndt objects to the use of instruments or song in church or at home. "No, rather it is St. Paul's opinion that everything should proceed devoutly, spiritually and from the depth of the heart, not that it should be only an outward noise or show."[175]

Indeed, while Arndt's *Vier Bücher Vom Wahren Christenthumb* give no evidence of strong musical inclinations, Arndt did endorse church music in a letter which connects the three types of writers mentioned thus far. Used by Frick as a preface to his *Musica Christiana*, the letter both praises Frick's discussion of music and suggests that he make mention of the hymns of "the most illustrious theologian Philipp Nicolai." Arndt would have been pleased to know that in Frick's second edition (published ten years after Arndt's death), Nicolai's "Wie schön leuchtet der Morgenstern" is cited. As for his own musical background, Arndt was reminded of his childhood, when after encountering the dry, sterile singing of the daily offices, he was powerfully affected by the singing of Psalms 51 and 103 in German tongue. "From this the opinion has always stayed with me that there is a peculiar force in hymns and in the singing of praise to God."[176]

Aside from recognizing the power of music, Arndt does not follow Frick in placing music at the foundations of the cosmos. Significantly, the building blocks which Frick needed for his structure are present in Arndt. When observing the natural world Arndt is fully convinced of the effects of the stars and the heavenly bodies on human beings. Just as human beings are made in the image of God, so the whole firmament is within. There is "a very mysterious and great consonance" between the microcosmic firmament and the macrocosmic.[177] In spite of the use of a musical term, however, Arndt does not pursue the metaphor.

Frick, on the other hand, also emphasizing the image of God in man, offers additional musical metaphors:

> Indeed when a human considers himself, he recognizes a glorious organ with its beautiful concord of all members....For humans were originally **in templo Dei**, like a glorious organ, well tuned according to the likeness of God so that a lovely concord was heard between the trio of the Holy Trinity and the duets of our first parents.[178]

The musical correspondence of microcosm to macrocosm is more than metaphor for Frick and Herberger, however. The triad is no more a human construct than is the Trinity, at least to the ear of Herberger, whom Frick quotes in this regard: "Music is God's gift. I am often amazed that in the whole keyboard no more than three keys harmonize together. The rest are simply octaves. Is that not a manifest mystery of the highly praised Trinity?"[179] Elsewhere Herberger marvels at the natural sense of consonance implanted in the human ear: "Is it not amazing that, when something is out of harmony in a song, one feels it in the ear at the same time?"[180]

As the obverse to Arndt's point that the significant parts of the human person are symbolized by musical instruments, both Frick and Herberger emphasize the potential of the human voice for praising God. Teleologically, it seems, the voice was created as a means of joining man to God, a purpose which is thwarted when the musical capabilities of the voice are not developed. In this passage by Frick, the human vocal anatomy is compared to one of the common reed instruments of the day.

> It is certainly a special work of art in human beings that they are so created that they can not only speak but also sing....Now it is an art work above all other art works that a person can take a song from all keys through his inverted shawm and can pitch it in the subtlest of semitones and execute it correctly.... How then can it fail greatly to please the master craftsman when everything is directed to his honor?[181]

Frick combines the Arndtian theme of the dwelling of God in the heart with the Herbergerian view of the human body as an instrument for praise:

> For the heart of a person should be God's dwelling; placed by God not far from the heart are the lungs, arteries, windpipe, mouth and tongue which make the voice and song. Thus when a person considers himself, he remembers that he should use all the members around his heart so that God, who wants to dwell in the temple of our heart, will be praised and addressed in song out of true thankfulness.[182]

Because of this integral connection of the external music sung through the human instrument and the internal harmony of the soul to God, those who misuse or fail to use their bodies as instruments of praise to God demonstrate that their souls are also out of harmony with God. The sublime harmonies of heaven are sinfully disgraced by unworthy music: "Therefore it is truly a sin and disgrace when one soils such holy heavenly harmony with frivolous obscene songs."[183] To be unwilling to sing in church, on the other hand, is external evidence that the heart is not in tune with God:

> Whoever is not stimulated by this and does not at all like to sing in the congregation but rather stands or sits there like a log, as if his mouth had been frozen shut, has—even apart from psalm and hymn singing—no desire or love for God the Lord, however much he may

> present himself as godly. He is not such a good Christian as he makes out, for the saying is, "I believe, therefore I speak." And Christ's words, "When the heart is full, the mouth overflows," also cannot deceive us.[184]

Hence, just as those who pursue music prepare themselves for heaven, so those who scorn it or sing the devil's music prepare themselves for hell.

> How then would it be possible for those to attain to such heavenly music who in one way and another scorn Christian and God-pleasing music or who give preference and support to the tiresome devil's hellish music? Rather it is certain that such people will for eternity cry dolefully with the hellish wolves and all the damned in that place where there is nothing but howling and gnashing of teeth....[185]

The thought process which led Frick to such a conclusion is logical enough, but the result is rather startling. What has happened to justification by faith alone when the failure to appreciate music can disqualify a person from heaven? Is not a doctrine of works being perpetrated here? Frick would undoubtedly deny this and insist that he never separates internal devotion from external activity. Yet the very fact that the two are inseparable for Frick supports the interpretation that we encounter here a reintegrating world view closer to the sacramentalism of the Roman Catholic church than to the fideism of the Reformation.

Whence, then, does this world view enter Lutheranism? Although we cannot know precisely what sources Frick read, it is illuminating to look to musical theorists whose writings or ideas might have had some influence, direct or indirect, on such devotional writers as Frick. Most obvious are the similarities to the thought of the prominent Italian theorist Gioseffo Zarlino (1517–1590) and to the German music theorist and theologian, Joannes Lippius (1585–1612).

Zarlino, like Frick and Herberger, argues in the influential work *Istitutioni Harmoniche* (1558) that music is necessary for eternal life. In addition to its comforting properties, it leads to contemplation of celestial matters. Not only is heaven itself populated by nine choirs of angelic spirits, but heaven and earth are united through harmony. This extends to the human body, which is a microcosm of the greater universe, as demonstrated by Aristotle's exposition of the harmonic relation of the parts of the human soul. There is in fact no good thing which does not have a musical disposition. Drawing on the authority of a certain Catholic theologian, Zarlino agrees "that music is necessary for the Christian, inasmuch as in knowledge of it is found beatitude. Wherefore I dare to say that those who are not knowledgeable in this science have to be numbered among the ignorant."[186]

Among German theoreticians the celestial choirs receive less attention than the Trinity of the Godhead. According to Benito Rivera, the first author to make the connection between a three-note chord and the three persons of the Trinity was Rudolph Schlick in 1588. Schlick emphasizes the beneficent work of God in creating and conserving individual things (he refers to the "universal machine of the world") and sees this symbolized in the properties of the major and minor chords (it seems Schlick was also the first to use these terms):

> Indeed this so represents the works and might of the Holy Trinity, that it bears an affinity to them; and all men are moved to declare with unanimous consent that this combination originated from the same fountain source....If the combination of three notes in either type of cantus deviates from the legitimate way, is mutilated, or ruined, you will see the entire harmony arising from it immediately disturbed, vanish, and utterly fall apart, just as everything contained in the expanse of the whole world would perish and return to nothingness, if it were bereft of the power and awesomeness of the Holy Trinity.[187]

Similarly, another German theorist, Cyriacus Schneegass, wrote in 1591 of musical triads as symbols of divine perfection: "Thus any concord (as long as it is full), made up of any three voices but in various keys (for octaves have no place here), foreshadows sweetly the three persons of Divinity. Indeed the consonance of three voices...is judged perfect."[188]

The importance of harmony in holding creation together was further developed by Joannes Lippius in the preface to his *Synopsis Musicae Novae* of 1612. Here not only musical intervals and the Godhead are considered internally harmonious but also all elements of the physical cosmos.

> There is a most beautiful harmony in God the triune original source of all, in the choir of good spirits, in the physical macrocosm, in heaven, in the elements, in mixed meteors, metals, stones, plants, animals and in the human microcosm. All things remain standing through harmony. In disharmony all things fall. Nor is anything raised, refreshed or restored unless it is called back to harmony. Hence the disharmonious devil will always at first cast one into a fall. Man, deceived by this, can rise up again solely through the grace of God, by which peace and justice are renewed and the harmonious image of God, which was wantonly lost in the first creatures, is brought back.[189]

Lippius' theory of harmony is all-encompassing in a way that Frick's is not. Frick was not interested in the harmony of meteors, metals, and stones, nor did he proceed, as did Lippius, to look for harmony in arithmetic, astronomy, geography, optics, mechanics, medicine, and all the other fields of human knowledge. But he did regard harmony as the proper term for describing the image of God in human beings. The loss of that image in the Fall is then appropriately described as disharmony. The devil and disharmony go hand in hand, as do divine grace and harmony.

Whatever the immediate sources of such a writer as Frick, the world view in which the person is the image not only of God through the soul but also of the cosmos through the proportions of the various faculties had become prominent in Lutheran circles.[190] Lippius had lectured on the harmony of the universe at the universities of Wittenberg, Jena, Leipzig, and Erfurt. Not to be ignored in this regard is the work of Johannes Kepler, *Harmonice Mundi* (1619), which, however, goes beyond the ideas of those mentioned so far to ascribe musical parts to the planets. Kepler thus distinguished himself from our devotional circle both through his interest in the "music of the spheres" and in his tenuous relation to Lutheranism.[191]

Another work of the same year, on the other hand, issued more directly from the circle of which Arndt was the dominant figure. The utopian vision of Johann Valentin Andreae, *Reipublicae Christianopolitanae Descriptio*, dedicated to Arndt, offers a model for the reform of society which has been called a "prelude of eternal life."[192] It depicts an auditorium to which those are admitted who have studied arithmetic and geometry and who from this background are capable of singing three tones "modulated in such an unspeakable and unending way that they excel not only over animals through their speech but also over birds through singing."[193] The music produced here "emulates heaven where an eternal musical play can be heard." Excluded is that frivolous music of the devil which eventually leads those who enjoy it to the place where "midst the feeling of the stings of death and the pangs of conscience the doleful howl of lament will finally have to be let forth."[194]

Final mention must be made of the work of another member of this circle, Josua Stegmann, some of whose hymns are known through their inclusion in the *Evangelisches Kirchengesangbuch*.[195] At first appearance the lengthy discussion of music in this massive *Icon Christognosia* (2125 pages) gives promise of being a major contribution to the theology of music, but closer examination reveals it to be largely derived from Frick. Many of the same anecdotes are cited and much of the structure and content of Frick's argument for music is copied without direct citation.[196] But by using Luke 2:14 as his text, Stegmann has opportunity to exploit the imagery of angelic music to its fullest. Perhaps because this verse testifies to angelic music being brought to earth, the music of the angels is for Stegmann even more clearly than for his predecessors a standard by which to judge earthly music. His chapter begins and ends with rhapsodic praise of angelic music, pointing to the angels as the source of our earthly music: "But more divine is our music which has heaven for a homeland and angels for inventors. O celestial source! O sweetness to be kissed!"[197]

To credit the angels rather than God with the invention of music is another step toward a literal understanding of the musical activity in heaven. Although Stegmann ascribes to angelic music the three functions of glorification, congratulation, and exultation, music is not understood as a mere metaphor for these functions. Heavenly music is more beautiful than any to be heard here, but apparently there is sufficient similarity to make comparisons possible: "O truly angelic melody which no Josquin, no Orlandus, no Gallus, no Praetorius, no Marentius, no Maxentius ever composed. Indeed it is a short song but it has long reverberations. It is short in words but rich in truths...."[198]

The apparent conclusion to this chapter might be at this point that the circle of devotional writers which best represent the new mood of seventeenth-century spirituality lent strong support to the composition and performance of church music as it was entering its golden age in Germany. The favorable mention of leading composers, the original hymns of the writers themselves, and the exuberant treatment of the importance of music both now and in the next life surely are evidence of their encouragement of musical activity in the churches.

Yet we must not forget the ambiguity inherent in the use of analogies of heaven. Retracing our steps back to Arndt, we can see that his mystical approach could easily lead in another direction. Such was the case with Johann Gerhard in a work written the year of Frick's *Music-Büchlein*.[199] Having chosen the Songs of Songs as a text, Gerhard had plenty of opportunity to expound on the importance of song. Instead, for the fifth Sunday after Easter, called "Vocem Jucunditatis," he moved in the other direction, using music as an analogy to prayer. The resulting meditation on the musical nature of prayer is an advocacy of prayer, not of music. Clearly the inward movement of the soul takes precedence over outward signs thereof.

Such an observation should also put us on guard in reflecting on the "new spirituality" as a whole. However broad the vision of the individual in relation to the cosmos or the saints in heaven, the intermediate relation of the individual to the church on earth is underdeveloped. To be sure, all the writers with whom we have been concerned were active churchmen and even ministers to congregations; but they did not reflect at length on the resemblance of the church on earth to the church triumphant. Even at a glance there is a striking contrast to Zarlino, who uses ecclesiastical terminology in his analogies of earth to heaven: "And just as in the celestial church, which is called triumphant, so also in our earthly church, which is called militant, the Creator is praised and thanked with nothing other than music."[200]

The neglect of the church militant is perhaps understandable in an age when earthly life seemed more evanescent than usual. But when the war came to an end and life seemed more stable, the weaknesses in the church militant became more apparent. A concern for church reform is the element which unites theologians writing about music in the mid-seventeenth century. The main elements of the Lutheran theology of music had already been formulated; the task of the next generation was to maintain or recover the vitality of Reformation faith within the institutional church.

SYNTHESIS AND ANTITHESIS

CHAPTER FIVE

JOHANN CONRAD DANNHAUER

The critique of Calvinism, the awareness of the psychological effects of music, and the emphasis on harmony and on the imitation of angelic music all meet in Johann Conrad Dannhauer, outstanding Strasbourg theologian of the mid-seventeenth century. This convergence of approaches to music, however, is more than a compilation of his predecessors' ideas. Dannhauer molded the elements into a very different configuration, primarily through his concern for that which the writers of the previous chapter tended to downplay: the church as an earthly organization.

Dannhauer's historical position has been blurred by the closer attention paid his more famous pupil, Philipp Jakob Spener.[201] Further, the variety of topics and genres represented in his many works prevents a simplistic characterization of the man. Popular preacher as well as erudite theologian, poet as well as philosopher, Dannhauer is perhaps best understood not as either orthodox or pre-pietist but as a man who stands in the middle of the century and looks both directions.

On the one hand, Dannhauer was as much a polemicist as those anti-Calvinist Lutherans we met in the first chapter. In the treatment of church music in his *Hodomoria Spiritus Calviniani* (*Foolish Way of the Calvinist Spirit*), he repeats many of the points used earlier in the century while adding others. To identify the Calvinist position, Dannhauer cites Beza at the Colloquy of Montbéliard and two later sources which by mid-century were beginning to be commonplaces: David Pareus on I Corinthians 14 and André Rivet on Exodus 15. Taken together, the citations present the Reformed position that Old Testament cultic music was a concession to a people less mature spiritually than Christians should be. Organ music is far inferior to the voice, which sings sacred words with purity of heart. Dannhauer recognized that Beza had called organ music an adiaphoron and had said, "Where there are still organs, one may use them if he wishes." Yet on the basis of Pareus' statement that God had indulged the stiff-necked and stupid people of olden times with reeds, horns and drums,

Dannhauer concluded that the continued use of organs in some Reformed churches had a similar negative motivation. "Today indeed the same organs remain in some places more from tolerance, connivance, and complaisance than from inclination and approval."[202] Hence, according to Dannhauer, the meaning of adiaphora was being denied. The Reformed operated not through the spirit of Christian freedom but by the "spirit of domination and belly aching."[203]

Far from being limited to Old Testament times, claims Dannhauer, organ music arose in Paradise as a twin of philosophy and poetry. Further, it was commanded by God in Psalm 150 and commended by the Apostle Paul in the New Testament. According to a fairly standard interpretation of the time, psalms were instrumental solos, as contrasted with hymns, which were vocal solos, and canticles, which were songs with instrumental accompaniment. The very definition of the words of Colossians 3:16 demonstrated that instruments as well as voices were used in the early church.

The authority of the early church fathers, on the other hand, had sometimes been used in the argument against instruments in church. Justin Martyr was said to have rejected instruments because of their association with "fools" under the law. In an ironic twist, the Lutheran Dannhauer uses the Calvinist Rivet's textual scholarship to deny the authority of this statement. Rivet, among others[204], had concluded that the work from which the statement was drawn had been falsely attributed to Justin Martyr; it stemmed instead from another Justin or from someone who wished to benefit from Justin's authority. As evidence in support of musical instruments, Dannhauer adduced the information from Joseph Scaliger[205] that the Ethiopian church from ancient times to the present continued to use cymbals, citharas, and other instruments. The fact that organs ceased to be used in the Roman church is a result of barbarian times, but after a long silence organs even began to flourish again there.

The effect of music on the listener is more than sensual pleasure, Dannhauer argues in opposition to Beza. Here again Dannhauer uses the Reformed to refute themselves, quoting Calvin on the power of music to change lives. Part of the citation might appear to be evidence of appeal to the senses, for Calvin notes that trumpets stir horses as well as men to battle, but he then refers to Plato's endorsement of music for changing the conduct of a city. Dannhauer also provides a reference to Hugo Grotius' commentary on I Samuel, in which further references illustrate the ability of music to change behavior in a positive direction.[206]

In his *Catechismusmilch*, ten volumes of collected sermons published over several decades (1642–73), Dannhauer discusses the psychological and spiritual benefits of music at greater length. Much of this is familiar to us already from earlier theologians: music drives away melancholy and counteracts the devil; it awakens the spirit and sweetens the word of God (it is "the sugar with which the divine medicine is coated"); it gives us a foretaste of heavenly joy.[207] Luther's songs are full of the spirit and awaken in the heart joy and comfort which spite the evil spirit. In times of suffering and death they have strengthened and prepared the dying for their entrance into eternal life.[208]

To a greater extent than previous writers, however, Dannhauer emphasizes the pedagogical value of hymns. Not only does the combination of music and words imbed doctrine deeper into the mind, but hymns are instructive for those who can neither read nor write. Great care must be taken to assure that hymns are free from doctrinal error (a reason to sing Luther's hymns rather than Lobwasser's psalms[209]), for they are a weapon stronger than sermons. Quoting the Jesuit Adam Conzen, Dannhauer asserts that "Luther's hymns and Beza's songs have killed more people than their sermons" (VIII, 544).

In spite, then, of his defense of instrumental music against the Calvinists, Dannhauer offers a relatively weak endorsement of instrumental music without words. Elaborating on the instruction to "teach and admonish one another with psalms, hymns, and spiritual songs," he repeats a fairly standard claim that strings and flutes, though without understanding in themselves, "awaken the spirit, encourage devotion, divert the mind and emotions from worldly cares, make the heart calm and capable of receiving the divine **afflatus** and movement through the accompaniment of the Word" (VIII, 547). What is clear here is that the sound alone only prepares the mind; the word is that which brings the divine movement. The music which the church should strive to imitate— the music of the angels—is a music with a holy text, fit for the majesty of God (I, 524). Likewise, "David's music was no lewd meaningless and textless barbaric ear-tickling" (VIII, 553).

"Majesty" is now added to "gravity" as a characteristic of sacred music. Frequently in his various sermons on church music, Dannhauer begins an attack against the instrumental music of his day with an exclamation such as, "Away with the textless and meaningless ear titillation." This applies in particular to French galliards, "pargamosca," courantes and "other fantasies." Nor does he approve of the "new ridiculous Italian jumps and siren songs which aim not at the joy of the spiritual heart but at wanton worldly joy" (I, 524).

Furthermore, humility is a characteristic of angelic music which is not shared by all church musicians. Where earlier writers had insisted on the integral connection between sound and heart, Dannhauer implies that this connection has broken apart in his day. Denying the validity of the external act without internal devotion, he writes, "God takes no pleasure in the mere **opus operatum**" (I, 525). Many singers are now more interested in showing their skill than their devotion, Dannhauer charges: "Away with the supposed nightingales who like to hear themselves, who sing for themselves, countering each other more in ambition than in fugues, who cannot be exalted enough for their art. What they are doing is not singing 'Gloria in excelsis' but 'Gloria in infernis'" (I, 524). Those musicians who are unemployed because of these abuses are rightly experiencing the judgment of God. Significantly, what Dannhauer cites from Augustine's *Confessions* is not the passage where music provided the impetus for conversion but the admission of a punishable sin in having been moved more by the music than by the text (I, 525).

Several factors come to mind as possible explanations for Dannhauer's more critical approach to church music. Probably the most important is that church music style and practice had undergone striking changes between early and mid-century. Dannhauer seems to become more critical of church music practice as the century progresses. Significant also is that Dannhauer was minister in Strasbourg, where the influence of Martin Bucer's church discipline may still have been felt. Further, Dannhauer's familiarity with Reformed writings may have led him to incorporate some Reformed ideas at the same time as he resisted others. His call for purification of Sabbath observance may be evidence of Calvinist influence. Indeed, Johannes Wallmann and K. H. Möckel assert that Dannhauer was influenced by William Ames, Johann Heinrich Alsted, and André Rivet.[210]

In any case, whether or not there was direct Reformed influence, Rivet's statement on the primary necessity for church music bears an obvious affinity to Dannhauer's pedagogical concern. Five pages before the statement on organ music which Dannhauer criticized came another which he surely applauded: "Especially in public worship it is necessary to give thanks to God not only with the heart but also with the voice in order that the faithful be mutually edified and that some be aroused by the example of the others."[211] Present here is a focus on the interrelationships among members of the congregation such as had been absent most particularly in the mystical writings of the "new devotion" but also in the polemically-slanted treatises of academic theologians. Like Rivet, Dannhauer sees music as a means of mutual edification. Just as a vibrating string causes sympathetic vibration in neighboring strings, so members of the congregation elicit faith and devotion from others through their vocal expression.

> "Teach and exhort each other among yourselves." Let each be the preceptor and instructor of another, each awaken the other so that in sympathy one heartstring may move the other as happens in natural manner when a song is heard: as soon as the other hears it he sings along or at least wants to sing. In this manner the prophecy of Jer. 31:34 would come true among you: "And no longer shall each teach his neighbor and each his brother, saying, 'Know the Lord,' for they shall all know me, from the least to the greatest, says the Lord." (VIII, 547)

Such a call for participation of the whole congregation does not in Dannhauer's thinking lead to elimination of choirs or art music. Old Testament temple music demonstrates the value which is to be placed on skillful church music. The large numbers of temple musicians reported in I Chronicles 23:5 and 25:7, a combined total of 4288, with 288 said to be trained, indicates that good music does not come without expense: "If you want to have and hear good music, you must first let the sound of money be heard, spend liberally, and thus make good appointments to the choir" (I, 551).

Not the simplest singable melodies but the most heavenly harmonic blend of voices should be the ideal form of church music, for Dannhauer drew also upon the trend of seventeenth-century Lutherans to regard harmony and heavenly, angelic music as the prototype for earthly music. In his sermons on the Third Commandment ("You shall not take the name of the Lord in vain"), Dannhauer treats music as part of the necessity and obligation to praise God. Thus, music is not merely a pedagogical or psychological device leading to a more spiritual state or inward unity with God. Rather it is an imitation of the perfect praise offered to God unceasingly by the angels. As their praise is characterized by holiness, burning love, humility, sweetness, majesty, and grace, so earthly music should strive through all the artistic skills available to attain a similar richness and beauty.

> We wish for a lovely echo or reverberation on earth, so that just as the parrot learns to copy human speech we might be able to imitate the song of the angels in heaven. We want to let the above-mentioned music be our example and tabulatur to demonstrate how our music must be constituted and formed if it is to be pleasing to God. (I, 520)

In the manner of Nicolai, Dannhauer then labels God "the principal conductor."

The ability of three-part harmony to express the mystery of the Trinity is another theme Dannhauer shares with the Arndtian circle: "...the great mystery of the Holy Trinity is presented and modeled by nothing so beautifully and clearly as by a lovely three-part piece of music (I, 521). As with Frick and others, this concord is built into the mathematical proportions upon which music is based. The loveliest music, as for instance that of David, results from the preponderance of such consonant musical relationships. "In the harmony and symphony that they sound together artfully and pleasingly according to mathematical proportions and consonances, they are joined and fitted into one another skillfully and sweetly so that it is a lovely resonance of unimaginable grace" (VIII, 548).

As is implicit, though less clearly stated, in the devotional writers of the previous chapter, this persuasion that earthly harmonies are metaphysically linked to spiritual reality does not extend to the physical heavens. "The delusion," says Dannhauer, that the planets moving in spheres give forth musical sounds, has long been refuted both by Aristotle and by Ambrose, who called it "an old fraudulent, absurd opinion."[212] Yet in a metaphorical sense it is true, for the whole **machina mundi** is constructed harmonically with many parts joining together without dissonance.

These similarities with the Arndtian circle make all the more striking the vastly different path which Dannhauer chooses from this point. The earthly analogy to the harmony of heaven and of the universe is not the individual human but rather the church. Showing little interest in the comparison of microcosm to macrocosm, Dannhauer instead compares the church militant to the church triumphant. The latter, far superior to the former, may be said to sing polyphonic music while the earthly choir produces only a chorale. Yet they are united to each other by "God the Holy Spirit, who as the principal conductor and lead singer directs and handles all pipes and tongues" (I, 379). Dannhauer is less interested in assigning parts in the heavenly choir than in forming an earthly community. The many gifts and temperaments of human personalities provide the diversity out of which a society is built. Both choral and instrumental music gain significance when compared to a well-diversified society. Taking as a point of departure Cicero's statement, "What the harmonic blending of voices is and does in music, noble unity is and does in a community and city,"[213] Dannhauer continues:

> Just as in vocal music different styles, notes, and tones (there are high, clear, fast, and happy as well as low, dark, slow, and sad voices and tones), so also in organ and pipework, indeed in all instrumental music, there are different types, voices, and resonances whose variety and multiplicity make the song graceful and charming. Similarly, in human life within all sorts of communities, organizations, and societies, there are differing persons, temperaments, skills, and gifts. Who can comprehend the many kinds of human countenances and lineaments whereby no one looks exactly like another? Who can explain the many gifts of nature, spirit, body, and members which God the Creator has distributed among us?[214]

Dannhauer's concern for unity and harmony in church and society is quite consciously opposed to the preoccupation with the union of the soul with God or the eternal salvation of the individual soul. He criticizes those who substitute the reading of Arndt or other devotional writers for attendance at worship or reading of the Bible.[215] It is a vice to neglect the hearing of the divine Word and instead to sit at home and wait for dreams and raptures. The joys of heaven must not be made so vivid in this life that earthly obligations are slighted. Specifically is this true in the relations of parents to children:

> Parents must cause no annoyance to the children by considering Christ's testimony that the angels always see the face of the heavenly Father; they are not so full of heavenly joy that they shouldn't also be present to the children to whom they are assigned.[216]

Although Dannhauer may have shared with his contemporaries a belief in the imminent end of the world and the Last Judgment, as Wallmann indicates,[217] the sense that this life is a vale of tears to be endured does not motivate his writings as it does Nicolai's or Herberger's. The fact that his references to music appear in discussions of the love of neighbor[218] and of the unity of the church[219] among other topics is an important key to the whole of Dannhauer's theology as well as a significant departure from previous writers.

Dannhauer's fifth sermon on the unity of Christian churches and the community of saints provides a point of contrast to Arndt. As with Arndt, music is here discussed as symbol rather than for its intrinsic value. The symbol, however, is applied at two very different levels by the two thinkers. Whereas Arndt sees the analogy of musical instruments to the individual heart, mind, and soul, Dannhauer sees "nations, classes, persons and languages of the church militant."

> In a well-sounding music there are differing voices, high and deep, clear and coarse, fast and slow, happy and sad, all mixed together, just as in organ and pipework there are differing tones, strings, and pipes, but they are brought into proportion by the composer and conductor, who rhymes the consonances—thirds, fifths, octaves, and double octaves—together and does not let the dissonances clash against each other. In this way the music becomes graceful, lovely, and pleasing. So it is in the society of the church. Within the church there are many nations, languages, gifts, classes, offices, temperaments, skills. In sum many hats, many heads; many heads, many opinions and thoughts. But they are rhymed together by the spirit of unity, God the Holy Spirit, according to the tabulatur of the divine Word. (VI, 406–7)

The dissonance which earlier in the century was interpreted as the sinful state of the individual soul here receives an ecclesiological significance. Those musical dissonances which result in "cat screeches" must be avoided, just as some persons must be removed from the church by excommunication (VI, 412–3). But interestingly (perhaps this reflects a change in musical theory or practice), some dissonance is unavoidable. The composer or director must simply avoid harsh sounds through pauses, semitones, "fast running fugues" and "coloration of tones."[220] Likewise in the church the goal should not be to attain complete unity through the extremes of either syncretism (that mish-mash of fundamentally different religions) or puritanism (the extreme purity and impossible perfection which finds fault with everything). Rather the ship of Christ sails down the middle, separating "middle things" from necessary, accommodating its weak members (VI, 413–4).

The doctrine of adiaphora, in such contexts, appears with some frequency in Dannhauer's writings. Polemical as he was in matters of doctrine, he was prepared to accept differences in church ceremony and organization. Among those practices which may vary according to different church orders, Dannhauer lists singing and organs (VI, 412). But just as any neutral thing can be good or bad depending on the circumstances, so functioning as musician for an "idolatrous Mass" is irresponsible (I, 61).

Nor does the adiaphoric status of church music describe more than its outward form. **How** one sings is not prescribed; **whether** one sings is, for to sing is to praise God.[221] This is a duty of all believers. To use the name of God properly, that is, to obey the Third Commandment, means "that first of all to sing with voices and thus praise God, whether with chorales or figural music, whether with simple or artistic voices, is not free but obligatory" (I, 521). Yet Dannhauer offers no threats to frighten the mute with hell-fire, as we found in Frick. In accordance with his ecclesiological concern for the weak and for the variety of gifts, Dannhauer offered exemptions to those who simply could not sing.[222]

Dannhauer's writings on church music were extremely influential during the debates which followed. Yet his combination of opposites—defense of skilled music and criticism of artistic ambition, emulation of angelic music and edification of ordinary people, command to make music and freedom for differences in worship—meant that he could be drawn in different directions. Like a seventeenth-century Augustine, his authority was useful for all who sought it.

CHAPTER SIX

THE ROSTOCK PRE-PIETISTS

A. JOACHIM LÜTKEMANN AND HEINRICH MÜLLER

If Dannhauer is significant for having woven together various strands of musical theology, the university theologians of Rostock around the middle of the seventeenth century are significant for having begun to unravel the delicate weave. One writer tugged at one thread, another at a second thread, and soon the fabric no longer held. When the participants realized what had occurred, they clung all the more tenaciously to the threads they had seized and refused to cooperate in any re-weaving attempt.

The most obvious protagonist in this scenario was Theophilus Großgebauer, whose *Wächterstimme aus dem verwüsteten Zion* set loose an impassioned controversy on church music practices. The animosities he aroused prevented the defenders of current practices from acknowledging any validity to his criticisms. From the time of his attack, the polemical defense of choir and organ music was no longer directed against Calvinists but against fellow Lutherans. The feuds between orthodox Lutherans and those who came to be called "pietists" can be traced to this point.

Prior to Großgebauer's publication, however, other Rostock theologians had advanced their own views on music in worship. Uniformly critical of the worship styles and attitudes of their time, they pursued one of two approaches to reform: intensification of personal devotion or practical liturgical change. These approaches clearly were not mutually exclusive; they arose out of a common sense of the superficial and perfunctory character of public worship. They were products of a theological faculty which, since David Chytraeus' leadership in the sixteenth century, had stood aloof from the polemical dogmatics of other universities and had dared to find value in certain Calvinist practices and scriptural interpretations.[223] Although dogmatically unassailable, such theologians as Chytraeus, Paul and Johann Tarnov, and the two Johann Quistorps were more interested in pastoral theology and practical scriptural exegesis than in confessional theology. Not surprisingly, such practical concerns and open-minded approaches led to considerable thought regarding worship, much of it deviating considerably from the polemically developed orthodox position.

Also not surprising is that one of the earliest members of the Rostock circle to comment on singing had been directly influenced by Dannhauer. Joachim Lütkemann (1608–55), who had studied in Strassburg as well as Rostock and Greifswald, was proud to regard Dannhauer as his teacher. He is reported to have compared him to Athanasius both for his erudition and for his godliness.[224]

The most obvious connection between Dannhauer and Lütkemann in the area of music is the insistence on congregational singing for the purpose of mutual instruction. The praise of God is not simply a matter between an individual and God but is also an example and means of influencing others. This is accomplished above all in corporate worship, "where Christians come together in a community, pray, sing, praise and thank God and thereby together encourage one another."[225] It is for this reason shameful to despise hymns or to refuse to join in the singing. The purpose of worship is not achieved when individuals read to themselves during the singing. Even if one cannot sing, one can still join in at some level.

> A large portion of the worship service depends on singing along in church. If one is of a god-loving mind, one will want to take part in the devotion and zeal of the Christian community. There one Christian encourages another; we instruct and admonish one another among ourselves with psalms, hymns, and lovely spiritual songs. If you can't sing along, just murmur and meditate on what is being sung by others.[226]

For the singing to have value for others, it must be comprehensible to them. This, according to Lütkemann, is the meaning of Paul's instruction to sing with understanding: "that is, with such a voice that others can hear and understand."[227] A comparison to the "speechless" birds singing in praise of their creator implies that human music can praise God without the means of a text. Yet Lütkemann begins to depart from Dannhauer by giving at least equal attention to the converse: those who cannot sing can praise God quite well by means of a text without music. Christ himself may not have sung when he praised God:

> If a person cannot sing pleasantly with his tongue, he should strive to sing to God all the more pleasantly in his heart. Children speak their song of praise before meals, and when parents listen to the prayer devoutly, they also speak the song of praise. So it is not necessary to hold that our Lord Christ sang when it is written of him that after supper he spoke the song of praise.[228]

When Lütkemann describes the activities of the angels, therefore, he focuses not on singing but on praise and thanksgiving: "For what is the occupation of all the angels if not to praise and give thanks to God without ceasing?"[229]

While the above quotations stress audible praise, whether spoken or sung, the overall emphasis in Lütkemann's writings is heavily weighted toward internal rather than external music. Aside from the sermon on Colossians 3:12–18, from which all but the last citation was taken, Lütkemann's references to music resemble those of Arndt far more than those of Dannhauer. Whereas in the Colossians sermon his concern is to ensure that understanding accompany external song ("One shouldn't think that everything here is accomplished only with the external voice"[230]), his sermon on Ephesians 5:15–22 makes external music a non-essential accompaniment to the music of the heart. Spiritual music begins in the heart and may or may not be expressed through words or music:

> External music pertains to the ears, while spiritual music presses forward to God; but it is kept in the heart, either alone or else with the mouth singing alone, since broken words are the best words. For in this rejoicing of the spirit in the heart so much is felt that words may not follow.[231]

Audible music, then, is most appropriate for expressing that which has occurred or is occurring in the heart. Under these circumstances it is a genuine outburst of praise and devotion. The best description for this situation is "spiritual drunkenness"—a concept which Lütkemann takes from Ephesians 5:18 ("Do not give way to drunkenness and the dissipation that goes with it, but let the Holy Spirit fill you: speak to one another in psalms, hymns, and songs"). Whereas the Arndtian circle had stressed the priority of the heart and had warned against outward noise and display, Lütkemann moves further in this direction, tending toward a dichotomy between music perceptible to the ears and that perceptible only within the heart. His sermon does not distinguish between instrumental and vocal music; they are both external and to that extent contrasted to spiritual music:

> When the world wants to have special pleasure with wine, it uses songs and stringed instruments. That is also true with spiritual drunkenness. For when the soul becomes full of the Holy Spirit, it raises up a song and jubilation in the heart.[232]

As noted above, the two endeavors may coincide, or they may be incompatible. To be spiritually drunk may mean that one breaks forth into song or else that one is incapable of expressing one's feelings.

Lütkemann does agree with all those who ascribed to music a power to stir hearts: "External music has a special and secret power to move humans."[233] In the context of this sermon, however, the implication is that it does not have this power unless it results from heartfelt devotion. He appears almost to be making a concession to those who wish to sing audibly when he pronounces the otherwise common injunction toward the cooperation of heart and mouth: "If one wants to use the mouth for song, one should first be sure that it proceeds from the heart."[234] The power, he implies, is in the heart, not the sound.

Another work by Lütkemann where one might expect a strong affirmation of music completes instead the conceptual dichotomy between internal and external music. His *Harpffe Von Zehen Seyten*, which consists of several meditations on each of the selected psalms, moves quickly from physical to spiritual harps. Without condemning musical instruments in church, Lütkemann stresses that the real significance of scriptural references to them is on a metaphorical level. Commenting on Psalm 92:4 he writes:

> A psaltery and an instrument which received its name from ten strings are among other instruments known and used during David's time. Now, to be sure, it is fine to use such instruments for the praise of God, but it does not produce the true hymn of praise that is pleasing to God. Still, your prayer and thanksgiving must sound to God like lovely music.[235]

Lütkemann adopts in this work the exegeses of the church fathers who, if for no other reason than that musical instruments were not used in the early church, resorted to allegorical interpretation of passages referring to instruments.[236] Common to Origen, Athanasius, and Augustine, for example, was the view that timbrels represented the mortification of the flesh, symbolized by the dried cowskin which was pulled taut to form the drumming surface.[237] Following this tradition, Lütkemann writes concerning the timbrels of Psalm 68:26:

> Whether the timbrels in David's choir were like ours, we cannot know. But they ought to signify to us the flesh which must be subdued beneath the spirit. For the timbrels are prepared from the hide of a slain animal, which is stretched out to a certain extent.[238]

For Lütkemann the lesson becomes one of moderation rather than of asceticism. If the skin is stretched too far, he notes, it breaks; if it is too loose, it gives no sound. By analogy, one must give the flesh its due without letting it run rampant ("One must give the flesh its due so that is does not become unruly and proud").

The patristic interpretation of the processional order described in this verse serves as the basis for Lütkemann's comments on this matter also. It should be noted that the verse has been variously translated. The Vulgate introduces princes among the singers: "Praevenerunt principes coniuncti psallentibus, in medio iuvencularum tympanistriarum." The German version with which Lütkemann was working mixes minstrels and maidens: "Die Sänger gehen vorher, darnach die Spielleute unter den Mägden, die da paucken."[239] Athanasius and Augustine agree in regarding the princes as the apostles who go before others announcing the gospel. The "maidens playing timbrels," following the above interpretation of timbrels, are the believing souls who, by means of their subdued flesh, fill the earth with the sound of praise.[240] Perhaps as a result of the differing scriptural versions, Lütkemann vacillates between the labels "apostles" and "preachers" in identifying the leaders of the choir, but the function is the same:

> When I preach I go in front as a singer; when others feel the power of divine preaching in themselves, they become minstrels. Then when the spirit begins to exert force on the flesh, the maidens play the timbrels. Thus the choir of Christ proceeds in proper order.[241]

The public function of this procession is clear in Lütkemann's interpretation. The maidens do more than testify to their own regeneration. By beating on the timbrels they produce a strong sound for the love of God which moves others to follow.[242] The next verse, "Praise God in the congregation," also gives Lütkemann occasion to emphasize that the gospel is to be preached in public gatherings, not in corners.[243]

Elsewhere, however, Lütkemann also stresses the devotional relationship of the individual soul to God. External observance of the Sabbath is an image of the true, inner sabbath of the heart.[244] To sing praise to God with a pleasing voice is to praise him in the spirit out of a fervent, believing heart. One can praise God in the heart at all times, and one may withdraw from all activities to spend time in quiet alone with God. Yet Lütkemann warns that this is not to be done in the expectation that God will respond by providing a taste of heavenly delights, for God does not owe these to anyone.[245]

The external world is therefore not to be abandoned in the pursuit of external matters. It is in fact of great value as a means of coming to know God. Among God's works are visible and invisible, heavenly and earthly, corporeal and spiritual creations, all of which have the ability to please and delight humans, leading them to praise and devotion. "There is nothing externally created which does not lead to the knowledge of divine goodness and wisdom and thus into the inner spiritual being of the Creator."[246] The Psalms appear to fit in this category as external means of arriving at a spiritual end:

> Here the Holy Spirit hands us the instrument we should play. Here he pours into our hearts the thoughts we should keep with us. Here he lays in our mouths the words with which we should praise God so that we should fittingly begin the holiday of the Lord with this psalm and thus arouse the soul.[247]

Music presumably can also serve this purpose, particularly when combined with the Psalms. As noted above, Lütkemann does to a certain extent subscribe to music's power to arouse devotion.

For the most part, however, music is regarded by Lütkemann not as part of creation or as divine gift but as a human response to creation. The mathematical proportions which give music its link to physical realities and which for other writers are accordingly a link to metaphysical reality are not discussed by Lütkemann. Yet the symbolic mode of thinking which linked music to other levels of being is carried on by Lütkemann. The result is that music no longer takes on sacramental overtones, for its physical reality is disregarded, but in the spiritual realm it is a symbol of psychological or spiritual realities. As with any other symbol, it is a means of expressing or communicating realities greater than itself, in this case the workings of the Spirit in the heart.

Lütkemann's views on music were transmitted with increased emphasis on internal devotion by Heinrich Müller, a younger colleague whose ten meditations on spiritual music prefaced his extensive collection of hymns, *Geistliche Seelenmusik*. Lütkemann's treatment of singing as an expression of spiritual drunkenness had particularly strong influence on Müller, who borrowed sentences from Lütkemann with minor changes of wording. Yet he takes Lütkemann's ideas one step further by placing not just priority of value but priority of sequence on internal devotion. For Müller, devotion should precede singing in such a way that the latter becomes a non-essential by-product. The proper order of events is outlined at the end of the Eighth Meditation ("On the Preparation of the Heart"):

> Therefore, dear soul, if you want to sing, first bow your knees and sigh with David: "Lord, open my lips, take not your Holy Spirit from me, sustain me with your joyous spirit." But if you feel spiritual thoughts, do not run away from them, do not resist them, for they are God's finger and a work of the Holy Spirit. Through spiritual thoughts your mind is drawn to heaven; from spiritual thoughts grow spiritual songs. If idle or sinful thoughts occur to you, know that the Holy Spirit is thereby grieved, so drive them quickly away. When you have finally finished your little song, thank the master and say: "Praise the Lord, my soul, who has made your mouth happy!"[248]

Because spiritual songs should be an outgrowth of thoughts evoked by the guidance of the Holy Spirit, to follow a particular sequence of psalm or hymn singing in accordance with some liturgical scheme is to have one's priorities backward. First the heart is moved, then the mouth—not vice versa:

> After the mind is moved, the mouth sings, sometimes a lament, sometimes a song of comfort. For this reason those who tie their devotion to certain times and words foolishly sing songs of joy in

times of sorrow or songs of mourning in times of joy, according to the order of songs they find in their psalm booklet. To be genuine, either the heart itself should create the words or, if one considers oneself unsuited for that, one should test beforehand whether the heart is inclined to joy or sorrow; then after such testing a song can be chosen from the book of psalms in which the heart with its movement is depicted in a timely and accurate manner. (112)

One of the drawbacks of public worship, therefore, is that the prescribed hymns may not be appropriate to one's devotional mood and thus cannot be sung sincerely. Another drawback is the total lack of devotion among some of those present. Such lack of devotion is a distraction and a hindrance to genuine worship:

But these days sadly church devotions are such a pitifully dismembered affair that I could cry blood. Most people do not go to church in order to stand before God in holy, fervent devotion with song and prayer, for they don't appear before the preacher steps to the pulpit. Thus they keep the cold and distracted heart which they had. That they go to church happens only out of custom or in order to display themselves in their colorful clothes. Through this the faithful are annoyed and kept from their devotions. If it happens that devotion is expressed by the faithful in gestures, words, and works, it is scorned by the style-conscious worldlings and even decried as hypocrisy. (138–9)

Müller's solution to this problem is one which none of our other writers had advanced: rather than fight impiety in the congregational battlefield, Müller advocated withdrawal. "One does better to build for himself a little church in his house" (139). The temple where God is truly present is, after all, not a building or a public worship gathering, but the chamber of the faithful heart. For this reason Müller does not ask that the spiritually filled person move outward in an evangelistic effort; the poor reception such a person would receive would not be conducive to the full expression of his or her experience. This is possible only in the quiet of one's isolation with God: "A spirit-drunk soul often locks itself up in its little chamber in order not to be scorned by the world when it behaves and speaks outwardly in accordance with its inner feeling" (193).

The power of spiritual singing to inspire others who listen is not denied by Müller, but his affirmations of this power seem more like carryovers from Lütkemann than original conviction. In writing of the three aspects of the spiritual art of singing, he notes the value of public oral confession for others: "The words also arouse the next person when they are full of spirit and life" (113). Elsewhere he urges those who have musical ability to sing for the sake of others: "If you have the gift of singing with the mouth to God, then sing with understanding so that others can hear and understand" (147).[249]

It is important to note, however, that the understanding referred to in the previous quotation is not of a primarily intellectual sort. Müller would deny that singing has instructional value because of the content of the text apart from the spiritual state of the singer. He is not interested in teaching the facts of Christian history and doctrine but in moving hearts to the love of God. The kind of knowledge which is of value in singing is not "dead cognition" but "living experience" (105). Only a person who has personal experience of faith can thus communicate it to others in song.

This is not to deny the power of musical sound to change moods and to prepare the mind for true worship. Müller asserts that "nothing leads the mind so quickly and sensitively to heaven as singing."[250] He recognizes the naturalistic power of music to drive away the melancholy spirit. There is, he notes, a "secret affinity" of the voice to the human spirit: "If one speaks plaintively, one is moved to sadness; if one speaks sternly and frighteningly, to fear; if one speaks sweetly, to love; if one speaks comfortingly, to joy" (85). While the speaking voice has this power by nature, the effect is increased when the powers of art are added: "That happens rather when art aids nature and makes everything in all aspects more stirring" (85). (We may note here that this distinction between art and nature had not been common among previous writers.)

The previous comments about the power of music are made by Müller under the rubric of "spiritual songs." The prevalence of worldly music, on the other hand, is a major hindrance to praising music in general for its beneficial effects. Only spiritual music, according to Müller, can exert positive influence. Whereas previous Lutherans had frequently criticized the raucous music of beer halls, they had not made a systematic distinction between spiritual music as good and secular music as evil.

The basis for such a distinction in Müller's thought can be found in the biblical commentaries of Johann Tarnov (1586–1629), an earlier Rostock theologian. With Tarnov, biblical exegesis in Rostock had already moved away from the polemical defense of Lutheran principles. He recognized the value of Calvin's position on musical instruments while at the same time contrasting it with that of the "more rigid sectarians and opponents of organs."[251] Nor did he feel compelled to include any positive words in support of the orthodox Lutheran position on church music. Instead, in commenting on Amos 6:5, where skilled musicians and inventors of musical instruments are associated with dissolute frivolity, Tarnov appeals to Calvin's exegesis in support of his own. Calvin seemed to reject the recreational use of musical instruments: "No doubt, David, when in a peaceful state, could also amuse himself: but he applied musical instruments to another purpose—to sound forth the praises of God in the temple, that thereby he and other godly persons might together elevate their thoughts to a religious devotion."[252] Similarly, Tarnov chastises musical revelers for appealing to the example of David, "as if he had used his musical instruments not for arousing devotion but for stimulating desire."[253]

The Amos passage came to be cited frequently in the Rostock circle to demonstrate that scripture did not give blanket approval to music. Müller also found other biblical references to music used against divine purposes. Nebuchadnezzar misled the simple people through trumpets, horns, and other musical instruments to worship the golden image (Daniel 3:4–7). Laban wanted to detain Jacob, contrary to God's instructions, by entertaining him "with mirth and songs, with tambourine and lyre" (Genesis 31:27). At the house of Jairus (Matt. 9), Jesus sent away the flute players before raising the girl from the dead (5–7).

These examples, according to Müller, all illustrate the spiritually deadening power of music. Just as spiritual music can sensitize the listener to the inner workings of the spirit, so worldly music can desensitize by awakening and distracting the external senses. Secular music, it seems, is not merely neutral but is an instrument of evil for drawing us away from good:

> Worldly music makes a person spiritually deaf so that he hears neither the sweet touches of God nor the sorrowful beats of his own heart....When the world notices that we want to draw out of her yoke, she makes her control over us pleasant with singing and playing....With this vanity it holds your senses, draws out your thoughts and disperses them so that your mind is unfit for inner attention to heavenly matters. (7–8)

In light of such distrust of music, it is not surprising that for Müller even spiritual music must be regarded with some suspicion. Augustine's dilemma of whether he was drawn more by the melodies than by the words reappears in a somewhat more complex form in Müller: not only might one be attracted by the music more than the words, but also by the artistry of the words more than their meaning:

> Many take delight in the artful poetic words or the passionate melody even though they do not feel the reality and power of the words in their hearts. It is as when one enjoys the pretty colors of a flower but pays no attention to its fragrance or vitality. (114)

For this reason Müller does not regard singing psalms or hymns as a value for its own sake but only for the sake of the heart which is awakened thereby: "The words are useful only to inflame the heart" (144).

Given all these potential abuses or misguided uses of music, Müller seems inclined to avoid talk of *using* music at all. While admitting its power to achieve certain effects, he prefers to regard music as a means of expression rather than as a means of creating a mood. Music can result from spiritual experience just as easily as, if not better than, it can induce such experience. It is, after all, the Holy Spirit who either moves the heart to sing or moves the heart to respond to music which is sung. Yet the workings of the Holy Spirit are not bound to the sound of the music.

There can be music without the Holy Spirit, but such music cannot be pleasing to God: "It is impossible for your song to please God if it does not proceed from faith....And how can you believe without the Holy Spirit?" (200). David's singing did not automatically carry with it the power of the Spirit; rather, he prayed each time before singing, "Lord, open my lips that my mouth may proclaim your glory." If the heart is not moved to God, the song is "cold and dead"; on the other hand, when the Holy Spirit moves the heart, the outward song is in accordance with the direction of that movement: "sometimes sad, sometimes happy, sometimes despondent, sometimes cheerful" (195).

Not all spiritual moods, however, are well expressed in song. Hence, while song must always be connected to the movement of the Spirit, the latter is not always connected to song. As with Lütkemann, external music is ultimately non-essential, a natural but not necessary expression of spiritual feelings:

> The power of singing does not lie in the words of the mouth but in the devotion of the heart. Indeed when the heart sings there follow either no words or only broken childish words....By the words you can discern the heart: by broken words a broken heart; by full and joyous words a full and overflowing heart. (143–4)

In sum Müller's theology is best described as individualistic mysticism. The believer is linked to God directly by means of the heart and the Holy Spirit. Corporate worship and audible singing have value only insofar as they contribute to or give expression to the soul's love of God. To be sure, Müller has not entirely lost the vision of the church militant united in praise of God:

> Indeed the public song of the temple is pleasing to God if spirit and devotion is in it. So all is fine and Christian when all Christian praise proceeds from the spirit and mouth...not to speak of the fact that such a gathering of many Christians praising God in the church militant on earth is a picture of the triumphant church in heaven. (138–9)

But he finds so little resemblance between the vision and the reality that he turns in despair to the only church he can depend on and recommends the same refuge to others:

> Yet in order that you may sing in all places—at home as well as abroad, with others as well as alone—draw nearer to God and build

his temple in yourself so that you may carry around your house of God everywhere; indeed it is you yourself.... (142–3)

Müller thus represents one form of what has been called "reform orthodoxy" in that, from within the orthodox Lutheran tradition he calls for an infusion of the spirit and a reform of hearts. Whether he was fully orthodox, however, is debatable. His view of the relationship between Spirit and Word tends toward a disjunction closer to spiritualism than to Lutheranism. The external means whereby the Word is conveyed are de-emphasized in favor of the unmediated workings of the Holy Spirit. The manner of preparation for the Spirit as advocated by Müller is reminiscent of medieval mystics. First the distractions of the senses must be overcome: "Thus a devout Christian must either choose for himself a secret place or else shut off the senses in public gatherings, cover the eyes, turn away the ears" (161). Then one turns into oneself ("Turn into yourself and seek your heart" [176]) to purify the heart ("Therefore first cleanse your heart before you begin to sing" [153]), for God will not come to an unpurified heart: "Where there is no purity of heart there is no light from God....God does not place his balm in an impure, stinking vessel" (152). When the heart is sufficiently purified, the way is open for God to enter: "Through devotion we open the door to Christ that he may enter the soul with all his goodness" (181). Without directly labelling a part of the soul a "ground," a "spark" or other term signifying an uncorrupted area, Müller alludes to this medieval concept through a metaphor for devotion: "Devotion lies hidden in the heart as a spark of fire under the ashes and is made alive through meditation on divine works just as a spark which is blown by the wind" (181).

By making God's appearance in the heart contingent on sufficient preparation, and by implying that God activates an already present spirituality rather than initiating the process, Müller moves away not only from Luther's position on justification but also from the **unio mystica** theology of Lutheran orthodoxy. As Christian Bunners notes, "Such inward-turning as preparation for singing from a level of devotion which corresponds to mystical union makes clear how Müller goes beyond the piety of Luther and Orthodoxy. In these the **unio** was identical with justification and for that reason preparation of the human soul did not come into question."[254]

If from our perspective Müller seems to have moved outside Lutheran orthodoxy, it should quickly be noted that this was not the judgment of his own time.[255] Müller was not attacked as heretical, nor were his works treated with suspicion. On the contrary, they were highly regarded and widely read. Müller's name figures prominently in J. S. Bach's library in the following century. The age was not one in which a piety bordering on Catholicism was likely to cause a stir. The stir was to be caused by those who bordered on Calvinism.

CHAPTER SEVEN

THE ROSTOCK PRE-PIETISTS

B. THEOPHILUS GROßGEBAUER

That Theophilus Großgebauer was moved by a spirit different from that which inspired Heinrich Müller has long been noticed. In his own day he was regarded by some as an anti-musical boor. In the nineteenth century, Otto Krabbe considered him lacking in basic understanding of Lutheran beliefs. The major portion of his *Wächterstimme*, Krabbe wrote, shows "that he was lacking in the deeper knowledge of the truths of salvation and that, even if he wanted to espouse the doctrinal position of his church, he was by no means firmly enough rooted in it to avoid deviating from it in many respects and entering into other basic outlooks and dogmatic circles."[256] Similarly, in our own day, Christian Bunners regards him as moving beyond reform within the Lutheran tradition which he professed. With specific reference to Großgebauer's views on church music, Bunners writes, "Großgebauer's proposals do not signify a reform of church music in the old Lutheran sense, but rather show a spirit largely alien to Lutheranism. Their result would have been to a great extent in formal agreement with the shape of church music in Reformed areas, namely the absence of art music."[257] Because Großgebauer died soon after the publication of his *Wächterstimme* at the early age of 34, we cannot know whether his thought would have moved closer to the center or further from the edge of Lutheran tradition. What we do know is that, in spite of the stamp of approval given his book by the theological faculty of Rostock, it had a more divisive effect in the discussion of the proper role of church music than any other work of the age in Germany.

Großgebauer's ideas were not entirely original, however. In spite of different approaches toward reform, he shared with his Rostock colleagues Lütkemann and Müller a concern for revitalizing religion in a time when outward observance seemed to satisfy many. More specifically, Großgebauer adopted many of the ideas of Johann Quistorp the younger, who in 1659 published a letter to the clergy of Mecklenburg ("Epistola ad Sacros Antistites Ecclesiarum ducatus

Mecklenburgici") advocating disciplinary and liturgical reforms. Republished in German as *Pia Desideria* in 1665, Quistorp's discussion of Sunday worship begins with the observation that most people don't come to church at the beginning of the service but wait until time for the sermon, thereby avoiding the singing of hymns: "On Sundays before the preacher mounts the pulpit, few come to church to sing spiritual songs along with the cantor. Rather, when the singing is over they finally come, all dressed up as if they were going to a wedding."[258]

There are some, on the other hand, who come to church mainly to hear or see something pleasant. They are the supporters of the instrumental and figural music which holds no value for the simple folk. Quoting Erasmus, Athanasius, and Augustine, Quistorp argues that music should not merely please the ear but also arouse devotion. The blame rests primarily on the cantors and organists, who "must answer for the fact that they and theirs (the common people excluded) sing unknown and Latin songs from which the people get no benefit."[259] Implied is also a criticism of the Lutheran church as a whole for not sufficiently reforming the liturgy: "Truly, to the great detriment of the church, we have kept most of the ceremonies that sprang forth from the papacy."[260] Quistorp sees a remedy in a hymnbook revision where attention would be paid to correcting those errors which had crept into congregational singing. People, especially women and peasants, were singing without devotion because the corruption of the texts had left the hymns without meaning.

Hymnbook revision was an idea whose time had come. The number of old, new, and revised hymns published in the numerous German hymnals of the late seventeenth and early eighteenth centuries is formidable. Ingeborg Röbbelen reports an increase from 276 hymns in the Dresden hymnal of 1622 to 2055 hymns in the Lüneburg hymnal of 1694.[261] Differing views on language, literary style, religious tradition, and Christian doctrine resulted in hymnals which represented different factions or viewpoints. For us to pursue the hymnological controversies of the day would be to venture into a dark forest from which we might never emerge. Important for our understanding of the theology of church music is the more general discussion of the comparative value of congregational singing and artistic church music. On this issue Großgebauer, more strongly than any Lutheran writer thus far, lent his support to congregational singing over against the music of professionals.

Großgebauer's discussion of worship begins in a manner similar to Quistorp's but with a much harsher tone. Labelling the "miserable, unedifying public worship" the eighth cause of the "ungodly, unspiritual ways of our churches," Großgebauer echoes the observation that the sermon is for many the sole reason for attending worship. "That preaching is the worship service is doubted by no one. Thus I have seen how in large cities the people storm into the church as the bell strikes the hour for the preacher to mount the pulpit; then when the sermon ends they storm out again."[262] Their language reflects their attitude and practices: rather than reporting that they have been in the "brotherly gathering," they say they have been "in the sermon." Relying on the report of the apostles in Acts 2, Großgebauer counters that worship consists not only in the sermon but in such works of brotherly love as "chastisement, ardor, compassion, reception, administration of communion, prayer and intercession, thanksgiving and songs of praise" (190).

These and other outward forms of church life are indispensable, according to Großgebauer, yet not for their own sakes but for attaining greater spirituality. The goal he shares with Lütkemann and Müller: through stillness in the soul, union with God is made possible or, in other imagery, the Holy Spirit fills the soul to the point of spiritual drunkenness. Such joyous spiritual heights, Großgebauer knows, are not achieved simply by exhortation or even by waiting for the movement of the Holy Spirit. Attention must be paid to the means whereby a congregation may be filled with the Spirit. It is not enough for preachers to instruct their hearers to be of good cheer; to do so would be as though a host invited guests to eat and drink but provided no refreshments: "But when I say to him, 'Eat, drink, be happy and of good cheer,' but give him nothing to drink and feed him with mere words, he would legitimately say I was making a mockery of him" (191).

What, Großgebauer asks, are the means provided by the Apostles for being filled with the Spirit? "None other than psalms, hymns, and spiritual songs. That is the sweet wine which the congregation must drink if it is to be filled with the Spirit" (191). It is good that the preachers annually preach on the text "Rejoice in the Lord....be fervent in the Spirit, be full of the Spirit," but when the means of attaining such joy are absent, the exhortation will be fruitless. Sermons cannot achieve the same results as singing: "You say, 'They have God's Word!' True. God's Word must dwell among us with wisdom. It is wisdom to bring God's Word into beautiful psalms and to pour the Word of God into the heart through the ears in pleasing melodies" (192).

Music's power to move hearts is explained in naturalistic terms through reliance on the description of the sixteenth-century Italian scholar J. C. Scaliger. Unscientific as the explanation may appear to our twentieth-century minds, it served in this period as a serious scientific effort to determine the physiological effects of music. By utilizing this theory, Großgebauer sets himself off from those who preferred to regard music's effects as a spiritual rather than empirical phenomenon.

> Because the little life-spirits which work in the heart conduct the vibrating and bouncing air into the breast and because the air is of the same nature as they, it unites with them. Then the other little mind-spirits in the other parts of the body follow and move the muscles or restrain them after the sound has moderated. This either increases with sharp strokes or quiets down with a well-tuned sound, and a slow beat also leads to rest. Just as when one string is played

on a violin or other string instrument the neighboring string vibrates, so the little spirits that are in the heart are roused after the external tone is moved; and as this happens much more quickly and easily than with the string, the union is that much greater. And this is the reason why when other people sing we secretly sing along even if we are not paying attention to them but to something else. (192–3)[263]

When Großgebauer then proceeds to declare that psalms, hymns and spiritual songs are the "means which the Holy Spirit uses as the wagon on which he pulls into hearts and fills them with all God's fullness" (194), his concept of **means** must be taken in a broad sense. His is not merely a doctrinal affirmation of the necessity of outward forms of worship over against a spiritualistic rejection of such forms. Beyond that, it is a psychologically based pastoral conviction that congregations need to be actively involved in worship in order to benefit therefrom. Only by involving the mind and emotions can the heart be moved. Rather than advocating withdrawal from distractions of the senses, as did Müller, Großgebauer seeks to change the sensory stimuli. Observing that music was used in war to turn humans into beasts and Christians into barbarians, he charged the church to use the same means to reverse the process.[264] If this group psychology can work for the devil among a battalion of soldiers, it can work for God in a congregation of Christians. The kingdom of God can be built on earth if Christians will sing not to themselves alone but to one another.

> When one sings psalms, as Paul says, "in the Spirit," that cannot edify the congregation; but when the whole congregation sings in the Spirit and at the same time one speaks to another through psalms, that improves and fills with the Spirit.
> No more beautiful harmony can be devised than this; and it is nothing other than a model and foretaste of the eternal gathering in heaven. (194)

If the congregational focus of attention distinguishes Großgebauer from Müller, they nevertheless share certain elements of mystical language. The end to which psalms and hymns are a means is "a quiet Sabbath of the heart." Through these external means, the "distracted senses are called back" and the now quieted soul can hear and understand God's word. External forms of worship are offensive to God if they do not lead toward this goal. Outward observance of the Sabbath, with cessation from worldly activities, was instituted by God to enable the soul to seek rest in God. In this stillness, the Holy Spirit can begin to "speak, sigh, pray, cry, praise, thank, work, inflame, move, drive," leading to the union of God with the soul and the spiritual fruits which result. "Then God goes into the soul, unites himself more and more with it, and works in it his works" (196).

Yet Großgebauer refuses to regard this goal as finally individualistic. He does not despair of attaining this state with the entire congregation. If the apostolic community could achieve the goal, it was still achievable:

> If you should say it would be impossible to arrange such a Sabbath, for everyone looks to himself, you would contradict the apostle of the Lord who commended this to the church not as an impossibility but as a possibility. Thus it is written: "Be full of the Spirit. Speak among yourselves with psalms, hymns, and spiritual songs" (Eph. 5:18). That applies to the congregation gathered together, as can be seen in I Cor. 14. (197)

The foretaste of heaven is experienced as a community, not as individuals. Public worship should be so designed "that, when the members of the congregation depart from one another, they go forth at the same time from the paradise of God and from the forecourts of the Lord full of divine consolation, joy, peace, love and compassion. And they should carry in them a foretaste of eternal life, as they have become full of the Spirit within the gathering" (197).

Großgebauer supports his emphasis on congregational singing by adducing evidence from the early church (200–204). The text which had been rejected by defenders of music because its ascription to Justin Martyr was questionable is introduced as "from the time of Justin Martyr." This early church source thus testifies to the removal of musical instruments from the community of worship. Augustine and Cassiodorus, on the other hand, are called on to witness to the power of singing among early Christians. The report of the latter that communities sometimes spent whole nights in singing and praying leads Großgebauer to suggest, with support from Philo, that antiphonal singing by different groups could serve well to refresh the tired. As Augustine had observed, alternation provides time to listen to and be inspired by the words of the other choir. Finally, Emperor Constantine was a precentor and began the singing in his congregation, saying it is not right to listen to divine teaching lazily.[265]

In Großgebauer's interpretation of church history, the decline of congregational participation coincided with the rise of clerical privilege and papal power. Already in the fourth century the church began to be brought under the "servile yoke" placed by the clergy. The Council of Laodicea decreed that only canons, or designated singers, should sing in church; nor were ordinary people allowed to read the Bible in church. It was a natural step from this to prohibition of the mother tongue in worship. All that was left for teaching people were the pictures of wood and stone, and the result was that "the people were almost changed into stone and wood" (205). Then the popes added more material objects for the people to see and hear. Appended to their already burdensome yoke were the "wooden, tin, and lead pipes of organs," which for Großgebauer were a symbol of lifelessness: "And such organ pipes are nothing but living pictures of a dead

Christianity; indeed they blare and cry with force but have neither heart nor spirit nor soul" (205). The people, consequently, are deadened by such sounds.

> With these [the pope] has made the people deaf and dumb so that they can neither praise God nor understand his Word; instead, deadened by the strange, splendrous music-making, they are drawn to amazement and tickled in the ears. (205)

With the Reformation all of this should have been corrected, Großgebauer asserts, for the German church cast off the yoke of the papacy. Yet the old habits were so well entrenched that the people did not make the most of their freedom. Much to Großgebauer's dismay, the old servitude to Italy was being reintroduced through the import of Italian music. His opinion of this Italian style is expressed in a lengthy passage which became the focus of controversy for the next half century:

> Oh, the miserable condition! What is happening? After the Reformation the community of Christ did indeed achieve her freedom from the Babylonian Captivity to the extent that she is allowed to sing some German psalms and to hear the prophecies and psalms in her mother tongue. But because at one time the Pope gave only the clerics the power to sing and make music it seems to us difficult to throw out such a human trinket through the command of God. Therefore unfortunately organists, cantors, town pipers, and musicians—for the most part unspiritual people—have control in the city churches. They play, sing, bow, and ring according to their pleasure. You hear the rushing, ringing, and roaring, but you don't know what it is, whether you should arm yourself for battle or whether you should withdraw. One chases after the other in concertizing and some contend with one another over which can do it most skillfully or which can most subtly imitate a nightingale.
>
> And just as the world now is not serious but frivolous and has lost the old quiet devotion, so songs have been sent to us in Germany from Italy in which the biblical texts are torn apart and chopped up into little pieces through swift runs of the throat; those are the warblers (Amos 6:5) who can stretch and break the voice like singing birds. Then it becomes an ambitious collective screaming to see who sings most like the birds. Now it's Latin, now German, only a few can understand the words; and even if they are understood they go in one ear and out the other. There the organist sits, plays, and shows his art; in order that the art of one person be shown, the whole congregation of Jesus Christ is supposed to sit and hear the sound of pipes. This makes the congregation drowsy and lazy: some sleep;

some gossip; some look where it isn't fitting; some would like to read but can't because they haven't learned how. But they could be well instructed by the spiritual songs of the congregation, which Paul exhorts. Some would like to pray but are so captivated and disoriented by the roaring and ringing that they can't. Occasionally everything breaks loose, and if an unbeliever should come into our gathering, would he not say that we were putting on a spectacle and that we were partly mad? (I Cor. 14:23). (208–209)

If the above passage pits congregation against musician, other passages pit ordinary people against the privileged. Even here current musical practices receive the blame: rather than giving expression to the suffering of the Lord, communion music has become an occasion to honor certain communicants:

Among us there is the custom that when a distinguished person goes to communion or a bride takes communion or a young woman goes to church, or the like, the remembrance of our Lord's death is set aside at the distribution of communion and something else is played and glorious music is made. And when the death of the Lord is supposed to be proclaimed, it is proclaimed that a distinguished person is going to communion or that a bride is among the communicants. Thus one idolatry follows another. (215)

For Großgebauer this is simply another means whereby a bit is placed in the mouth of the congregation, as if they were mules. To thus single out individual members of the congregation is to counteract the purpose of communion, which is that through proclamation of the Lord's death the community of believers be moved to follow in his steps in works of love and mercy. If the nobility are truly interested in extending the kingdom of God, they could contribute by furthering the worship of the congregation. Specifically, they should provide for better religious and musical education for ordinary people. Boys and girls in schools, villages, and towns should be led to knowledge of God and to the custom of singing in order that "through human voices" God might be praised and the congregation be filled with the Spirit (217). As things stand, both the nobility and their subjects go to church for the sake of the sermon and are never filled with the Spirit.

Far from hating music, then, Großgebauer regards music as the key tool for raising the spiritual level of worship. Nor does he want all musical instruments removed from the church. Yet they must always be subordinate to the singing of the community. Only human voices can appropriately praise God; instruments can assist but cannot themselves glorify God. Any instruments may be used in church, but their use must not eliminate the singing of the people. Whether in Großgebauer's view they must always accompany singing, or whether they might be allowed short solo interludes is not entirely clear: in any case, lengthy instrumental pieces would be excluded.

> Should one wish to direct the psalms and spiritual songs of the congregation—and also to provide greater encouragement for them—by the playing of organ and stringed instruments, that would do no harm. It would put into effect that which is in the last psalm: "Praise him with trumpets; praise him with psaltery" (Ps. 150). When the spirit and the mouth of the congregation of God praise the Lord, trumpets, psalteries, and harps may also ultimately be used. But when the trumpets, psalteries, and harps are supposed to praise God and the congregation is deaf and mute, that may just be blaring and a damnable praise. (218)

Although Großgebauer's proposals are more drastic than had been heard previously among Lutherans, his analysis of the problem is in keeping with the church order which had been in effect in Mecklenburg since the beginning of his century. The *Revidirte Kirchenordnung* of 1602 suggests that organists had already begun to expand their role in the services. The intent of the church order, in contrast to Großgebauer's, was to preserve the prerogatives of the preacher: the organist must not intrude on the preacher's time. Yet it also shows concern for maintaining the interest of the congregation:

> In order that on Sundays these ceremonies not last too long and the people grow weary of them, especially in those places where the organ is used, the organist should adjust his playing according to the time. In order that the preacher begin at the usual hour, the organist should not play too long between the psalms and the other songs before and after the sermon.[266]

Organists, according to the church order, must also submit to the authority of the preachers in the choice of music, playing pieces fitting with the psalms, chorales and motets and avoiding worldliness and frivolity. These indications of organists' insubordination are evidence of the importance which organists in North Germany had achieved already by the beginning of the seventeenth century. Organists in Rostock were more highly respected and better paid than cantors.[267] They were also more highly skilled and more creative; in contrast to other areas of Germany, the organists in North Germany were more likely to compose music than were cantors. Although Daniel Friderici, as cantor of St. Mary's and capellmeister for all the churches of Rostock, is still recognized as a significant composer, other notable names of Rostock musicians are those of organists, preeminently Nicolaus Hasse and Heinrich Rogge.

The higher status of organists in comparison to cantors reflected the comparatively low priority accorded to music in the schools of Rostock. In contrast to many cities of Germany, the cantors of Rostock were not members of the teaching faculty proper, nor were the hours of music instruction part of the regular curriculum.[268] The university faculty also questioned the educational value of the practice of music and sought to limit instrumental music as much as possible and to move vocal instruction outside lecture hours and off university premises.[269] One might expect, given Großgebauer's harsh criticism of musicians, that he would share this suspicion of musical instruction, but, in a school sermon of 1647, he points to music's decline in favor as the key to the problem. Music has ceased to be an activity for all classes of society; city councillors and mayors whom Großgebauer had heard sing in other cities in earlier days would no longer dare to engage in such activity publicly. Forty or more years previously, the nobility were not ashamed to learn to sing, but those, Großgebauer notes, were the times of "simplex et germana Germania," of simple and German Germany. Now that Germany is no longer German but Italian, vocal music is scorned and avoided by all but the poor pupils whose singing provides financial support. Even among them, Großgebauer predicts, music will gradually lose its position.[270]

Großgebauer's antipathy to Italian influence should not be taken as xenophobia, however. His orientation was simply to the Protestant North rather than the Catholic South. He exhibits familiarity with English Puritan writings and even appends the text of the communion service from Edward VI's Book of Common Prayer to his *Wächterstimme*. Whether his use of English sources and his emphasis on regeneration are evidence that the basis of his theology was not truly Lutheran is subject to debate. He was by no means the only Lutheran preacher reading English works; Lewis Bayly's *Practice of Piety* amd Immanuel Sonthom's *Golden Gem* had been available in German translation since 1632.[271] Karl Holl rejected the view that the reform movement introduced ideas foreign to Lutheranism through the use of such texts. With regard to Großgebauer's emphasis on community over against individualistic worship, Holl sees no difficulty in the possibility that Großgebauer was stimulated by Reformed writings. What he presents, Holl believes, are "in the final analysis genuine Lutheran thoughts."[272] In general, Holl sees Großgebauer and others who criticized the churches of their day as seeking to recover the original Reformation impulse. Johannes Wallmann, on the other hand, sees Großgebauer as moving with puritanical strictness beyond the realm of that which was consistent with the Lutheran tradition.[273] Opinions regarding Großgebauer were as divided in his own day as in modern scholarship; had he not had support within the Lutheran camp, his book would not have been attacked with such vehemence.

Whatever judgment is made regarding the orthodoxy of Großgebauer's theology, surely his appeal was not that of an innovator but that of a conservative. For those who saw the world changing around them too rapidly, Großgebauer's call for a return to good German ways was attractive. In another work, Großgebauer launched out against the intellectual novelties which were being brought back from foreign lands into Germany. Doubts about the authority of the Bible were being spread by Jesuits. Doubts about the existence of God were widespread in Paris. The reality of the second coming was being debated elsewhere. The sons of the wealthy and the nobility were eagerly adopting and importing such ideas from their travels in France, Spain, and Italy. The poor and suffering, Großgebauer says, have never doubted the Bible or sought to resist the will of God.[274]

Großgebauer's identification with the poor over against the rich, the German over against the foreign, old ideas over against new appealed to the discontents of the lower classes. For this reason, it is somewhat beside the point to debate whether his view of music was truly Lutheran. The point is rather that the music being used in the Lutheran churches was beginning to represent the taste of the upper social classes. That Großgebauer may have been inconsistent by saying that the people become sleepy during organ music while also saying they are astonished by the wondrous ear-tickling sounds is also not the issue.[275] The problem was that the new music was foreign and therefore meaningless to ordinary people. Unable to comprehend the organ and the sounds it emitted, the overstimulated would-be worshippers withdrew from the service mentally because they could not concentrate.

Großgebauer's musical stance, therefore, reflected the pastoral concerns of a preacher who sought to represent the majority of the people. He perceived, perhaps more clearly than anyone up to this point, how the adiaphorist teaching had been turned against its original purpose:

> In the beginning of the Reformation it happened that middle things were employed out of love and for the improvement of the weak; but what was then a free matter in the good hope that those who had such ceremonies would turn to us is now compulsory and almost an article of faith which we cannot change. (225f.)

The possibility of a healthy self-examination within the church, which the liberating nature of the adiaphorist doctrine should have furthered, had succumbed to anti-Calvinist fervor. Granted that Großgebauer's ideas would have led to the virtual elimination of art music in the church and that his tone was not conciliatory, still he was unfairly lumped together with those Calvinists or Zwinglians who opposed organs or choral music on principle. His was a critique of contemporary musical styles, not a fundamental rejection of artistic music. The fact that his words continued to be quoted well into the following century by both enemies and allies indicates that some portion of the truth was to be found on both sides.

CHAPTER EIGHT

HECTOR MITHOBIUS: CULMINATION OF ORTHODOXY

The first major response to Großgebauer's *Wächterstimme* was only partly conceived as a counterattack. Although the *Wächterstimme* may have provided the motivation for publication, the group of sermons published as *Psalmodia Christiana* by Hector Mithobius in 1665 had their origin with Mithobius' father, also named Hector. The elder Mithobius had preached a sermon on music in Böblingen in 1633, which was delivered with minor changes by his son to his own congregation in Otterndorf in 1661. The fact that the second and third sermons were preached within five days of each other the following year indicates that they were conceived jointly as a response to Großgebauer. Rather than adopting a purely defensive pose, however, he presented in the second sermon a systematic analysis of the basis for church music, leaving the polemical counterattacks for the third sermon. The result can be seen as a *summa* of Lutheran orthodox music theology. As Bunners notes, "Mithobius is not attempting an individual view and judgment of church music but rather a presentation of the orthodox Lutheran standpoint."[276] Most of the writers we have met thus far reappear in the footnotes of Mithobius' pages, demonstrating that what seem to be divergent emphases of devotional or theological groups were regarded as components of a harmonious tradition. Mithobius, writing in the middle of the century, marks the culmination of the theological developments which preceded him and the last major attempt at a synthesis of this tradition.

Most of the conflict between Mithobius and Großgebauer results from their opposing points of departure. Whereas Großgebauer's theology was anthropocentric, focussing on psychologically and pedagogically effective means of communicating the gospel, Mithobius' approach was theocentric, with humans playing a subordinate role in a God-centered universe. For Mithobius the main purpose for music was not to arouse devotion but to praise God. Mithobius' universe is hierarchically conceived with God on his throne in the heavens surrounded by angels and saints who perpetually sing his praise. His subjects on earth are far below, beneath the patriarchs and prophets who now belong to the church triumphant.[277] As in the time of the Old Testament kings, God expects to be glorified in the manner appropriate to his supreme majesty. Using the analogy of an earthly king being honored with the most splendid music possible, Mithobius argues that God likewise is to be praised with all resources available. "So one should many thousand times more apply all skill, wit, sense, reason, and understanding to the music of the king of kings...who alone is wise, indeed is himself the highest wisdom."[278] This argument is interpreted in a very literal manner as entailing the implementation of all varieties of musical form at the highest level of musical skill.

Elsewhere Mithobius acknowledges that a lack of skill should not prevent one from singing, or at least joining with the heart rather than the voice. "But when the devotion is good, God pays no attention to the voice, even if it is cacophonous or sounds bad, as Jerome writes [in his Ephesians commentary]. For the song of praise by stammering Moses was just as dear to God as what his sister Miriam sang with other women, who by nature usually have a more pure, sweet, and pleasant-sounding voice than do men" (162). Nor is an outward performance sufficient without proper devotion or spiritual understanding: "Therefore in our singing we should also think diligently about this and use our hearts as well; certainly the large majority in the church or congregation and elsewhere only sing with the mouth while their hearts are far away and contemplating nothing of what is being sung" (162).

Yet music in church does not have as its primary purpose the stimulation of devotion; such a purpose requires an accommodation to the musical level of the congregation. Rather, music is a response to God's command, performed in loving and obedient service to him. Accordingly, appropriate to his dignity, the biblical command to praise God demands the most artistic, happiest, loveliest music available. "But the words of our text [Eph. 5:19] reveal that this command of God can in a certain way be understood to include artistic figural music, which is best and most elegantly arranged with many voices and many kinds of alternation according to the notes and rules of the singers" (179).

To some extent this connection of elaborate music with the command to praise God is based on Old Testament example and the Psalm references to numerous instruments. To that extent, however, it could be rejected by some, especially Calvinists, as an aspect of Old Testament ceremony which could be regarded as surpassed in the more spiritual days of the new covenant. Mithobius argues that the New Testament also admonishes the use of full artistic skills: whereas others read Paul as emphasizing spiritual gifts or the "song of the heart" over the "song of the mouth," Mithobius regards the phrase "with all your heart" (Eph. 5:19) as entailing "all powers of body and soul." The variety of genres listed by Paul (psalms, hymns and spiritual songs) is for Mithobius an endorsement of all available modes of singing and playing, and the instruction to converse with one another involves mutual stimulation: "With one's gifts one should arouse, stimulate and encourage the other to bring about the most artistic, happiest and loveliest music to the praise of God, so that a voice and a choir compete and contend to see which can do it best" (179). Similarly, the Colossians passage so often used to support the primacy of inward feeling over outward song is interpreted by Mithobius as a call for beautiful, skillful music. The "wisdom" which should dwell richly is taken to apply to figural music, and, in the phrase "singing with grace in your hearts," the grace is connected first of all with the singing and only through that with the heart. "Figural singing is a great wisdom and art; through it the most beautiful texts and sayings of divine Holy Scripture are movingly repeated and implanted by various means in the mind. In this way a sweet, glorious, and beautiful loveliness, charm, and harmony or concord is heard" (180).

The New Testament passage (I Cor. 14:40) which served as the basis for the doctrine of adiaphora in the Formula of Concord, that worship be organized "for the sake of good order and decorum" is likewise seen by Mithobius as fulfilled through artistic music.

> Whatever provides for the adornment and well-being or worthy order of the church should be promoted eagerly and diligently....If there is anything which adorns a church, it is fine figural music, says a distinguished theologian [Dieterich], for it sounds indeed lovely when many voices and choirs sing together in the church to the glory of God in an artful work of harmony. (180)

Even Jesus is found to be a supporter of instrumental music, though the argument is an undocumented claim that "the son of God himself and the apostles and evangelists in the New Testament again and again commended the Psalms of David to us" (182). That this entails instrumental music is based on an exegetical and etymological tradition extending back to the early church whereby the verb *psallein* meant to strike strings. According to Hilary of Poitiers, "There is a 'psalm' when the voice rests and only the playing of the instrument is heard."[279]

Given these readings of the New Testament references to music, the adiaphoric position of music as ceremony is no longer adequate. To be sure, music meets the minimum requirements of contributing to good order and decorum in worship. Yet the reasons for singing go far beyond music's ceremonial utility. Like many writers before him, Mithobius listed several reasons for singing, first of which was "the command of God," followed by "example of the saints," "the duty of the servant to the lord," "benefits to us," and "the harm of neglect" (173–4).[280] With greater care than previously, Mithobius attempted to reconcile "the command of God" to sing with the ceremonial freedom to omit music. This he does by distinguishing between what is absolutely and what is conditionally necessary. Music is not absolutely necessary—the church does not stand or fall on whether there is figural or organ music—, but on the basis of the above reasons it is conditionally necessary.

When Mithobius discusses the conditions which make music necessary, he sometimes applies the utilitarian principles by which adiaphora are judged and sometimes turns to the larger moral question of Christian liberty. According to the first, as formulated by Dieterich in a church dedication sermon, the result of using a ceremonial element must be compared with the presumed result of abandoning it. In the case of music, Mithobius says, there can be no doubt that its use is "far, far better" than its omission (299). Further, the principle which was formulated in times of conflict may also apply here: when the opponent attempts to remove something that is theoretically non-essential, it is necessary to defend its use. "We do not let ourselves be forced to remove the same, and we thus promulgate our freedom, lest we be imprisoned" (248).

Treated under the rubric of Christian liberty, singing is like any other action which has been commanded by God. With the coming of the Gospel, Christians are freed from the law, but freedom is not a release from obligation; rather, the faithful joyfully and voluntarily do the works that please God out of gratitude for the salvation which has been freely bestowed. The commands of the Old Testament are not abrogated, however. The fact that there are fewer commands to sing praise in the New Testament than in the Old does not indicate any change in the wishes of God or in the demands of being faithful. It merely reflects the decreased need for commands as Christians respond out of love toward God (188).

In relation to the love of neighbor, the principles of ceremonial freedom and Christian liberty intersect. Elements of outward ceremony which might not be important for one's own spiritual growth may nevertheless be vital for others. Whether the freedom to remove a ceremony should be invoked depends on whether the removal would offend those weaker in faith. On this question the difference of opinion between Großgebauer and Mithobius rests not on the theory but on its application. For Großgebauer, the concern not to offend the neighbor would mean, in practice, the omission of any music too complex or sophisticated to be understood by everyone. Mithobius' application of the principle is diametrically opposed: to omit artistic music would prevent many from experiencing the joy of festive celebrations. "What a fine Christian freedom it would be if one were to omit [figural] music on high feast and festival days and thereby withdraw the means of spiritual joy from many faithful hearts, thus causing much harm and offence!" (190)

Mithobius thus professes to be as concerned for the common folk as was Großgebauer, but he disagrees entirely with Großgebauer's analysis of their feelings. It is not true that they dislike organs: on festival days they crowd into church to hear the joyous music, "for they sense its hidden power" (261). Nor is it true that they cannot understand the words sung in motets and concerted music: most of the texts are in German and consist of familiar passages from the Scriptures which through repetition have been implanted in people's hearts (261). Furthermore, the people even understand and joyfully sing the Latin phrases which have been retained in familiar hymns such as "In dulci jubilo" and "Surrexit Christus hodie" (262). Repetition, therefore, not removal, is the solution; the more the people hear a piece, the more they like it. But it is not necessary that everyone join in the singing of everything that is sung (265), nor is there evidence that singing always accompanied instrumental music in Old Testament times. Moreover, it is unlikely that in David's time everyone could have understood the text of temple music with all the strings and 120 trumpets being played at the same time (259). But instrumental music is not directed at the understanding; rather it appeals to the senses and the affects, and any listener can discern what mood is being conveyed (258–260).

While Mithobius thus expects the common people to be inspired by the music, he does not expect music to serve as an instrument of inner healing, either spiritual or psychological. Mithobius scorns Großgebauer's use of the supposedly naturalistic explanation of the spirits working through the harmonic resonances of the body. It is futile, he asserts, to attempt an explanation of music's "divine, secret and hidden power" (283). Großgebauer's examples of music driving people to madness are an attempt, Mithobius believes, to show that music is of the devil. True, different modes have different effects, but the effects depend on the object, just as the sun warming different objects may produce either a sweet or putrid smell (283). Not music, but the listener, is either good or bad, and the response will reveal which.

An example both of Mithobius' disinterest in naturalistic investigations and his belief that the results of music depend on the hearer is found in his explanation of the devil's dislike of music. Far from equating Saul's evil spirit with melancholy or spiritual turmoil, Mithobius turns to witchcraft literature for an explanation more suited to his cosmology, which, incidentally, includes more than one devil. Quoting Bernhard Waldschmiedt, he explains,

> The reason devils cannot stand music is that they are well aware of having served God and praised his divine majesty unceasingly before they fell, when they were good angels. From this they know well how very dear and pleasing it is to him; and because the extreme loveliness of the heavenly music stills hovers in their memories, they consider how they must be deprived of it for eternity. Even nowadays, whenever they hear us humans making such a musical song of praise, they remember their original glorious circumstances and thus scorn it. These evil spirits become so angry that they must retreat from humans who are making music from the bottom of their hearts. (226)[281]

Although Mithobius does not explicitly reject the view that the Holy Spirit uses music for his own ends or that music is an instrument of the Holy Spirit, his thinking does not consistently move in this direction. Using as his sermon text the verses of Ephesians 5:18–19, "Be filled with the Spirit and speak among yourselves of psalms, hymns, and spiritual songs," he does say that the way one becomes "full of the Spirit" is through these forms of singing, "which come from the Holy Spirit and awaken a spiritual joy in the heart" (155). Yet more often he implies that the singing or lack thereof results from a given spiritual state which is either receptive or resistant to the influence of music. Just as the fallen angels show their prior sinfulness through their dislike of music, so people's willingness to sing reflects their existing relationship to God. If one is filled with the Spirit, one will gladly sing; if not, one's hardness of heart will be displayed by a closed mouth. At one point he even suggests that non-singers may be possessed by the devil: "For such a person, especially when he sits in church and will not sing, either out of pride or other vicious causes, thereby lets his mouth be shut by the devil; then he is dumb and possessed by him like that poor man in Luke 11:14" (166).

More than previous writers, Mithobius makes a point of encouraging women to sing and, as quoted above, regards female voices as more naturally pleasing. Yet when they are reluctant to sing, he does not look sympathetically to a long tradition of discouraging women's participation but to their sinful obstinacy: "It is an indication that many women are not full of the Holy Spirit but full of pride, folly and sin when they do not want to sing along in the psalms and hymns in church and laugh at those who exhort them to do so" (159).

Mithobius, then, does not dispute the charges such as those of Quistorp and Großgebauer concerning people's tardy entrances into church calculated to miss the music and hear the sermon. He is simply much less sanguine about the possibility of effective reform measures. Previous authoritarian efforts have been fruitless: "This godless, sinful, condemnable habit unfortunately cannot be completely broken among us by zealous sermons on the law, by frequently reading and repeating a command of the authorities, or by occasionally making an example of someone" (176). Not inclined to change worship in order to meet the needs of the people, Mithobius intends simply to defend the right as he sees it: "…for now we simply want to remain with this apostolic admonition to them, as our office requires, whether they hear or refuse to hear (Ezekiel 2:5,7; 3:11)." In sum, the congregation are to blame if the music has no effect on them; they could get involved if they tried. As Conrad Dieterich advised, the people could lift their hearts to devotion and joy rather than impassively sitting during the organ music like bumps on a log (309).

Be this as it may, cantors and organists have much to answer for. In fact, when Mithobius begins assailing them, one could almost believe Großgebauer was the author. Much as the two would refuse to admit it, they are in substantial agreement on the abuses of music perpetrated by church musicians. Although Mithobius responds vehemently against Großgebauer's attack on ungodly church musicians, this is a defense of the **office** of church musician against Großgebauer's assertion that the **office** is a remnant of popery (302). In actual practice, Mithobius is far from satisfied with the current crop of cantors and organists. If not ungodly, many cantors are at least lazy. Mithobius shows himself to be an exasperated pastor unable to get his musicians to produce enough music on the main feast days of the church year (198). Comparing the amount of time the Levites spent in liturgical praise (2 Chron. 30:21), he resents the attempts of musicians to reduce the expected three days of festival music while being willing to provide eight days of music for a wedding, where "day and night they serve people's sinful pleasures" (195). The lack of choirboys on feast days is not a persuasive excuse; the cantor can still sing alone "*voce sola* into the organ" (219). There is plenty of music available in this form, and in any case the Italians consider it the best. Aware that more money needs to be spent to provide for good church music, Mithobius nevertheless has no sympathy when those who are employed to do the Lord's work do not perform:

> It often happens that the preacher's life is embittered on high and happy festival days; in order that the music not fall short, he always has to drive those who are employed to perform music like stubborn mules with much vexation and even to the point of death. May those who are slack in the work of the Lord be cursed! (Jer. 48:10.) (219)

Even if they are in their place during the service, they often take advantage of the seclusion of the organ loft. Calling to mind Dieterich's complaints, Mithobius notes that such high places in the church as the choir and organ lofts have nearly become market-places for those who prefer to chatter rather than to pay attention to the service. They cause offense to innocent youths and sincere believers by their "tomfoolery, mischief, pranks, roguery, laughter and gossip" (273).

Not only is it difficult to keep the musicians working; it is also difficult to get appropriate music out of them. Instead of "holy, devotional, spiritual music" they bring into the church a "wanton new, strange, dissolute, overly embellished, indeed irreverent worldly manner or style of singing" (234). Quoting Dannhauer,[282] Mithobius threatens God's judgment on them: if their jobs are eliminated because of the worldly music they perform in church, they have only themselves to blame. Mithobius' images of the punishment God metes out for blasphemous music are not, like Frick's, of the lightning bolt variety, but they are dramatic enough: the Turks, who were threatening the imperial residence in Vienna and were reported to have destroyed the musical instruments of a delegation from Francis I to Suleiman, might be God's punishment for the abuse of music in Germany (235).

As one who so adamantly defends figural and instrumental music against Großgebauer's criticism, Mithobius' own musical conservatism is something of a surprise. In disputing with Großgebauer he defends the value of Italian music: "Thus the nicely and reverently set Italian pieces based on Scripture are not to be rejected, for from them [Italians] we may also learn what is good and use for our benefit the gifts which God bestowed on them more than on others" (305). When not directing his wrath to Großgebauer, however, his complaints about church musicians are remarkably similar to his opponent's. Tracing the history of style criticism based on morality from Plato and Aristotle through Clement of Alexandria, Jerome, and Bernard of Clairvaux to Luther, Hunnius, Balduinus, and Stegmann, Mithobius finds uniform support for rejection of a worldly style of music:

> The *Genus Chromaticum* or the wanton, frivolous, confused and overly ornate manner of singing and playing, with all too many startling coloratures and strange runs where everything is fighting and simultaneously laughing and hopping in and through everything else as if one were in a pleasure house or worldly gambling house, has never been praised by honorable people, much less by upright Christians. (269-70)[283]

His instructions to cantors call for "nothing but reverent, graceful, serious, heart-warming pieces" and avoidance of those instrumental pieces which "are comprised...only of worldly, galliardic hops or other modes of wedding dance" (276). Organists are advised not to show off with "unusual runs, now here, now there" and to avoid "all unfitting and frivolous fashions with courantes, passamezzos, and dances." In words scarcely distinguishable from those of Großgebauer, Mithobius warns against interfering with people's devotions:

> Therefore it is also a sin when the organists, through their untimely playing and their runs, hinder and halt devotion rather than furthering it. For example, when the congregation is supposed to sing along, they cut apart the Psalms and spoil them through their strange running interludes before each verse and their long, irregular pauses after every line. In this way they deter and distract the congregation in their devotion when they could easily play along unnoticed in a most pleasant and harmonious manner. (276)[284]

The musical style which Mithobius favors, then, is by no means the latest import from Italy or France but rather the uncontroversial German motet style. More specifically, the composer who epitomizes church music for him is Andreas Hammerschmidt, who is always introduced whenever Mithobius wants to demonstrate a kind of figural music to which all people can respond: "So also examples are well known to us in this congregation when the music on high festival days has been especially delightful: when Hammerschmidt's six-part piece, 'Who will roll away the stone?' was sung on Easter, godly women poured out many tears from heartfelt devotion" (306).[285]

Mithobius, then, is not a partisan of church musicians any more than he is of the congregation. His perspective is that of the pastor, who as head of the church is ultimately responsible for the music. Pastors and musicians should confer about the music so that the music and the sermon are in harmony (302–3). This means that pastors should be musically informed, and in his preface he holds up his father and grandfather as models of clergy who knew music and took an active part in the planning of the music in their churches (45ff.).

Although this ideal hardly differs from what one might read in a manual for church music in our day, Mithobius's image of the church reflects the Age of Absolutism. Not only does he believe in authority and order within the church, but political authority bears a responsibility for providing for the religious needs of the society. Mithobius' 24-page dedication of the book to Anton Gunther and Sophia Catherina, count and countess of Oldenburg and Delmenhorst, praises their examples and expounds the importance of piety and patronage on the part of the nobility. The princes on earth should emulate the princes in heaven, that is, the angels, and make it their concern that the praise of God carried out in glorious manner. A Baroque vision of the hierarchies of heaven and earth combines here with Luther's fear of societal disorder to identify outward ceremony as crucial for maintaining a civilized society: "When the authorities do not faithfully embrace worship, it falls away and with it all outward adornments, while sheer disorder and barbarity prevails, as the books of Kings and Chronicles and other histories and experiences from all ages teach and testify" (12).

From a practical standpoint, Mithobius' aim was to persuade the nobility to spend money on church music rather than on secular entertainment. As model patrons of church music, Mithobius recognizes King Manuel I of Portugal, Emperor Maximilian I and Johann Georg I, Elector of Saxony.[286] Recalling a precedent for his own situation, he notes that Matthias Hoe von Hoenegg, court preacher for the Elector of Saxony, had praised the Elector for engaging the services of such excellent musicians as Michael Praetorius and Heinrich Schütz (10).[287] Through his properly submissive and lengthy book dedication, Mithobius expresses his gratitude to Anton Gunther and Sophia Catherina for their support of good music and urges its continuance.

This solicitous attitude toward the nobility is diametrically opposed to that of Großgebauer, who in another work had harshly berated court preachers for supporting their employers' military campaigns.[288] Not surprisingly, then, Mithobius defends the custom of including the patrons' favorite pieces among the music played or sung during their presence at communion. This is not "respect of persons," as Großgebauer calls it, and no one should ever think that individuals are being honored in communion. But when a person who is entrusted with oversight of the church comes to communion, "why should one not serve them with the same means which are ordered for the church as a whole?" (319). If the piece awakens devotion in them, it will do so for the whole congregation.

If to this extent Mithobius shows himself to be politically astute and Großgebauer lacking in social graces, still there are substantive differences in their view of communion music. Against Großgebauer's complaints that music during communion often expresses something other than the death of Christ, Mithobius responds that to proclaim Christ's death "does not mean specifically his suffering and dying only but also in general his whole precious work, which finally led up to his death" (314). During Advent the focus is on Christ's coming, during Christmastide it is on his birth, and so forth. In general communion is a joyful celebration of Christ's redemptive work, not a penitential remembrance of his suffering.

The different emphasis in communion is rooted in a very different ecclesiology. Whereas for Großgebauer the visible church with all its outward forms is a means of preparation for a truly spiritual future existence, for Mithobius the visible church is an imperfect representation of and participation in the more glorious existence of the saints and angels. The institution and its outward forms are for Mithobius not merely a temporary shell from which a very different life form will emerge; rather, the divinely instituted body of the church is modelled after the original heavenly body. While for Großgebauer music is useful only insofar as it furthers the spiritual transformation of the congregation, for Mithobius it is already a participation in the life of the spirit. Mithobius' concern for the church and its harmonious ordering as an institution is therefore not an accommodation to political power or practical efficiency but is based in the conviction of the unity of heavenly and earthly structures. From this perspective, Großgebauer was a threat not only to church music but to the concord among preachers and among the three estates of Christendom. What Mithobius refused to admit was that his vision of the church was tied to one particular era in earthly history. By idealizing the status quo, he stubbornly resisted changes even in areas where he recognized serious problems. He was disturbed by sinfulness and lack of devotion among those who attended church and those who provided the music, but he offered no solutions other than to maintain the outward forms of worship. This is not to say that the outward forms were empty ritual. His recollections of his grandfather, father and a beloved cantor and rector (45–54) are moving testimony that deep inward devotion was possible within Lutheran orthodoxy. But in his attempt to avoid a spiritualism which retreated from the institutional church, Mithobius denied the legitimate concerns of those who sought change. To his mind, the Lutheran church was the *ecclesia reformata*, not the *ecclesia semper reformanda*.

FROM PIETISM TO THE ENLIGHTENMENT

CHAPTER NINE

WORSHIP AS EDIFICATION

The emergence of Pietism in the last three decades of the seventeenth century marked a significant change in theological approaches to music. Yet because Lutheran Orthodoxy also underwent changes, it would be fallacious to contrast Pietist thought of the late seventeenth or early eighteenth centuries with Orthodox thought of the mid-seventeenth century. In some respects the concerns and outlooks of the time provided greater common ground than did a theological label applied across several decades. So many misleading and negative interpretations of Pietism have been advanced, especially in relation to music, that one is tempted to avoid using the term altogether and instead simply to focus on individual thinkers.[289] Furthermore, the complexity of the subject and the disagreements among scholars concerning the definition of Pietism make it difficult to use the term with any precision.[290] Yet to make any contribution toward clarification of the concept and correction of misinterpretations, it is necessary to confront the difficulties.

For purposes of this book, I am concerned only with those Pietists who remained within the institutional church. Because the term was applied in the late seventeenth century to Philip Jakob Spener and his followers, I believe the definition of the phenomenon should emerge first of all from an examination of their position. Antecedents and influences should be identified through direct personal or textual connections, not by abstracting concepts and looking for shared ideas. Above all, the inclination to equate such general phenomena as mysticism, subjectivity, and sentimentality with Pietism must be resisted unless specific forms thereof are represented by individuals who were in their own time identified as Pietists.

Our treatment of Pietism here will, as has been the case with Orthodoxy, be limited to writings **about** music, specifically church music, and will leave hymn texts and melodies for others to study. No attempt will be made to answer Martin Geck's question, "But what is the music of Pietism?"[291] His efforts to draw connections between the music of Buxtehude and the spirituality and theology of the Pietists have not been found persuasive,[292] but his brief discussion of "The musical views of early Pietism"[293] is a useful clarification of Pietists' basic attitudes toward music.

That the Pietists were opposed to elaborate church music is generally known, but, as we have seen, even defenders of artistic music were critical of musical showmanship and irreverence. What is necessary is to understand the larger framework within which the criticisms are expressed. As Geck explains, "Edification with the goal of regeneration is the **positive** content of pietist devotion."[294] Over against the types of sermons and church music which many people heard without understanding, Pietists asserted that comprehension was crucial. People could make no progress in faith if they were ignorant; the many errors which had crept into hymn texts revealed that people did not understand what they were singing, if indeed they were singing at all. Far from substituting new individualistic hymns for recognized, congregationally-centered hymns, the Pietists sought to fulfill the original Reformation ideal of a singing congregation.[295]

Just as it is a mistake to set up a dichotomy in which Pietism focusses on the individual and Orthodoxy focusses on the congregation, so it is a mistake to associate Orthodoxy only with intellect and Pietism only with feeling. As we have seen, orthodox theologians had consistently demanded the involvement of the heart when singing, while they had said little about involvement of the mind on a cognitive level. Pietists, on the other hand, while opposing metaphysics and arid intellectualism, stressed the need for understanding the faith as a prerequisite to living it.

The Pietist view of worship, and indeed of all activities, was summed up in a 1672 treatise written by Christian Kortholt, professor of scripture in Kiel, for Spener, who had it published in Frankfurt. Referring to Paul's advice to the Corinthians in chapter 14, Kortholt notes, "He wants everything in the Christian gathering to happen for [the purpose of] improvement."[296] This chapter was one of the most important for Pietists writing about worship and music because it stresses intelligibility. The pragmatic question, "Can the people understand it?" was for Pietists the first test of music's acceptability for public worship. Not satisfied with the standard response of Lutheran Orthodoxy, "It is enough if they understand its **genus**," Pietists demanded textual comprehensibility. For this reason, they repeatedly objected to Latin texts, choral music where the words could not be discerned, and organ music which conveyed no meaning.

All of these objections had been raised by Calvinists, of course, but in Calvinism they tended to spring from theological principles such as the subordination of the senses or the superiority of the New Testament. No such principles are raised by Kortholt, who is not opposed in theory to either choirs or instruments, as long as they are "correctly used and applied."[297] In fact, singing hymns in a pleasant voice with instrumental accompaniment can bring tears to the eyes and increase devotion[298]; but if the words are in Latin or the text is chopped up, there is no benefit, even if the sound is pleasing: "Such may serve for pleasure and delight but not for edification in Christianity."[299]

The congregational focus of Kortholt's treatise is indicated in its title, "Of Public Worship." Like the Rostock theologians, Kortholt was concerned about the common practice of coming to church only for the sermon. To those who say, "we can sing and pray at home," Kortholt responds with the words of Chrysostom, "You deceive yourself, my friend, and go far astray.... Your prayer will not be heard so easily when you call upon God by yourself as when you pray together with your brethren."[300] With respect to singing, Kortholt appeals to the words of Luther, who extolled the benefits of the Psalms "especially where the crowd sings along."[301]

Even when the music of the choir is comprehensible, therefore, the singing of the whole congregation is preferable. This is clearly stated three decades later by Christian Gerber, who was under attack from Georg Motz, a defender of artistic music:

> Furthermore I can assure [Motz] that the singing of a whole congregation, which he scornfully calls "a vile chorale clamor" is far more pleasing to the Highest than an artistic piece where the listeners can understand nothing because of the noise of the instruments or else hear a word only now and then. I do not deny that God's deeds can be praised also in lovely and reverent [figural] music if it is rightly arranged for edification. But through the singing of chorales it happens just as well and even better, because the whole congregation is praising the greatness of God with one mouth.[302]

It is significant that Motz was a cantor and school music director at Tilse, not a preacher or theologian. After Mithobius, the major defenses of music came from musicians or music theorists. This fact has tended to distort the understanding of Pietism in relation to music, for the presumption has been made that the position of Orthodoxy was represented by these defenses. As we have seen with Mithobius, however, musicians could cause grievance to Orthodox preachers, and on this subject both critics and defenders of the musical status quo could agree.

This is also true on the subject of the relative importance of hymns and figural music. Samuel Schelwig (1643–1715), one of the most virulent theological opponents of Pietism, admitted in his *Cynosura Conscientiae oder Leit-Stern des Gewissens* that in the practice of the time figural music overshadowed congregational hymn-singing. The first reason to reverse this emphasis, he argued, was that, here as in the secular arena, the adage applies, "Salus populi suprema lex esto." Secondly, the combined force of many voices in prayer or song is more pleasing and more effective with God. Even when the choir sings, the sound should be as of one voice directed to God.[303]

Because of the importance of hymns for both parties, the temptation to attribute to Pietists all the hymnological innovations which occurred during this period should be avoided.[304] Quite apart from the tenets of Pietism, changes were taking place in musical and literary style which interacted with changes in church and society in ways much too complicated to explore here. Without analyzing the actual hymns and melodies produced by those who might be labelled "Pietist," we can say with certainty that it was not the intention of leading Pietists to abandon the traditional Lutheran hymns. On the contrary, the prevailing disposition among Pietists, as well as other theologians, was to preserve the tried and true and regard novelty warily.

In the preface to the hymnal he was publishing in 1686, the pastor of the German church in Copenhagen Johannes Lassenius, who is best classified as Reform Orthodox, launched out against the predilection for innovation. Underneath a godly appearance much godlessness was being introduced, "because people have itchy ears for all kinds of innovations."[305] He considers it his duty to warn against evil and to test whether the inspiration for new hymns came from God. Not that there is any reason in principle to oppose them, for Luther himself urged others to write hymns. But there is now, as Lassenius sees it, a preference for artistry over spirituality. Although the new hymns may be more artistic, Luther's are more spiritual. Regretting that people will not be satisfied with singing the new hymns privately and that they have been accepted in public worship, Lassenius is willing to allow scripturally based new hymns as long as preference is given to Luther's hymns.[306]

By 1697 the variety of hymnody which had made its way into different churches was so great that Spener, for the sake of uniformity, called for a return both to the traditional hymns and to the traditional forms of those hymns. His favorite hymn-writer was Paul Gerhardt, whose poems deserve preference because of their great "power and spirit."[307] In order to assure that the original hymns be retained for public worship, Spener recommends that there be two types of hymnals, one for church and one for home.

As concerning the relative importance of congregational and choir singing, so on the introduction of new hymns into public worship, similar sentiments are found among both Orthodox and Pietist. In 1715 the Orthodox theologian Ernst Salomon Cyprian wrote a treatise "On the propagation of heresies through songs," in which he raised the problem of the reception of new hymns into the church. With the Psalms of David and the hymns of Luther, there hardly seems any need for the new hymns, which in no way excel over the old. Because of the dangers of heresy, new hymns should not readily be accepted; there is no reason for the private to be made public.[308]

If both theological camps agreed on the need to dam the flood of new church songs, it may be necessary to look elsewhere for points of dispute. Evidence suggests some conflict concerning the relationship between the patron and the pastor in matters of church music. In legal commentaries there is some ambiguity concerning this relationship. Johann Brunnemann (1608–1672) had recognized the responsibility of the "Ministerii Sacri" and the "Magistratus Politici" to provide music for public worship, not further specifying how directly involved the magistrates should be.[309] Benedict Carpzov (1595–1666) distinguished in theory between the internal and external areas of ecclesiastical authority: princes and political estates were to be responsible for propagation of religion, ecclesiastical jurisdiction, and care and defense of the church, but were not to interfere in the preaching of the Word, administration of the sacraments, or the power of the keys. In defining these areas of authority, however, it becomes clear that music in different ways falls on both sides of the distinction. The magistrate has the duty of confirming appointments of cantors and organists and warning or removing them in cases of improper behavior; moreover, he has the right to suspend instrumental and figural music in times of public mourning.[310] The difficulty in maintaining the balance of power was demonstrated in the Großgebauer–Mithobius debate: Mithobius stressed the pastor's authority over the choice of music and hymns but was willing, within limits, to accommodate the musical tastes of the secular authorities who provided the external support for music, whereas Großgebauer was offended by such incursions of secular rank into sacred worship.

Johann Muscovius (1635–95), following in the line of Großgebauer, was sufficiently disturbed by what he perceived as intrusions on the rights of pastors that he laid out a procedure for musical suggestions by patrons. Citing Carpzov, he first specified that the right to choose music did not belong to ecclesiastical jurisdiction or to the rights of the patron but to the office of pastor. Because the texts of the music should be in keeping with the subject matter of the sermon, the secular authorities cannot in good conscience bypass the pastor in requesting music. By appointing the pastor, the patron has entrusted to him the care of souls, and this includes the choice of hymns. Thus Muscovius suggests,

> But when [a secular official] has a special intention to sing this or that hymn in church, this is first communicated to the pastor or minister in order that no new hymns be introduced which are composed from a worldly spirit or are otherwise suspect. The pastor will listen to him and afterward indicate to the cantor or schoolmaster what is to be sung. Thus one proceeds in orderly fashion.[311]

The importance of procedural orderliness in bringing about changes in externals of worship is strongly emphasized by Spener. Rather than pitting clergy against political authority, however, Spener recognizes the interests of all three estates in these matters. Because special consideration is to be given to the weak, neither a preacher nor a prince has the right single-handedly to introduce new forms of worship, even if they are more edifying than the old ones.[312]

Singing in Latin is a case in point. Although there is no doubt in Spener's mind that it would be preferable to eliminate all Latin singing, this should only be done through a gradual and orderly process of discussion and persuasion. Latin can, after all, be understood by some, but singing in Latin is a sinful remnant of popery when it takes time away from the singing of German hymns or causes people to stay away from church. This should be explained by the pastor to the council, and he should not cease trying to bring about the elimination of Latin singing, but it is not his right to change ceremonies without permission. Neither should the secular authorities be stubborn, especially when the congregation expresses its grievances, for the edification of the community is, after all, the goal of worship.[313]

To pursue the discussions of the protocol for liturgical change is a task for another study,[314] but some provisional generalizations are possible. The fact that the extent of political authority in liturgical matters was debated indicates that at least some rulers sought active involvement in the shaping of worship life in their territories. As the issue did not emerge as significant until the latter part of the seventeenth century, it appears to coincide with the rise of absolutism in the German principalities.[315] Muscovius notwithstanding, the level of acquiescence to the rights of princes within the church appears to have been fairly high among those who chose not to separate from the state church. Stated differently, one of the marks of separatists was the unwillingness to accept such shared authority.

The practical result of this situation for church music was that the adiaphoric status of organ and choral music was highlighted by theologians of all stripes. Whereas church music in general was defended against Quakers, fanatics, and Pietists who, correctly or incorrectly, were said to oppose it, not even Orthodox theologians were inclined to assert that music was necessary or to argue for the importance of organ music.

Schelwig, for example, after presenting reasons in favor of singing, acknowledged that instrumental music was "less to be tolerated" and that he did not consider it necessary. In Old Testament times it was indeed customary and even expressly commanded, but as an essential component of temple worship it ceased to be obligatory when the temple was destroyed.[316]

Similarly, Johann Ernst Schulenburg, writing in 1711 against the "fanatic abuse" of Christian freedom in matters of external ceremony, appealed not to divine command but to ecclesiastical order and authority as reasons not to abandon ceremonies. Like Schelwig he admitted that the Levitic cult was lifted and no obligation remains, but organs and other instruments may be used on the basis both of Christian freedom and also the evidence of music in worship since the time of the early church. However, using a scheme of historical evidence which had become standard during the late seventeenth century, Schulenburg noted that the early church fathers had been opposed to organs and that Pope Vitalian in the seventh century had been the first to introduce them to worship. Thus not the intrinsic correctness of church music practices but the fact that the church in its freedom had long held to these practices makes them worthy of retention: "Accordingly, what was introduced long ago with the approval of the whole church is by no means to be set aside through the self-willed fantasy of novices."[317] The "fanatics" who so rashly attempt to change these traditions out of their unmoderated freedom are thus opposing Christian rulers who, like Constantine, Theodoricus, and Justinian, are responsible for good order in the church.[318]

The role of princes in matters of adiaphora was discussed at length in a debate at the university of Halle involving Christian Thomasius (1655–1728), leading rationalist professor of law. Citing Brunnemann but without mention of the clergy, Thomasius states that instrumental music in church is a matter for the prince to arrange. While quoting several criticisms of theatrical and worldly music in church, he seems to prefer to leave the resolution of this controversial matter to the prince.[319] Although no one, he claims, will deny that abuse is rampant—many cantors imagine they are contributing greatly to the honor of God, but their minds are far from religion—, it is still an adiaphoron. A century after the development of the Lutheran Orthodox stance, music was indeed being treated as an adiaphoron.

Although their attitudes toward political authority might differ somewhat, it is nearly impossible to distinguish non-separatist Pietists from late Orthodox theologians solely on the basis of liturgical theory or attitude toward music in worship. Among theologians of the late seventeenth and early eighteenth centuries, I have found none who, like Mithobius, put primacy on the doxological purpose of worship. Both Pietists and Orthodox point to edification or improvement of the worshippers as the justification of all aspects of worship. Of course, none would deny that God is to be honored in all that is done, but the verse which provided direction for them was Romans 12:1, which in the translation then in use recommended "reasonable worship" ("vernünftiger Gottesdienst"). Most saw this as best fulfilled musically by hymns sung by the congregation with understanding.[320] Elaborate music, particularly instrumental music, was surely less reasonable and contributed less to the understanding or moral improvement of the people than did music with comprehensible texts.

To be sure, Pietists were more negative than the Orthodox in their judgments of organ and figural music. They appealed frequently to Großgebauer and to the Dutch Reformed theologian Gisbert Voetius, who had devoted a lengthy section of his *Politicae ecclesiasticae*[321] to the question of the legitimacy of organ music in worship. With this source material Samuel Stryk came close to demanding ouster of organs as remnants of a papist yoke. They were not in keeping with the spirit of the New Testament, they were superfluous, useless impediments to worship, and they encouraged the superstition that humans could promote the glory of God in this way. Even Stryk, though, had no objection if instruments were used to accompany unison singing.[322]

Systematic exclusion of organs and figural music from worship was never a tenet of Pietism. With perhaps more honesty than those who had previously recognized music to be an adiaphoron, Pietists truly regarded music as something which could contribute to worship in a positive way but which could also be misused in a variety of ways. No dogmatic position could be taken regarding music in the abstract. In many particular settings of the time, however, music was detracting from worship. Rather than merely complain and criticize, as many preachers had done, Spener suggested a practical alternative: those who want to hear figural music should have a separate time when they can listen to it without the interruption of the sermon; with it removed from the main service, those who are not interested in it will not be tired out while waiting to hear the sermon.[323] Marcus Steffens, also a practical man, felt that the money spent on organs would be better spent in feeding the hungry.[324] Still, instrumental music was not a matter of conscience but a free "Mittel-Ding" so long—and here Steffens summarizes the Pietist attitude—as in the gathering of Christians it is not ruler but servant.[325]

While the emphasis of this chapter has been on the similarity of attitude among Pietist and Orthodox on the role of music in worship, it should not be assumed that there were no remaining adherents of the celestial harmony approach or the doxological perspective. These lines, as we shall see, had been taken over by music theorists and were developing independently. Nor should it be concluded that Pietists were not involved in bitter controversies with musicians. But, as we shall also see, these had less to do with music than with the character of the musicians. There was, finally, a clear doctrinal distinction between Pietists and Orthodox in the matter of music, but it lay not in the importance of edification but—and here we come finally to the second major concept in Geck's summary—of regeneration.

CHAPTER TEN

THE REGENERATION OF MUSICIANS

That music in worship should serve to increase devotion was agreed by all. That what was sung with the mouth should be believed in the heart was also uncontroversial. The point of controversy arose when the devotion or belief became a prerequisite to the use or performance of music. Luther had regarded music as a means by which God stimulated faith. For devotionally inclined writers of the seventeenth century, the perspective was often reversed: the outward song should issue from the inspired heart, and the allegorical use of musical terms in writers such as Johann Arndt tends to place audible music in the position of a non-essential byproduct. The interior state was by far the most important, and the impurities involved in public worship sometimes led the devout, such as Heinrich Müller, to esteem private devotion more highly. This form of subjective individualism is the mark of the mystic. Pietists shared the insistence that music express what is in the heart but combined it with an evangelical conviction that the faith of others might be increased through song. Although the mark of the Pietists may have been the exclusive gathering of the regenerate in the **collegia pietatis**, those with whom we are concerned did not abandon the attempt to rid public worship of impurities. This attempt, in the view of some of their contemporaries and later commentators as well, introduced a form of ecclesiological purism tinged with the heresy of Donatism. In their own view, the goal was to recover the energy and vision of Luther's Reformation. As in most theological disputes, there was some validity to both claims.

Two articles of the Augsburg Confession are important to note as background. Article 8 condemns the Donatist denial "that the ministry of evil men may be used in the church" and affirms that "the sacraments and the Word are effectual by reason of the institution and commandment of Christ even if they are administered by evil men."[326] Article 24, on the other hand, condemns those abuses of the Mass which have resulted from regarding it as an automatically efficacious outward form. Melanchthon, describing this viewpoint in his *Apology*, used the phrase **ex opere operato** to indicate the external observance of a sacrament without faith. As Erwin Iserloh and Vilmos Vatja point out, this term as understood by the Catholic church referred to the position which was affirmed in article 8, namely that the "the sacrament is valid regardless of the dignity of those who administer it."[327] The Reformers apparently misunderstood the anti-Donatist term **opus operatum** and applied it to a kind of ceremonial works--righteousness.

When Pietists used the term, they too referred primarily to the undue emphasis on outward forms without regard for inward meaning. One of the more radical Pietists, Gottfried Arnold (1666–1714), saw the cause of the retention of Latin singing to be financial corruption, just as Melanchthon had seen this to be the cause of private Masses. Although simple, edifying hymns had been introduced early in the Reformation, music fell again to the **opus operatum** of endowed cathedral choirs. Giving the example of the Freiberg cathedral, Arnold finds "entire responses by which the Latin bawling of the canons has been declared good and orderly and even canonized, though undoubtedly some gifts of such endowments have contributed greatly thereto."[328] Organ music also had contributed greatly to hindering devotion, and the abuse had reached such a high point that it foreshadowed a fall.[329] In Arnold's view, the Reformation had gone awry; the Lutheran churches were in need of another major reform. Music as it was being practiced in Lutheranism was no closer to fulfilling the demands of Protestant worship than if the Reformation had never occurred.

Because Arnold limits his discussion of music to the criticism of Latin singing and organ playing, the issue of Donatism does not emerge. The reason, however, is not that Arnold wanted to avoid heresy,[330] but that his demands were more radical than most. In his view, the forms of worship themselves needed a thorough overhaul. Unreformed worship practices could not be improved merely by raising the moral level of the musicians. Arnold believed his time was like that of Luther: only radical institutional changes would enable the gospel to be preached and heard.

Less radical Pietists tended to place less blame on structures and more on persons, but the difference is a matter of degree. When, for example, Johann Muscovius bemoans the **opus operatum** which has flooded the church, he appears to have in mind both perfunctory church attendance on the part of the people and moral inadequacy on the part of musicians. Most directly, to be sure, he is referring to the empty externalism of a service in which the parishioners listen to glorious music and even to the sermon but continue unrepentant in their godless ways.[331] This faithless ceremonialism is like that described by Amos, and God's condemnation falls not only upon the mode of making music but on those who bear responsibility for it. Thus the preachers who want to save their own souls should be zealous in combatting this evil and should "warn those fleshly minded musicians of the threatened woe which is again and again cried out in scripture on the godless."[332] Muscovius proceeds to an impassioned and vivid description of the torments which await these sinners.

Significantly, what is being condemned here is both an internal and an external godlessness. The issue is not that reverent music is being sung or played without a fitting interior disposition; rather, the music itself is irreverent and, given the power of music to change behavior, as recognized by Plato and Aristotle, it produces only ill effects. Thus while the worldliness of the musicians is greatly to blame, the major change should be in the style of music. As things stand, the music often sounds like the crows of a rooster or the cries of battle or of a hunt. There ought to be a difference between church music and drinking music, Muscovius charges; appealing to Ezekiel 42:20, where the sacred space in the temple is marked out, he writes, "God wants the holy to be known and held as different from the unholy."[333] Alluding to the view of music as expressing affects, Muscovius urges good Christians to judge worship not according to the affects which proceed from corrupt flesh but according to the Word of God out of the spirit; they should recognize that "fleshly church music is neither pleasing to God nor does it edify the congregation but only tickles the ears of the world, robs the time set aside for true worship, grieves the simple and thus brings great harm."[334] Muscovius reports that this style of music was introduced 40 or 50 years previously (i.e., c. 1650) and had become increasingly elaborate and obtrusive.[335]

As with Arnold, Muscovius' position avoided the problem of Donatism because the issue did not involve conflict between inner disposition and outward means of grace. Though perhaps more open to choral and organ music than was Arnold, the two agreed in demanding changes in the external character of the music. Music's ability to serve as a means of grace, according to their understanding of worship, entailed its power to evoke serious, uplifting thoughts. Music which evoked laughter, disgust or confusion could hardly qualify.

The donatistic charge has more validity, ironically, when applied to a more moderate Pietist such as Christian Gerber, who complained of two ways in which outward forms conflicted with interior devotion. First there are the Italians who perform in Lutheran churches but are themselves adherents of a "false and idolatrous religion." They have no qualms about earning money for their singing, but they scorn the form of worship and think they will be contaminated, so they leave the church as soon as they have sung and spend their time drinking and courting women until time to sing again. Secondly, there are musicians who belong to the church but are whores, adulterers, or drunkards. They think everything is fine, no matter how un-Christian their behavior, as long as they play or sing well. Gerber tells of a cantor who preferred drink to prayer and claimed he composed better with a glass of wine in the company of friends.[336]

In a later publication Gerber introduces a contrasting figure named Bartholomew Ziegenbalg, who had become a missionary to East India. When at the age of sixteen Ziegenbalg had attended a session of the Collegium Musicum, a fellow student remarked to him that music was indeed a glorious art but that it could only be used correctly by those who were in harmony with themselves and with God. This harmony is a reversal of the effects of the fall whereby human nature was totally confused.[337] What is at issue in this example is not whether the unregenerate should sing in church but whether they should sing at all: will not abuse of a good thing result when handled by the unworthy?

Strictly speaking, because sacramental validity is not at issue, this is not an instance of Donatism. Music, after all, is not a sacrament, even though at times it seemed to assume characteristics of a sacrament. As an adiaphoron in worship, it was to be judged as good or bad depending on its contribution to good order and decorum. But whether sacrament or adiaphoron, Gerber in his first two examples is judging a liturgical activity according to extra-liturgical standards; to this extent he indeed adopts a position which could be considered donatistic and thus not in accordance with Lutheran teachings.

This is, in effect, the response of cantor Georg Motz, who responded to Gerber so vehemently. Applying the orthodox teaching on the office of priest to that of musician, Motz states, "The office of priest is and remains holy, even if he himself is unholy and godless. And thus singing and making music is likewise good in and of itself, even though sometimes the person who sings and makes music is evil and godless."[338] Pointing out that the church will never attain purity, Motz notes that there has always been corruption.[339] The demand for purity would also mean omitting chorales because of the sinfulness of the people in the congregation. But because no one can look into another's heart, we must continue to keep external observance as commanded by God.[340]

In all this Motz indeed represents the position of orthodoxy over against Gerber's apparent heterodoxy. But in other respects Motz shows himself to represent a new, if not deviant, viewpoint. Defending composers against Gerber's charge that they compose out of a "worldly spirit," Motz counters that artistic compositions come from the Holy Spirit.[341] But contrary to ordinary Lutheran expectations that the Spirit comes by means of Word or sacraments, the claim here is that the Spirit comes directly to the composer's mind. Whereas for Luther music served as an instrument of the Spirit by stilling the affections and thus preparing the mind for hearing or preaching the Word, for Motz music is equivalent to the Word, for God is the "highest Harmonicus of all" and has created the world harmonically.[342] Preaching and composing are very similar, requiring withdrawal from distractions to be with God. Thus Motz agrees with Gerber that a composer could not write music of and through the Spirit while drinking wine with friends.

When they use the same image of harmony to describe the state of the person in right relation to God, however, they understand this in very different ways. For Gerber it is a metaphor for the state of the soul which has been shaped anew by God. For Motz it is a fundamental reality of the universe which is implanted into the soul as well as into leaves, trees, birds and planets.[343] The music of heaven is not a metaphor for eternal joy but is the source of the music which the composer hears and recasts for human ears. The gifted composer can provide a foretaste of heavenly joy which is more vivid and memorable than any mere speech which uses words alone.[344] For those such as Gerber, who believed worship should be "reasonable," to exalt music over speech was unacceptable. "We should sing like reasonable humans, not like birds."[345] If Gerber believed harmony existed in subordinating passions to reason, Motz believed disharmony existed in refusing to praise God joyfully in song. Like Luther, Motz associates sadness with the devil, but one senses that Motz never experienced Luther's struggles with the devil. Motz's musical theology begins with Luther but ends in a view of artistic inspiration more mystical than Lutheran. The essential connection of music to ultimate reality enables the composer to tap a source of revelation other than the historically revealed Word.

As with others who lay claim to immediate revelation, a certain element of elitism reveals itself in Motz. The artist is not meant to be subject to the congregation, for they may not understand or appreciate his work. In an interesting twist to the David–Saul story, Motz cites not the passage where Saul was calmed by David's music but the incident where Saul was provoked to throw a spear at him for his singing (I Sam. 18:10–11). "Such is the recompense which the world gives for all faithfully performed services," Motz concludes.[346] Composers are bound to use their best art and skill; those who scorn it are scorning not only the composer's God-given skill but also God himself, who commanded the music.[347] It is not the fault of the composer if his music does not fall on fertile ground any more than preachers are to blame if the Word of God falls on deaf ears. The responsibility for listening with the right intention rests on each member of the congregation.[348] By regarding the roles of musicians and preachers as parallel, Motz also implies an unwillingness to be subordinate to the authority of a clergyman in matters of music; the musician's authority, it seems, comes directly from God.

From a strictly dogmatic standpoint, Motz's view of the church is orthodox on the question of Donatism, whereas Gerber's is heterodox. However, one wonders if Motz was not too eager to advocate the mixed composition of the visible church to protect his own position and that of his musical colleagues. The issues of job security and a living wage were not far below the surface in any of these theological debates: Steffens and Gerber had brought it to the surface by suggesting that less money be spent on organs and more on feeding the poor.[349] Motz responded by bringing scriptural evidence of the financial support of musicians in Old Testament times (Num. 18:26, 30–1; Neh. 12:44); even though there was corruption then also, God provided for the musicians to be paid.[350]

There is some evidence that the lack of money was at the root of all musical evils. Church musicians who did not earn enough in their church jobs supplemented their income in the entertainment industry, as it were, thus drawing charges of contamination on themselves. Or the good artists could earn a better living outside the church, leaving the church with unskilled musicians who gave music a bad name. Organist and music theorist Andreas Werckmeister, who was more willing than many musicians to admit the musical abuses prevalent in the church, called upon the authorities to provide sufficient funds to hire qualified personnel: "Removal of this abuse falls among the duties of the authorities....But as the salaries sometimes are so desperately low, no solid candidate is to be found on such terms."[351] It is no wonder, he recognizes, that music is scorned as a result of the way it is botched by the unqualified: "For there are in many places such bunglers that they cannot play a song or a right note on the keyboard, they pay no attention to meter or pulse—in other words music is greatly disgraced and must necessarily fall into disrepute."[352]

Even though money is the key to the solution, the abuse is no less damnable. Not only does Werckmeister render harsh judgment on the inadequate performance of church music, but he also castigates those who take their music into taverns. Those who abuse "this costly gift" by working as "beer fiddlers" not only sin themselves but cause others to sin also. They are thus unworthy to be called musicians. Whether, when they then play in church, their music can be considered pleasing to God or a service to him, Werckmeister leaves to others to judge; but he considers their playing sinful, for "such people have no faith in God, and whatever does not proceed from faith is sin."[353] To this extent Werckmeister seems to come close to the Pietists in demanding the ouster of faithless musicians from church, and in one instance he even uses the word "regenerate" ("wiedergeboren") to refer to the person who receives the gift of harmony directly from God. In an earlier work, he had also, in a manner similar to Pietists, scolded those who seek honor or fame through their music.[354] As a gift from God, music was to be used for the glory of God, not for personal ambition; to belittle or detract from others' talent is a vice, for God gives more or less talent as he wills. Virtue comes from using it diligently to honor the giver.[355]

Werckmeister in this way avoided the tinge of elitism we observed in Motz as well as the implication that music is a form of special revelation. On the contrary, as music is based on numerical relationships which are found in nature, it is a form of general revelation available to all. By thus revealing himself in the "light of nature," God assures that there can be no excuse for godlessness. There are, of course, some who are particularly gifted in music, but this must be regarded as a basis for serving others, not a pretext for startling them with innovations: "We are human beings, and each is obliged to serve the other with his gifts."[356]

Had all musicians insisted on such selflessness and purity of motivation, they might have avoided attacks both on their music and on their character. Indeed, the words of Gotha gymnasium rector Gottfried Vockerodt, who most extensively defended the Halle-Pietist view of music in education, might well have been those of Werckmeister: "They take up their profession with the intention of thereby fulfilling their lusts, enjoying the good life, achieving riches, praise, and human favor; ...through wonder and esteem for their art they become insolent to the point of looking down on other professions in comparison to theirs."[357] Both writers would agree that music, even outside the church, must always be in keeping with the glory of God.[358]

The points of agreement between Werckmeister and the Pietists, nevertheless, should not obscure some fundamental differences. For Pietists music is essentially a tool for achieving moral purposes; as we observed in the preceding chapter, it belongs to the category of neutral things which can be used either for good or evil. Musical skill and the moral order are essentially unrelated but become related through the motivation which leads to application of the skill. As with theology, so with music, there is no virtue in the knowledge of theory but only in the practice. Accordingly, Vockerodt's primary criterion for good musicianship is right intention, not thoroughness of learning: "I shall consider to be solid musicians those who have learned their art not from the theory but only **per praxin, imitationem,** and **usum** as long as they make music only to the glory of God and do not abuse their art."[359]

For Werckmeister, on the other hand, intention and knowledge were as inseparable as music and the moral order. Werckmeister had been strongly influenced by the cosmological approach to music as represented by Johannes Kepler and Robert Fludd. As we observed in an earlier chapter, Lutheran theologians who stressed the harmonic concord of heaven and earth resisted the theory of the music of the spheres, but this was not true of music theorists of the Lutheran tradition. Relying on Kepler as well as the 38th chapter of Job, Werckmeister asserted not only that the stars and planets are arranged harmoniously, but that they influence music on earth. The regenerate person may receive music directly from God, but God provides it indirectly through the stars as well: "I will not deny that humans are also ruled and moved to the art of music through the order of relations of the stars and their movements, which cause many sorts of shapes, conjunctions and harmonious appearances."[360] These astronomical changes are the explanation for changes in musical style from one era to the next: through the influence of the stars, new forms of composition are made possible and old forms seem less pleasant. Although all aspects of music have an inner spiritual meaning—and Werckmeister does not claim an audible music of the spheres—nevertheless external music is not to be eliminated. Given God's immutability, what he commanded in Old Testament times remains obligatory for all time.[361]

To try to separate internal devotion from external music or knowledge from practice is therefore to disturb the unity of creation. The musician whose soul is in harmony with God naturally produces God-pleasing music, yet knowledge and skill are crucial for the proper exercise of his art. These enable him to express in melody the appropriate music for a particular text. If he tried to set a penitential text to a melody of praise, the result would conflict both with nature and art. Those who have just taught themselves to play a few pieces have not acquired this knowledge and are not rightly called musicians. In sum, Vockerodt's minimal demands of "practice, use, and imitation" for producing qualified musicians are for Werckmeister quite inadequate.

To analyze all the differences between Werckmeister and Pietists would lead beyond our present topic into a more thorough study of Werckmeister's theology and its relation to the Lutheran tradition. Clearly Werckmeister's metaphysical orientation and his allegorical interpretation of the Bible were inimical to Pietist anti-philosophical pragmatism and the historical search for the true church. A comparison of the two world views would produce a long list of contrasts without common points of departure. Nevertheless, their common concern for the imperfections of the church and its members prevents them from being on opposing sides. Their agreement consists in the belief that no aspect of life (or, for Werckmeister, of the cosmos) lies outside the realm of faith. In Werckmeister's vision of the universe, the harmony of the whole is echoed throughout all the parts. Similarly, the Pietist image of the regenerate person is reflected in every action which proceeds from faith. What the two positions are united in opposing is a secularism which, either in theory or in practice, considered some areas of human activity irrelevant to faith. They resisted the attempt to legitimate the secular areas of life as positive in themselves rather than as dependent on religious legitimation.

The issue of moral impurity among musicians was, then, only part of a larger issue of moral impurity in society. From the outset, the Protestant principle of justification by faith alone had produced conflicts and confusion about the role of moral acts in the life of faith. Clearly, Pietists placed greater demands for moral improvement than at any prior point in Lutheranism. In testing the Pietists' degree of orthodoxy against the background of Luther's teaching, it is important to recognize that the doctrine of sanctification was now being preached not to a people burdened with the legalistic demands of an authoritarian church but to a people well imbued with the teaching that faith alone was essential to salvation. What was necessary now, as the Pietists viewed the situation, was to eliminate all vestiges of **opera operata** in order finally to achieve an **ecclesia reformata**.

CHAPTER ELEVEN

MUSIC AND ADIAPHORA

Although the primary focus in this book is on music in worship, the attempt to define a Pietist theology of music necessarily takes us outside the church. It was not religious music but recreational or theatrical music which aroused the greatest controversies involving Pietists and most clearly pitted Pietism against Orthodoxy. Acting out of their belief that life outside the church was nevertheless not outside the realm of faith, Pietist preachers attacked aspects of secular culture which they found to be inimical to Christian faith.

This application of moral concern to secular musical culture began in 1678 with pastor Anton Reiser's attack on the Hamburg opera. The history of the controversy has been studied in depth from a political and literary standpoint[362] and lies for the most part outside the scope of our study of the theology of music. Beyond the particular issue of operatic entertainment, however, the dispute brought into the open widely differing views on morality and culture in what is sometimes called the "second adiaphoristic controversy." The stakes in this debate were broader than in the earlier adiaphoristic controversy which was restricted to matters of ceremony: now the modern world view, with its recognition of the autonomy of the arts, was emerging against the protests of the theocentric tradition. To be sure, the Hamburg opera dispute was at one level a matter of purely local concern, but in succeeding decades the ethical positions supporting each side were more extensively developed. Unfortunately, this aspect of the opera debate has received very little scholarly attention and can only be summarized here.

When the question of the moral legitimacy of operas was submitted for resolution to the theological and juridical faculty of Wittenberg, the decision was that operas were adiaphora; as such, they could not be condemned but were to be considered "permissible entertainment" subject to the discretion of the magistrates, who were responsible for this and other adiaphora.[363]

Far from regarding operas as truly indifferent, however, the professors proceeded to emphasize their value in presenting examples of virtue and vice and thus leading to edification of the audience. They understood the term, then, in the sense in which it had been applied to liturgical matters as containing potential for beneficial use; but by extending its application to operas, they moved from the area of liturgy to that of ethics.

This shift is noted by Leipzig preacher Albrecht Christian Rotth (or Rothe), primary defender of the orthodox position on adiaphora against the Pietists, when he reports that "this word through previous usage 'commonly' refers more to matters left free in worship than to other optional matters in affairs of the world."[364] Adopting the broader application to human behavior Rotth also draws explicitly on Stoic philosophy and prefers the Latin *res indifferens* to the Greek term *adiaphora* or the German term *Mittel-Ding*, even though he is writing in German.[365] In defining the term he does not cite the Formula of Concord or the passage of I Cor. 14:40 on orderliness in worship, for the issue now has nothing to do with worship; rather, the term applies to "every human affair which, considered in general and only according to its nature, is neither expressly nor by a good inference either commanded or forbidden by God."[366] For him it does not apply to neutral objects which could be used for good but instead to areas of human behavior which are considered ethically neutral. Rotth defends the existence of adiaphora on the premise that there is no biblical expectation that every act be done "positively and immediately to the honor of God."[367] This extreme formulation fails to deal with the real issue of whether seemingly insignificant actions may **indirectly** honor or dishonor God, and because he does not discuss recreational music explicitly, we can only assume that he found it morally indifferent.

The main Pietist writer involved in both the dispute over Christian ethical theory and the controversy over theatrical music was the educator Gottfried Vockerodt (1665–1717), who as rector of the prince's school in Gotha was concerned about the relationship between his students' musical activities and their moral development. Closely associated with August Hermann Francke, Vockerodt shared the Halle vision of education as a process of molding lives.[368] As we saw in the previous chapter, Vockerodt placed a higher value on the practice of skills by regenerate persons than on the attainment of a high degree of theoretical knowledge. His position drew resistance not only because of the moral demands placed on musicians but also because of the perceived relaxation of musical standards. As would be the case with Johann Sebastian Bach and Rector Ernesti, eighteenth-century educational values were strongly resisted by those musicians who sensed the dislocation of music from the center of the curriculum.[369]

The occasion which drew Vockerodt into controversy was a school presentation in 1696 by three of his pupils which used the Roman emperors Caligula, Claudius, and Nero as negative moral examples. Their failings, according to the pupils' talks, were attributable largely to an overriding fascination with music and theater. Vockerodt, a teacher of ancient languages, regarded the study of emperor's lives as useful for demonstrating the dire results of turning one's attention in the wrong direction. Caligula, for instance, was murdered while talking with some of the boys who had been brought from Asia to appear on stage. Nero's mind was so obliterated by musical and theatrical arts that he was incapable of ruling and was driven to suicide. Claudius' failings had less to do with the arts than with an immoderate desire for useless study, but the potential for abuse of study was less prominent in the presentation than were the dangers of the arts.

It was not without cause, then, that the program was interpreted as an attack on music. Three defenses of music hit the press shortly thereafter. That of Weissenfels court concertmaster Johann Beer, *Ursus murmurat (The Bear Growls)*, was the most polemical and direct, gaining most of Vockerodt's attention. Johann Kristof Lorber's *Lob der edlen Musik* (Weimar, 1696) is a 66-page-long poem drawing on a long tradition of musical encomium and is of less interest for our purposes. Johann Christoph Wentzel, rector at Altenburg, raised some significant issues, if we are to judge by Vockerodt's response, but to my knowledge the publication itself is not extant. Vockerodt replied to all three writers in *Mißbrauch der freyen Künste insonderheit der Music (Abuse of the liberal arts, especially music)* (Frankfurt, 1697). Beer continued the debate by writing *Ursus Vulpinatur, List wieder List, oder Musicalische Fuchs-Jagd (The Bear plays the Fox, Cunning vs. Cunning, or Musical Fox-Hunt)* (Weißenfels, 1697), to which Vockerodt replied in *Wiederholetes Zeugnüs der Warheit gegen die verderbte Music und Schauspiele/ Opern/ Comödien und dergleichen Eitelkeiten Welche die heutige Welt vor unschuldige Mitteldinge will gehalten wissen (Repeated Testimony of Truth against the Corrupt Music and Plays, Operas, Comedies and such Vanities, which the world today wants to be considered Innocent Indifferent Matters)* (Frankfurt and Leipzig, 1698). At this point Rotth entered the fray to defend the concept of "Mitteldinge": without referring directly to any of the preceding, Rotth published two general works entitled *Höchstnöthiger Unterricht von so genanten Mittel-Dingen (Highly Necessary Instruction concerning so-called Indifferent Matters)* and *Wiederholter und ferner ausgeführter Unterricht von Mittel-Dingen (Repeated and further elaborated Instruction on Indifferent Matters)*, both printed in Leipzig without date of publication, presumably in 1698. In 1699 Vockerodt answered Rotth with *Erleuterte Auffdeckung des Betrugs und Ärgernisses So mit denen vorgegebenen Mitteldingen und vergönneten Lust In der Christenheit angerichtet worden (Elucidated Exposure of the Deceit and Offence wrought in Christendom by assertions of Indifferent Matters and Permissible Pleasures)*, a work published by the Halle orphanage press. The prolixity of these writers precludes a summary of all the arguments; our main concern will be to contrast Vockerodt's position on *adiaphora* with that of his adversaries.

Against the charge of being a despiser of music, Vockerodt responded both with biographical and theoretical evidence. Whatever one's interpretation of the school program, he writes, his actions demonstrate that he is no enemy of music. The choirs at the school are in better shape than when he took over; there are more hours of singing instruction. Citizens notice the change in quality and contribute 100 Taler more than before. He has encouraged not only the poor boys who earn scholarships for singing but all boys to learn the rudiments of music; older pupils who need to develop clear speech are exhorted to practice singing. Even instrumental music has been permitted to those who notify the rector. Both vocal and instrumental music are used at official ceremonies of the school. In his own youth he was introduced to music and is not a hater of music.

Indeed, his references to the history of music theory demonstrate familiarity with the Pythagorean-quadrivial tradition as well as the more recent works of Marin Mersenne and Athanasius Kircher. His frequent citations of Kircher's *Musurgia universalis sive ars magna consoni et dissoni* drew criticism from Beer, who pointed out that Kircher was not a professional musician. Nevertheless, as Ulf Scharlau has pointed out, Kircher's influence extended not only to the musical laity of the seventeenth century but also to music theorists such as Werckmeister and Buttstedt; even those such as Beer and Johann Mattheson who found Kircher outdated were not totally free of his influence.[370] Surely the different perspectives on music theory were only a minor factor in the controversy between Beer and Vockerodt.

For Beer, who was not only a musician but also a novelist and satirist, personal temperament was a significant difference between himself and Vockerodt. After expressing thanks that he had been born in the bosom of the Christian church, he also gave thanks that he had been given a cheerful disposition, implicitly arguing that one need not be somber to be Christian. He regarded Vockerodt as one of the "grumpy melancholics and misanthropes" who saw music as not fitting for a prince, thus following in the line of the Precisionists of Holland "who take everything so strictly and precisely."[371] Indeed Vockerodt's belief that every aspect of life was to be taken seriously was perhaps the biggest obstacle to reconciliation, but for Vockerodt it was not a matter of temperament but of theology.

Turning to what he regards as the substance of the argument, Beer accuses Vockerodt of throwing out the baby with the bath water, or, as he also puts it, tearing out the whole organ because of one pipe.[372] He interprets Vockerodt as opposing music altogether, an interpretation which could justifiably be drawn from the text of the school program. Thus Beer persuasively argues against rejecting music because of abuse any more than one would abolish schools because of students' misbehavior or printing presses because of obscene publications.[373] It was not the music which ruined Nero and others but their evil nature. He does believe music can aid and strengthen rulers, but for the most part he does not regard it as shaping character. Just as it is abused by those of bad character, it is pure for those who are themselves pure. The music itself emerges as beyond criticism, neither good nor evil, an *adiaphoron*. As in an Aristotelian conception of virtue, what is decisive is whether one uses it in moderation or in excess. Just as medicine can be poisonous in too large a dosage, so too music used in excess can produce insanity rather than the comfort which moderate usage provides.[374] Music practiced in moderation enhances the majesty of honorable lords and is therefore good.[375]

Beer challenged Vockerodt to respond and clarify his position, which he did with great thoroughness in 162 pages of text with appended statement of support from the theological faculty of the university of Giessen. What he opposes, he insists, is not music, but the abuse of music. No Christian teacher will deny, he writes, that the abuse of music is "the most dangerous crag to which many a young person is drawn as if by the Sirens, falling into dissolute and ungodly living and suffering shipwreck in both temporal and eternal salvation."[376] Because these pupils are being trained for positions in schools and churches, it is evident what damage could be done to society if in their youth their consciences were ruined by godless activities. If they develop bad habits while young, these will follow them into adulthood. The legislation requiring students to get permission from the rector for playing musical instruments was already on the books when Vockerodt arrived, but his implementation of punishment for offenders has caused him to be decried as an enemy of music, he argues.

What Vockerodt opposes is not something as innocent as secret music-making in students' rooms. Rather, some students have played instruments for dancing and drinking in public bars forbidden to students, and others have played at secret orgies and in suspicious corners. Still others have run around with the town musicians. At times brawls have resulted, especially at church dedications. Those who fall into this form of behavior can seldom be brought back on track, and, what is more, they are likely to mislead others.[377]

Vockerodt cannot understand why truly honorable members of the music profession should defend such musicians. Nor does he comprehend why they should scorn those pupils who diligently and devoutly pursue music in his school. If they truly loved music so much, they would love the devout musicians, who know music thoroughly. Instead, they defend those the rector punishes and make them appear to suffer for the sake of music. He can only explain this approach as based on personal animosity and suspicion of Pietism, a charge which Beer denies.

Vockerodt then proceeds to a more theoretical discussion of the value of music in which he recognizes its mysterious effects and close relationship to the order of the universe. It is in fact its marvelous power for good that makes him all the more wary of its potential for abuse. "Just as the best wine gives the sourest vinegar and the best and strongest medicine brings a spoiled nature first to its downfall, so also the best minds, when they are misused, bring about much harm and trouble."[378]

Thus music can only properly be learned and practiced in faith. Referring to Romans 14, Vockerodt argues that, in music as in other adiaphora, one needs the certainty of the Holy Spirit working within in order to assure that music will not be abused. The goal of life and of education is the salvation of souls, and if musical knowledge and training do not further this goal they are of no value. As rector, Vockerodt sees himself charged with the cure of souls perhaps more than with the education of minds. "And how would we preceptors come off on that day if we did not show the right path to those youths entrusted to our souls and if we didn't try as hard as we can to save their soul?"[379] There can therefore be no abstract defense of music apart from the performer; the spiritual state of the musician is determinative. The only proper use of music is through faith.

Beer's response takes the anti-Donatist tack we encountered in the previous chapter, implicitly likening music to a sacrament. Insisting on a distinction between music in the abstract and any concrete examples of its practice, Beer argues that the person who uses or abuses music does not affect the substance of music. For him the situation is the same as that of the priest whose powers are not diminished by unholy living. One could be a good musician without being a good person. "It is one thing to be virtuous and another to be a virtuoso. Both can stand together or both can come separately without any harm to music."[380] Music in the abstract, in its substance, is "always pure, always good, always praiseworthy, always a gift of God."[381]

Yet Beer goes on to say that there is no abstract use of music. The time, place and occasion where music is played are the accidents which do not change the substance but can change the effect from good to bad. Trumpeting, for example, is a noble art, but if it is done on Good Friday in the town marketplace, then it is abused. Or if a spiritual melody is given a worldly text, the power of the music is weakened and good is turned to evil. In defending only music in the abstract and admitting concrete abuses, Beer believes he has made agreement with Vockerodt possible but that Vockerodt stubbornly insists on disagreeing.[382]

Indeed, the two positions seem very close but entail a significant difference. In his examples of abuse, Beer is concerned with the suitability of the setting or with the integrity of the musical genre, not with the motives of the performers. The wrong time or location for music cannot be made right through right motives; nor is there a kind of music which is bad in itself but which could be made good through right motives. Similarly, the right music at the right time in the right place cannot be made wrong through wrong motives. In effect, music for Beer is not truly a neutral matter, an adiaphoron, but something good in essence yet subject to misuse.

For Vockerodt also music in its substance is unaffected by its particular application, but he refuses to label it good or even to discuss it in the abstract. "It is not necessary to differentiate music itself into good or evil," he writes, but to distinguish between good and evil effects.[383] Significantly, the evil effects are to be attributed to the artists, not to the art, nor to the situation. In this respect, Vockerodt regards music as more truly neutral than does Beer, for the fault does not originate in the music; and yet there is no neutral application of music because there is no neutral human activity. Anything which is not to be sinful and displeasing to God must be learned in faith and exercised in faith.[384] Through faith an activity which for most would be harmful can be beneficial; everything depends on the goal.

> If an unbelieving musician sets fleshly pleasure as a goal and tries to awaken it through certain modes of singing, even these could direct a believing musician to the praise and love of God, if there are no other sinful circumstances, and could be conducive to joy in the Holy Spirit. Indeed, a believing musician, who always has with him the true singing master, the Holy Spirit, is always taught by the same and reminded how he should use the otherwise dangerous and lewd modes of singing at the right time and apply them for moral improvement.[385]

For Beer, on the other hand, faith is not relevant to every human activity. To go walking in the pheasant garden of Weissenfels, for instance, does not proceed from faith, so, mocking Vockerodt, he concludes one shouldn't climb on a bench and sing a lovely song in the garden.[386] Vockerodt's position is based on a limited understanding of adiaphora, Beer argues. Like the Dutch Precisionists, Vockerodt "makes virtues and arts into vices, changes the permissible into sin and makes everything a matter of conscience."[387] Beer is more sympathetic to the Preacher's line, "There is a time for everything." Accordingly, dancing, comedy, and opera are approved in their own time, which is to say, in moderation or for recreation. Only those who indulge themselves excessively or make recreation their obsession cause it to be sinful. For others it is not a matter of conscience.

This distinction, based as it was in an Aristotelian view of virtue as the golden mean, did not satisfy Vockerodt. In his next book, *Wiederholetes Zeugnüs der Warheit Gegen die verderbte Music u. Schauspiele*, he responded by introducing a distinction between acceptable and unacceptable recreation. After repeating his previously stated distinction between a virtuous use of music, which is intended for the praise of God and the improvement of oneself and others, and a sinful use thereof, which aims at personal glory, pleasure, or material reward, Vockerodt adds a further distinction which excludes the possibility of a neutral use. Music used merely to pass time is far different from music used to refresh the spirit after work or to awaken the heart toward the praise of God. "You also abuse music who use it only for amusement, seeking not so much a fitting revitalization following work and an awakening of the heart toward praise of God as pleasure and stimulation of your fleshly desires."[388] Adiaphora, as referred to in 2 Cor. 6 are not to be equated with useless activities but with those activities which can contribute to good order, Christian discipline or evangelical well-being. Accordingly, Vockerodt does not even approve of what might be called a secular use of music, that is to give honor to humans: they also abuse music, he writes, who "flatter people and pay court to them with serenades or use music in some other manner where God's name is not sanctified."[389] If the purpose of life is to glorify God and work toward eternal salvation, then anything which does not contribute thereto takes time away from achieving those goals: "For one already does enough evil when one is not doing anything good and is losing the time on which eternity depends."[390]

Beer, who enjoyed the friendship and sometimes the hunting companionship of the duke of Sachsen-Weißenfels, could scarcely have sympathized with Vockerodt in this social criticism. Yet one wonders whether Vockerodt could avoid a feeling of righteous vindication when Beer met his premature end as a result of a hunting accident.

Even before Beer's death in 1700, however, Vockerodt had turned his attention to Rotth, who as a theologian at least shared his frame of reference if not his opinion. Whereas Rotth embraced the changed definition of adiaphora, Vockerodt regarded the shift in meaning and application as a betrayal of the Lutheran symbolic books. During the Augsburg and Leipzig Interims the term referred to matters of ceremony, or "ecclesiastical" adiaphora, Vockerodt writes, but since then it has come to refer to matters of behavior, or "political" adiaphora. The concept of Christian freedom, as interpreted through the scholastic and Aristotelian philosophy of seventeenth-century theologians, has allowed the introduction of the category of indifferent activities, which are taken to include drinking, dancing, and other forms of entertainment.[391] But, as Vockerodt sees it, the symbolic books, by teaching the total corruption of human nature through original sin, leave no room for indifferent behavior. There are, according to scripture, only two inner drives or principles of action, flesh and spirit; thus all desire is also of two sorts only, that is, either sinful or holy, leaving no room for a middle ground of indifferent actions. Only through the scholastic concept of **pura naturalia**, or sinless natural powers, could Vockerodt find any basis for a third source of action; but this comes "from the old heathen philosophers and the Pelagian school" and led to the "papist works-righteousness which... destroyed Christ and his saving grace."[392] The Lutheran concept of Christian freedom, as Vockerodt describes it, is not a fleshly freedom or a freedom with regard to external activities, but a freedom of spirit and of conscience. The adiaphorists' concept of freedom, on the other hand, "is fulfilled in the flesh and puts the conscience to sleep."[393]

Vockerodt's analysis of the reasons why Lutheran theologians strayed from the teachings of the Lutheran Confessions is revealing. In the first instance he blames Balthasar Meisner, who was so intent on defending Lutheran customs against the Calvinists in his *Collegii Adiaphoristici* that, contrary to his own conscience, he spoke in favor of dancing and comedies because Calvinists had forbidden them. This was a dangerous step and has proved to be a stumbling block. Secondly, following the Council of Trent, Lutherans felt the need to adopt the weapons of the papacy in order to do battle with them and hence turned to Aristotelian and scholastic philosophy. In this way the Christian teaching of the renunciation of the world was replaced by the Aristotelian teaching of moderation.

Vockerodt's second charge was, and, I suggest, still is, less controversial than the first. Widespread as Aristotelian thought was at Lutheran universities in the seventeenth century, still it was not the criterion by which adherence to orthodox belief was judged. Evidence of affinity to Calvinism, on the other hand, could be damaging to one's reputation. Beer, for instance, while showing on the one hand a rationalist's aversion to theological controversy, blamed Vockerodt for fraternizing with the Calvinist enemy. He concludes his *Ulpus vulpinatur* with a satirical dream in which Vockerodt's army shot sausages to the enemy in order to prevent them from starving, the enemy responded with a similarly friendly gesture, and both sides went away laughing. No pacifist where Calvinists were concerned, Beer did not like Vockerodt's praise of Voetius: "One should, to be sure, praise virtue in one's opponents and enemies, but never in my life have I liked to see or hear a confessing Lutheran approve doctrines of the Reformed."[394]

Even today fears of puritanism make an impartial evaluation of Vockerodt's theology difficult. One of the most controversial questions in Pietist scholarship is the extent of Reformed influence on the theology of leading Pietists. It cannot be denied that Vockerodt was familiar with and favorably inclined toward the writings of Voetius. Nor can it be denied that Vockerodt endorsed a standard of moral rigorism not common among Lutherans. But that his teachings were further removed from Luther than were those of Lutheran orthodoxy has yet to be demonstrated.

Against the charge that he was advocating a form of asceticism based on dualism of matter and spirit, Vockerodt defended himself in his response to Wentzel. The meaning of "crucifying the flesh with its lusts and desires" had been distorted, Vockerodt claimed. To "forswear nature" does not mean to regard the natural order created by God as sinful. On the contrary, those who follow this path "eat and drink, take wives and beget children, and use all natural things for their needs as do other people; least of all do they hate music."[395] Not the natural activity being engaged in but the disposition of the heart determines the spiritual value of the act. In keeping with Luther's anthropology, the "natural man" is under the power of sin, whereas the regenerate man is led by the Spirit. In contrast to Luther, however, the Holy Spirit seems to take up residence in the heart and to make inward sanctification possible rather than to work externally, leaving the justified person still in essence a sinner. As a result, Vockerodt does not envision the Holy Spirit using music to change hearts or to drive away the devil except as the music issues forth from a person moved by the Spirit. David's psalms were not produced in his natural, sinful state but out of the new heart and spirit given him by God: "with natural song and music he would never have driven the devil away, because the devil can endure and indeed likes to see music used to make the natural man happy and prepare the path for him."[396]

Music, then, was indeed removed by Vockerodt from its special place as an instrument of the Spirit. Powerful as it was when used for good purpose, it was equally powerful in working evil. More consistently than previous Lutheran writers, Vockerodt regarded music itself as an adiaphoron. Neither it nor any other object or activity could be judged good in the abstract, apart from actual use. Conversely, operas could not be declared sinful in the abstract, but in actual practice they were being used for ungodly purposes.

Vockerodt's refusal to consider music in the abstract ("Extra usum Musices non agnosco Musicam ut Musicam") was the major sticking point for Beer. Among musicians of the time there was division over the relative importance of practice and theory in music. Beer, as defender of the primacy of theory,[397] undoubtedly saw Vockerodt as a threat to the tradition of education which accorded music theory a central role in the curriculum. Indeed, Vockerodt shared the pragmatic pedagogical theory of the Halle Pietists which was to be the wave of the future.

From Vockerodt's perspective, on the other hand, Beer represented a new and undesirable movement toward the separation of religion and the arts. What to modern artists was emancipation was to Vockerodt, in Heinz Krause's formulation, a sign of decline (*Untergang*): "the humanization of art, hand in hand with the divinization of the artist, and the increasing autonomy of art."[398] Such a formulation emerges from a more distant perspective than that available to either Beer or Vockerodt, however. While the dispute was, as Krause asserts, a "Kulturkampf" between two different world views, the differences must not be exaggerated. The struggle for artistic independence was in its infancy, and there was as yet no thought of removing art from its metaphysical foundation. Beer shared with other music theorists the cosmology of harmony as sustaining principle of the universe,[399] which by now had been virtually abandoned by most Lutheran theologians in favor of a less metaphysical, more biblical approach. It was not, however, Beer's metaphysics which was so objectionable to Vockerodt but rather his refusal to take life seriously in every detail.

CHAPTER TWELVE

THE CANTATA DEBATE

In the year 1700 Erdmann Neumeister, preacher and poet, took a daring step for the history of Lutheran church music. In the face of Pietist criticism of operas, Neumeister openly embraced an operatic style of music for the church. Consciously drawing on the structure of opera librettos, he introduced the cantata as "a portion of an opera composed of stylo recitativo and arie together."[400] While the "Neumeister Reform" is a recognized event in church music history, its significance may have been underestimated. For while scholars pay tribute to this new merging of the sacred with the secular on the one hand, they treat it on the other hand not as a new merger of former rivals but as a marriage of lifelong companions. Günther Stiller, citing passages of a dissertation by P. Brausch, writes that Neumeister "'was generally looked upon as the founder of the new style while he was still living,' even though 'he did not provide anything new at all,' but 'merely took the last step on a pathway already walked before him.'"[401] Alfred Dürr did recognize the revolutionary impact of the cantata form ("We today can hardly any longer imagine what an epoch-making innovation it represented to take up the most modern of all forms for the music of the church"), but thought only Pietists were disturbed by it: "As much as this alleged secularization is attacked from the side of Pietism, still Orthodoxy itself takes no offense at it."[402] Dürr sees the new form as a highly appropriate application of Luther's principle of keeping worship in touch with the times ("Aktualisierung des Gottesdienstes"). The monumental weight of the historiographical tradition which places Bach at the end of a continuous musical development since the Reformation seems to force scholars to depict a major innovation as no more than a minor glitch.

Setting aside any musicological debate about precursors, it is plausible to assert that Neumeister's innovation was a turning point in the theology of music. For over a century Lutheran theologians waged a losing battle against the incursions of secular style into church music. Suddenly embracing the enemy, young Neumeister and his companions proclaimed it was time to wage common cause. Not surprisingly, those of the older generation who had known nothing but separation resisted the prospect of unity. The truce in fact was short-lived, but it made possible such a glorious era of peace that most later observers forgot the war. Discussing the history of Passion music, Basil Smallman says matter-of-factly that "In Bach's time Opera and Oratorio were virtually indistinguishable in musical structure and in their use of highly stylized idioms; and consequently the techniques of the theatre—recitative, aria and dramatic chorus—could be used in Passion composition without any gross violation of the restraints of the church liturgy." Only after Bach's time was there "a stylistic separation between the two."[403]

Typical as such analyses are in our day, the unity of styles was not taken for granted in the early eighteenth century. Neumeister knew from the outset that there would be opposition. In the preface to his first year's cycle of cantata texts in 1704, he wrote, "it might almost be supposed that many would be vexed in spirit and ask how sacred music and opera can be reconciled, any more than Christ and Belial, or light and darkness."[404] His response was that, when dedicated to the service of God this kind of poetry could be sanctified, as had worldly songs which had been converted into spiritual songs. Clearly, many were persuaded by the argument, but many others had doubts. Gottfried Ephraim Scheibel reported in a 1721 commentary on the state of church music that a cantor had asked him to have a composer at a certain university write a cantata on the passion of Christ. Scheibel made the request, specifying that the work should be in theatrical style. The composer responded that he could not do this, "because there is such a great difference between theatrical and church music."[405]

Scheibel himself admitted that there was a general consensus to this effect, and "the best musicians and composers have affirmed and believed that church music must appear different from worldly music" (34). Indeed, much of the opposition to the stylistic merger came not from Pietists but from musicians. Johann Kuhnau's novel, *Der Musicalische Quack-Salber*, ends with instructions to "the true virtuoso and happy musician" in the form of a letter from a minister but presumably expressing Kuhnau's views: "An honorable virtuoso takes care not to approach this holy place with any of the vanities which may find favor in the theater or in high society. If he is a chapel music director, he should avoid the luxurious style as much as he can and instead arrange everything with nice expression, devotion and in general with movement" ("fein pathetisch/ andächtig u. sonsten beweglich").[406] Johann Heinrich Buttstedt is well known to have resisted the new stylistic innovations; writing against Johann Mattheson's use of a Luther citation, Buttstedt argued that Luther did not have in mind the "rubbish which is used today in musical pieces in the theater as well as in private music societies and also in pieces for church."[407]

More open-minded than Buttstedt but still hesitant, Friedrich Erhart Niedt endorsed a "serious and modest" style which avoids "foolish fads." Musical styles change as do clothing styles, he admits, but the fact that Italian music is in vogue does not mean that everything Italian is acceptable. The recitative style ought to resemble speaking more than singing and thus the range should be limited to a sixth, but many absurd jumps, hops and runs have been included in recitatives by those who are more nearly buffoons than judicious composers. He himself has adopted the cantata style as suited to the taste of his congregation but modified by eliminating runs and Italianate antics unfit for the German language. Niedt admits that his sober approach to the new styles has caused him to be classified as a Pietist; to this he responded that it was a shame values had become so distorted that genuine heartfelt devotion to God would no longer be endured by the gallant world. In spite of Niedt's adoption of cantata style, therefore, the limitations he applied and his principle of modesty and seriousness place him close to those who opposed the new form.[408]

Given this evidence and that introduced in chapter three, it is puzzling that so many learned Bach scholars insist that there was no stylistic distinction between sacred and secular music in Lutheran tradition in the time up to and including Bach. Christoph Wolff, for example, seems to be handing down musicological tradition rather than drawing his own conclusions when, after citing Christoph Bernhard's style classifications, he claims there was no attempt to glorify or sanction the old polyphonic vocal style as the true church style.[409] Similarly, how can Ulrich Meyer interpret Bernhard as representing stylistic monism (though "not completely unlimited") after citing Bernhard's indications of the usual settings for the three styles?[410] More accurate is Kerala Snyder's report that Bernhard's style classifications have to do with composition, not sociology.[411] It is also true that they have nothing to do with theology. Meyer surely reads too much into Bernhard's brief comments when he writes that Bernhard "characterizes three different manners of composing and assigns the middle one without reservation and the other two to a lesser extent to all areas of musical practice, sacred as well as secular."[412] The assumption that the use of different musical styles in church reflects a theological openness to artistic innovation has led to further confusion.[413] Bernhard, in the first place, merely reported current practice; he did not propose norms. More importantly, he was not a theologian and must not be used as a spokesman for Lutheran theology.

Others writing about the ease with which Bach transformed secular pieces into sacred music look to a Baroque world view or a Reformation doctrine of vocation. Andreas Marti, relying on the work of others, says simply, "A differentiation between the two spheres [sacred and profane] would be meaningless for the Baroque view of the world and of humanity."[414] Christhard Mahrenholz appealed to the Lutheran concept of office and vocation, "which separates the concepts 'churchly' and 'worldly' in the practice of executing one's office but not in the principles of responsibility for the office."[415] The fallacy in both of these approaches is the assumption that Bach's practice represented a continuous development rather than a radically new compositional procedure. Evidence from his contemporaries, on the other hand, shows that both advocates and opponents considered the theatrical style of church music and the parody practice which accompanied it to be an innovation in their time. Indeed, for the first time we find preachers embracing artistic innovation. Gottfried Tilgner, editor of the 1717 edition of Neumeister's cantata texts, praised Neumeister for introducing a poetic form which could excite the interest of the best composers of the time and thereby keep church music in the artistic mainstream.[416] More significant for our purposes is that the theological reasoning which underlay the new form was not that of the Reformation nor the Baroque but of rationalist empiricism.

Johann Mattheson was the most famous theorist to advocate the new style, but his direct involvement in the cantata controversy came a few years after the publication by Scheibel. Yet Mattheson's influence on Scheibel is unquestionable, and it might be most logical first to focus on Mattheson and mention Scheibel briefly as a less important ally. This study, however, has dealt with theologians' writings on music and has introduced writings by musicians for purposes of comparison only. Scheibel, who identified himself at the outset as a non-musician and was identified by Johann Gottfried Walther as "Candidatus Ministerii," is a better spokesman for the circle of preacher-poets who produced cantata texts. It is in itself significant that no influential theologians took part in the debate. As theology became more practical and "reasonable," the theology of music was increasingly written more by musicians than theologians. Scheibel claims to be neither but rather to present himself "comme un Philosophe," alerting us at the outset that he is a man of the Enlightenment.

Accordingly, Scheibel's definition of music contains nothing of the Baroque concept of harmony or the Reformation idea of a divine gift; instead, focussing on an aspect which had become increasingly more central with the influence of Kircher's *Musurgia*, Scheibel writes, "Music is an art which shows us how one can move the affections by changes of tone" (3). For further information he refers the reader to Kircher, Marcus Meibom's *Scriptoribus Musicae Antiquae*, and Mattheson's *Orchestre u. Organisten Probe*. His historical survey, in contrast to those which idealized either biblical or Reformation worship music, depicts church music as reaching its pinnacle in his own time because of increased understanding of the theory of affections. In a comment reminiscent of Luther's confidence that Augustine would agree with him, Scheibel excuses Zwingli for rejecting church music:

> At the time of the Reformation, Zwingli especially wanted to have music removed. But I believe if he had lived in our day, now that musicians have better understood the doctrine of the affections, he would have judged otherwise. In his time music was still poorly executed; it's no wonder that it couldn't please everyone. (8)

His view of the purpose of church music is by no means new—it is a means of honoring God and edifying the congregation—, but the rationale is less biblical than naturalistic. Aware that religions are characterized by some form of outward worship, he regards this as a natural outgrowth of inward devotion: "It is based in nature that when a human being recognizes God he will as a consequence honor Him outwardly with words and deeds" (19). The seventeenth-century premise that God had commanded music is not to be found in Scheibel's thinking, but he is confident that "God himself takes pleasure in music" (8).

Scheibel's view of what is meant by edifying the congregation likewise combines familiar content and new perspectives. Like many orthodox writers, Scheibel regards church music's goal as "to bring minds to attention and encourage devotion" (22). But never does he connect music to the workings of the Holy Spirit; rather, the effects of music are physiologically based. His explanation of the movement of the affections draws entirely on the ancient physiological theory of the four humors as explained, for instance, by Kircher.[417] Because of different humoral constitutions, music affects people in different ways. The cold, thick blood of melancholiacs is averse to quick movements, for example, so that their musical preferences incline to slow tempos. Used as a medicine for the spirit, though, music can produce moods contrary to the natural disposition, as when light-hearted music cheers a melancholiac or when a lament brings tears from a person of sanguine temperament (17).

If music has such power and can bring pleasure through secular genres such as opera, this same power should be used to effect spiritual pleasure. Admitting that music is not in the strict sense essential to worship, Scheibel argues that an "abstract" service which consists only of the essentials—a few hymns, a sermon and communion—is not appealing to the ordinary person. (Scheibel, as was common in his time, writes of "music" in the sense of figural music as distinct from congregational hymnody.) The unregenerate, specifically, find nothing to engage their attention in such a service. To be sure, too much ceremony may induce superstition, but too little ceremony fails to encourage belief: he reasons that the cause for so much atheism in Holland and England must be the barrenness of worship among the Reformed (31).

Scheibel, then, wants to launch an outreach campaign for the church through music. If the opera houses are drawing in the crowds, the way to compete is to offer the same attraction in the church: "And perhaps not so many people would run after worldly performances if they could hear music as well and as movingly performed in the houses of God" (32).[418] Even if they come to church just to hear the music, they may well be sufficiently moved that they can last through the sermon. Scheibel reports of "a certain place" where a Passion was to be sung before and after the sermon on Good Friday. He is convinced that people came in such numbers and so promptly not because of the preacher but because of the music. The musical text was the passion story from one of the gospels mixed with numerous chorales and some arias. Scheibel was amazed "how eagerly people listened and how devoutly they sang along, to which the moving music contributed the most. And although the service lasted over four hours, everyone remained inside until it was over" (31).

Against the commonly held belief that the music of the church should be of a different sort from that of the theater, Scheibel asserts that the affections which are to be aroused are the same in each case; it is the object of the affections which differs. The text is thus crucial for communicating the intended object of the affection; the music may be identical. To prove his point, Scheibel takes some operatic aria texts and suggests religious parodies which convey the same affection. The first two examples are taken from Telemann's opera "Jupiter and Semele" (Act I, Scene II) as presented in Leipzig five years earlier.[419] In her first aria Semele sings

> Ich empfinde schon die Triebe
> Die der kleine Gott der Liebe/
>   Meiner Seelen eingeprägt.
> Ach wie kan sein Pfeil erquicken
> Und die süße Glut entzücken
>   Die er in mir hat erregt.

Appealing to the memories of those who heard the opera, Scheibel suggests that minor textual revisions could transform the same piece into a sacred aria:

> Ich empfinde schon die Triebe
> Die mein Jesus/ der die Liebe
>   Meiner Seelen eingeprägt.
> Ach! wie kan sein Wort erquicken/
> Und des Glaubens Glut entzücken/
>   Den sein Geist in mir erregt. (36)

The second example comes from the following aria of the same scene:

> Meine Flammen sind so schön/
> Daß ich mich von aller Pflicht
> Durch ihr sonderbahres Licht/
> Kan hinfort befreyet sehn.
> Wo ein Gott verliebt will sprechen/
> Müssen andre Bande brechen. (37)

Scheibel's parody follows:

> Meine Flammen sind so schön/
> Daß ich aller Fleisches-Pflicht

> Durch des wahren Glaubens-Licht
> Mich kan fort befreyet sehn.
> Wo Gott wil von Liebe sprechen/
> Müssen irrd'sche Bande brechen.

Scheibel's third example is taken from the Opera "Artaxeris" translated from Italian and set to music by "Mons. Vogler" in Leipzig:[420]

> Oeffnet euch/ ihr schönen Augen/
>   Lasset euren Wunder Schein
>   Meiner Seelen Pharus seyn
> Haltet die beflammten Blicke
> Länger nicht von mir zurücke
>   Denn ihr Glantz hemmt meine Pein.

The reference could easily be transferred to the situation of doubting Thomas, leaving the same affect in the music:

> Oeffnet euch ihr Glaubens-Augen/
>   Lasset Jesu Friedens-Schein
>   Eurer Hoffnung Pharus seyn
> Haltet die beflammten Blicke
> Von der Lust der Welt zurücke
>   Denn ihr Ansehn bringt nur Pein. (37–38)

Apart from whatever intrinsic value these experiments may have had, they shed light on some questions of scholarly interest. Whereas the term "parody" is in common usage among Bach scholars to identify his practice of re-using compositions in another context, the applicability of the word has been questioned.[421] That Scheibel used the term is in itself worthy of note, but that he also explains the procedure and the theory behind it is of considerable significance for our understanding of Bach. We do not know whether Bach read Scheibel's book, but Scheibel's words could have served as a prescription for Bach's own parody practice:

> I take a secular composition from a cantata, make a parody of it from religious material and express just the same affection which the composition brings with it. Thus this affection will be moved just as if it had a secular object to which it was directed, and therefore it will not lose its force. (35)

The reason that secular compositions were transformed into sacred is simply that it was the theatrical style which was being appropriated for church use, not vice versa. But far from denigrating church music by adapting secular models, Scheibel, and presumably Bach, aimed at appropriating the best music for the nobler cause. Scheibel wanted composers of church music to be competitive in the larger musical arena so that the church would also be as competitive as the opera house.

> I don't know where operas alone get the privilege of extracting tears from us. Why shouldn't that apply to the church?... It is sometimes said that this or that composer can write a good piece of church music but doesn't succeed at other things. I turn it around: if a composer can move the affections in theatrical and secular music, he will be able to do so in sacred matters, as the examples of Monsieurs Kayser, Mattheson, and Telemann bear witness. (40)

For the first time in our tracing of the Lutheran theology of music, we find in Scheibel, as a spokesman for the Neumeister reform, the insistence on the unity of sacred and secular music which has so often been attributed to the entire Lutheran tradition up to Bach. Even then, of course, not everything is equally suited to the church: "I gladly grant that minuets, gigues, gavottes, passepieds, etc. are not suited to churches, for they produce idle thoughts in the listener" (41). But most of those who come to church already have idle thoughts, and the importance of music is to draw their thoughts to spiritual matters through music which moves the affections in the right direction. "So long as their affections have been moved just once by well-performed harmony,...they can easily last through the sermon because they have already been prepared for it" (29). For Scheibel, then, church music has an evangelizing purpose; only by meeting the worldly halfway can the church expect to have any influence.

In a later book Scheibel modestly expressed pleasure that his first book had been well received, especially by "one of the greatest and most learned musicians of this century."[422] But the matter was not settled. In 1726 a book appeared from the opposing camp, written by Joachim Meyer, who was at different times cantor, professor of music, and professor of law and history at the Gymnasium in Göttingen.[423] The book, *Unvorgreiffliche Gedanken über die Neulich eingerissene Theatralische Kirchen-Music*, was not a response to Scheibel but to the cantata movement as a whole. Whether Meyer is representative of a group is unclear; although he defended Vockerodt against charges he considered unfair, there is little evidence to connect him with any Pietist circle. As a former music teacher, he may have been motivated to preserve the integrity of music more than to espouse a theological position. We need not assign a label; for our purposes he serves as spokesman for the resistance to a new theology of music.

The accommodation to popular taste which resulted in the cantata style was a questionable approach, according to Meyer. It had been used in the ancient church by heretical sects, he claimed, thus spreading their weeds into the church.

Although Meyer regarded the edification of the neighbor as one goal of church music, his emphasis lay on the glorification of God. For this purpose "honorable, devotional, and edifying music"[424] should be employed. Recent innovations, he felt, were better suited to the theater; they were more conducive to dancing than to praising God.

Meyer cannot grasp the argument that theatrical music becomes sanctified by being dedicated to the glory of God (69). The borrowing of secular melodies for spiritual songs does not bother Meyer, because, he claims, most people are not aware of it. The theatrical manner of singing and playing, on the other hand, is recognizable to everyone and gives rise to worldly and frivolous thoughts. This is particularly true with instrumental music, which is not marked as sacred by a text; but because most sung texts cannot be understood, it applies also to vocal music. Meyer is particularly concerned lest biblical texts be altogether displaced by the new poetry. He insists that he does not oppose cantatas entirely, but he disapproves of the innovating mentality which would abandon "a far more edifying and comprehensible form of music" (69) based on biblical texts for poetic invention.

In addition to misgivings concerning the comprehensibility and appropriateness of the texts, Meyer is uncomfortable with the musical rhythms and tonalities in the new music. He observed that the ancient Greeks had chosen modalities appropriate to the mood of the text: for example, love songs were set in Phrygian mode, laments in Lydian mode (35). They used the **genus chromaticum** in the theater but rejected it for the temple as insufficiently serious. The **genus diatonicum** or Dorian was best suited for temple music because it was the most moral and conducive to devotion (28–29). In matters of tempo, also, there were distinctions between temple and theater music. Eighth, sixteenth, and thirty-second notes were unknown in temple music, which was generally restricted to whole, half, or at most quarter notes (31). Meyer also turned for support to ancient Hebrew music; while admitting that we cannot know how it sounded, he was confident there is enough evidence to know that their worship music contained "nothing frivolous or histrionic, but was modest, solemn, and edifying" (13).

Appropriate to his argument, Meyer's book is moderate in tone and without polemical fervor, but its clear-cut defense of distinctions in musical style provoked an enraged response from the most prolific musical commentator of the time, Johann Mattheson. Perhaps correctly perceiving Meyer's little book as a major impediment to the maintenance of a professional class of church musicians, Mattheson undertook a counter-attack which aimed at everything from Meyer's grammar to his major thesis. By admitting not an iota of truth to Meyer's arguments, Mattheson refused even to acknowledge any connection between cantatas and operas. Because of its polemical nature, this work of Mattheson, *Der neue Göttingische Aber Viel schlechter, als Die alten Lacedamonische, urtheilenden Ephorus*, is not entirely consistent with his other works, as another respondent attempts to point out.

On the matter of textual comprehensibility, Mattheson countered that the solo voices in cantatas were far more comprehensible than the many voices of counterpoint. To be sure, some singers have faulty diction, and in some churches the singers are placed so far from the listeners that they cannot be understood. But in such cases neither the text—whether biblical or modern—nor the musical style—whether cantata or motet—would matter; the only way in which the text of vocal music will always be understood is to distribute it in printed form.

As for the strictly musical issues, Mattheson saw no validity to any of Meyer's points. Meyer should know, he argues, that all melodies of his day belong to the **genus diatonicum**. Further, note duration is irrelevant: there is more seriousness in church cantatas which use 32nd and 64th notes than in rigaudons, gavottes, and bourrées which use only quarter, half and whole notes.[425] But dance rhythms in themselves are not necessarily unsuited to church. Gottfried Tilgner had written, "In truth, whoever sings of the painful suffering of our savior according to the melody of a folie d'Espagne or wishes to celebrate his joyous resurrection and ascension with the rhythm of a courant or gigue, would fairly be considered a very simple-minded worshipper of divine mysteries if not a godless scoffer."[426] Mattheson responded that the rhythm of a courant is not to be rejected from church music, as it is the most serious that one can find. Nor is a gigue rhythm unsuitable for worship, even though no one would think of using a gigue itself (102).

For the most part, the disagreements voiced thus far have to do with perception and practice rather than theology or theory. The authors' more fundamental differences, I would argue, concern the range of emotions which could be identified as religious. Mattheson, agreeing that the true and final purpose of church music is the praise of God, labels contrary to reason the belief that this is only to be accomplished through a "respectable, serious, and emphatic" manner of music-making (82). When asserting that to rejoice in glorifying God is the purpose of creation, he employs the word "Belustigung" with its more secular connotations of amusement, entertainment, or diversion rather than "Freude," which was the more usual term for religious joy. Meyer sensed that the scope of Mattheson's joy was too broad and responded to the point in his next book, *Der anmassliche Hamburgische Criticus sine crisi*: "Joy in God does not extend to the fleeting and trifling...; when joyfulness in God is based, as it should be, on something solid and enduring, there is indeed something delightful but nothing fleeting or trifling about it."[427]

Although Meyer gives fewer clues than does Mattheson, it appears that their differences arise from fundamentally different views of the relationship between body and soul and, on a larger scale, between the divine order and the natural world. Meyer regards the natural, physical world with suspicion. Because ears are corporeal, that which is sensed by them is incorporated, so to speak, by the body; if music has no text to be grasped by the mind, it can scarcely rise above bodily appeal to a spiritual level. Referring to Augustine's scruples concerning the aural delights of the music heard in church, Meyer asks if one does not fall into mortal sin when the ears alone are gratified and the mind is untouched.[428] Meyer criticizes Mattheson's use of the term "natural" as a defense of theatrical music. Clearly, "natural" does not have positive connotations for him; "one should," he warns, "be wary of such things as are all too natural and come straight out of life."[429]

Mattheson, by contrast, represents a newer, more empirical philosophy in which the physical world is the opening into the spiritual realm. The senses are not elements of a corrupt corporeal nature but means whereby the soul is awakened. Hearing, in his view, is not a characteristic of the body but of the soul. If the hearing were not meant to be flattered into praise of the creator, "why would God have attached to it such extraordinary artistic sensitivity? Why did Paul write with such excellent rhetoric?"[430] It is not essential, therefore, for music to pass through the understanding in order to produce spiritual effects. Because the senses are no longer regarded as impure bodily elements in need of control by the mind but rather as direct channels to the soul, music can convey spiritual power directly.

> Harmony has a secret power, and in order to sense this it is not always necessary to understand it thoroughly....Who understands or grasps the special manner by which foods taste good and nourish us? Yet we sense their good effects even without knowledge of them and their characteristics or of their origin or of their power....In sum, all things, even those which we don't understand or grasp, redound to the greater glory of God.[431]

With this formulation Mattheson has slightly but significantly modified an argument which proponents of organ music in Lutheran worship had used since the end of the sixteenth century. Against those who argued that only music with a text was suited to elevate the mind to God, the Wittenberg theologians of the 1590s had insisted that purely instrumental music could be understood as belonging to the genus of spiritual music and thus could lead the worshippers to devotion. Mattheson leaves out the middle step of identifying the music's genus and relies on its immediate power to affect the listener. The senses, no longer to be considered easily corruptible without the guidance of the intellect, are now, under the influence of Locke and the new "Physico-Theology," the empirical means through which any knowledge of the divine is to be obtained.[432]

It is this new philosophy which gives significance to the debate between Mattheson and Meyer. Except in the heat of debate the two did not differ radically on the distinction between theater and church styles nor on the importance of understanding sung texts. Martin Heinrich Fuhrmann, who brought the debate to a conclusion with his *Gerechte Wag-Schal* of 1728, mediated the two positions by pointing out that Mattheson never approved of the "luxurious theatrical style" for church; by denying that operas were the source of cantatas, he intended to make a clear differentiation: "I am of the opinion that Herr Mattheson understands by his 'moderate and restrained theater style' nothing else than that in church cantata style there should be **suavitas et gravitas**, lovely and serious compositions, light and heavy movements, in order to give satisfaction both to the clever and the half-witted."[433] As Fuhrmann viewed the issue, both writers had missed the crucial factor: the ability of the singers. Mattheson had presupposed capable singers, whereas Meyer had failed to see that the comprehensibility of a text depends on the skill of the singers. Had he recommended that cantatas be performed only in churches where there were capable singers, Fuhrmann claims, Mattheson would have felt no impulse to respond.

Meyer was apparently not satisfied with Fuhrmann's attempt at mediation and responded again, this time to both Mattheson and Fuhrmann, in a treatise entitled *Der abgewürdigte Wagemeister*.[434] Whether or not any copies of this are still extant, it is not to be expected that any new insights would be gained from examining it. What would be important to locate is not another work by Meyer but one by an acknowledged Pietist debating the cantata form. Philipp Spitta, in his Bach biography, listed three categories of cantata opponents: Pietists, conservative musicians, and serious minded laity and dilettantes. For the second category he gave Buttstedt as an example, for the third category Christian Gerber and Joachim Meyer. For the first category, he names no names. Who, then, are the Pietists who opposed the cantata form, and what were their reasons? In the absence of textual evidence, Spitta, using nineteenth-century categories, patronizingly wondered why two movements toward subjectivism could not recognize their own allies:

> It is often strange how little mutual understanding exists between tastes and tendencies which are really identical in aim and feeling. As if, in point of fact, the endeavour to express personal emotion on the boards of a theatre differed in essence from the transcendental subjectivity of the hymns in the devotions of the Pietists themselves![435]

Following Spitta's lead, Martin Dibelius made a similar point a half century later:

> Pietism lacks sensitivity for the fact that those they attack are in a certain sense pursuing the same cause. Now for the first time poets and composers have the opportunity to develop those subjective feelings on which Pietism places such value in the reading of the Bible.[436]

Tied to terminology from their own era, neither Spitta nor Dibelius considered that subjectivism was not a useful criterion of differentiation for the eighteenth century. If, as Walter Blankenburg noted, the devotional literature of the entire era was characterized by subjectivism and emphasis on feelings,[437] then one could not expect those who lived in such an age to identify either their friends or their enemies by means of these categories.

Further research may in fact demonstrate that Pietists placed less value than did others on subjective feelings. In their theology, to involve the affections did not in itself bring one closer to faith; if God is the active agent in conversion, then human efforts to prepare the heart are of no consequence. In an unredeemed state the natural affections are sinful and cannot even cooperate in the process of repentance and regeneration.[438] For this reason Spener rejected the kind of religious meditation which cultivated a form of emotional empathy: "The proper art and fruit of meditation do not consist in one's considering that he must suffer and empathize with Christ in his great suffering or weep over him and his suffering....There is much greater worth in faithful joy than in natural compassion."[439]

The musical doctrine of the affections, then, is, theologically speaking, a form of semi-Pelagianism, for it presumes that by the physiologically based effects of music the soul can be prepared for God's Word. The orthodox Lutheran view, by contrast, regarded music not as a naturalistic force but as a means used by the Holy Spirit to prepare the soul. Furthermore, the affections were unruly elements needing to be tamed, not pure faculties needing to be cultivated. To be sure, with the physiology of the humors, music may likewise be used to counteract natural dispositions. But to put the power to control affections in the hands of the composer is to displace divine power. Not the style of music but its source, then, is the real point of contention. An emotion-laden aria which is the expression of authentic religious feeling (i.e., a response to God's workings in the soul) may not sound different from an aria skilfully composed to evoke a similar feeling, but the latter is, for the Pietists, an imitation only. If the art of stimulating emotion which had been developed in the theater was allowed to be introduced into the church, worship, they feared, would be as fictitious as opera.

Significantly, it is not the music but the superficiality of the emotional stimulation to which Christian Gerber objects. A revivalistic preacher is open to the same criticism: "A year ago we saw here in the area how the preachers of repentance who were then traveling around here frequently moved people to tears with their theatrical performances; but a large number of these people went immediately thereafter to the pub, got themselves drunk, and continued on where they had left off."[440] Far from arousing genuine devotion, the musical doctrine of the affections turns religion into outward show; one might as well return to popish ceremony, as far as Gerber was concerned. "O whoever knows just the first letters of Christianity is disgusted by such theatrical affairs and seeks instead to change the theater of his heart and to found Christianity inwardly in his soul."

FINALE

JOHANN SEBASTIAN BACH

A MUSICIAN, NOT A THEOLOGIAN

To include Johann Sebastian Bach in a history of the Lutheran theology of music is to risk succumbing to the same confusion which has given rise to the Bach legend. However well informed Bach was in matters of theology, he never took up the pen to argue a theological point or to support his music with theology. He was not a trained theologian. In the previous century, it had not been uncommon for a cantor to advance to the position of pastor, as the academic training for both posts was similar, but Bach's lack of formal theological education would not have qualified him for such a switch. Whether he was even a church musician by profession or a musician who happened to land in the church has been a subject of much controversy.[441] The important point to be made in the present context is that in addition to the different theological positions of Pietist, Orthodox and Enlightenment theologians or pastors regarding music, musicians represented another theological perspective within Lutheranism.

Bach was not, however, one of the formulators of the musicians' theology of music. As defined in this study, we are concerned with texts **about** music, not texts **of** music. The latter are the focus of much theological research on Bach, but must be declared out of the bounds of this study. What remains are a few short comments scattered in letters, biblical annotations, and prefaces to musical compositions. Given the paucity of evidence, the most striking aspect of Bach scholarship is that so much has been written about so little. Just as the Luther legend distorts the historical evaluation of his theology of music, so the Bach legend has attributed more religious significance to him than is historically warranted. The veneration which is rightly due his musical compositions has been transferred with less justification to his person. As we have seen, however, both musicians and theologians recognized at the time that talent did not necessarily cohabit with virtue. Until twentieth-century scholars endorse the Pietist view that regeneration takes priority over skill, they must admit that great religious music need not be written by a saint. To be sure, few can ignore Bach's squabbles with authorities, but generally these are attributed to righteous indignation against amusical villains.

It is not my aim here to reverse the stakes but merely to plead for a historical rather than a hagiographical picture of Bach. If evidence is thin, it should be supplemented with other contemporary evidence, not with speculations based on assumptions about his personality drawn from his compositions. In his article on Bach research since 1965, Walter Blankenburg asked the question, "Do not person and work determine each other? Is not Bach's music in the end only fully comprehensible through the circumstances of life and above all the philosophy of life of its creator?"[442] To that question I wish to answer, "no, not necessarily." I would point out that the contemporary defense of church music against Pietism rested in part on the distinction between person and work. Johann Beer insisted on judging the work, not the person: "Indeed, though I should be silent, my position could be strengthened by a thousand examples of many famous artists, who, alongside their glorious art, experience, and knowledge, have been the most dissolute scoundrels of the world."[443] Surely no one would wish to drag Bach so low, but neither is it necessary to elevate him above the level of ordinary mortals.[444]

Even if we can piece together Bach's world view or theology, we cannot know the depth of his religious motivation. The fact that he began his compositions with S.D.G. or J.J. is not meaningless, but from that we can discern nothing more about his faith than if we were to observe a Catholic making the sign of the cross and genuflecting upon entering a church. Because it was not an unusual practice, it does not distinguish Bach from his contemporaries.[445] No matter what differences we have discovered among the musicians of the time, all have endorsed the view that music should first of all serve the glory of God. If the musicians of Germany had anything in common, it seems to have been a fundamentally religious understanding of music.

The fact that the religious inscription was applied to both sacred and secular pieces may or may not be significant. In the preceding chapter I argued that the practice of borrowing from secular pieces for sacred compositions was based in an eighteenth-century view of the affections which had not previously been part of the Lutheran tradition. But that is a specific issue in the relationship of sacred to secular music and does not respond to the question of religious inscriptions on secular music. I see no basis for explaining this as an expression of a Lutheran concept of vocation or office; there is far more contemporary evidence for explaining it as a reflection of the natural theology which we have encountered among music theorists and which, as Blankenburg states, was "by no means limited to the Lutherans among them but was rather a general interdenominational and international phenomenon."[446]

This theology of cosmic order and harmony was first encountered within Lutheranism in the early seventeenth century, where it seemed to combine elements of Italian music theory with mysticism and popular devotion (see chapter 4). By the beginning of the next century, however, little remained that could be construed as specifically Lutheran. The most frequently cited sources in Buttstedt's *Ut, Mi, Sol...* were such non-Lutherans as Robert Fludd, Athanasius Kircher, and Agostino Steffani. Indeed, the belief in uncreated and eternal harmony allows Buttstedt a perspective beyond temporary confessional differences; his proof of harmony's eternity is limited to the doctrines of the Trinity and Christ, which were not divisive issues for the three forms of Christianity familiar to Buttstedt. In their expectations of the afterlife, furthermore, "every Catholic, Evangelical, and Reformed Christian" believes with Job that with the fleshly proportions of our earthly members we shall see God.[447] Although this natural theology was thus not perceived to be in conflict with biblical revelation, nevertheless the musician, as we have seen with Motz and Werckmeister, was privy to another means of revelation. Through music the composer was attuned directly to God and had a foretaste of heavenly joy. If indeed Bach shared this world view, as seems likely,[448] he must have felt that all his compositions required divine inspiration and fulfilled a divine purpose. But, whether or not he recognized it, he was in this respect more a musician than a confessional churchman.

To say this is by no means to accuse Bach of hypocrisy in his church work or to claim that he would have preferred a court to a church position. It is, however, to question the unswerving institutional loyalty which some have asserted.[449] The phrases "regulated church music" and "well-appointed church music" ("wohlbestallte Kirchen Music") have, so far as I can tell, nothing to do with liturgical order but rather with artistic excellence. As we observed from Scheibel, "wohlbestellte Kirchenmusik" consistently refers to the skilfully composed and attractively presented music which was being offered by the talented musicians of his day. Bach's use of the term "final purpose" ("Endzweck") in relation to "a regulated church music" does not, after all, appear as an impartial statement concerning his personal goals; it is offered in a letter of resignation to his Mühlhausen employers as a highminded reason for switching to a better paid position. Under the circumstances, the term "regulated church music" deserves far less attention than it has been given, but in any case it refers to a kind of music that money can buy.[450]

Those who perceive Bach as a thoroughly committed churchman tend to explain away or to theologize evidence which leads in another direction. The formulation "zu Gottes Ehre und Recreation des Gemüths" has, accordingly, been interpreted as two more or less synonymous ways of expressing Bach's single sacred purpose. The word "Recreation" is broken into its etymological components ("re-creare") to give music the task of renewing the spirit. Thus, for Marti, both "for God's honor" and "for recreation of the spirit" are "in the end identical, as music renews (re-creation!) hearts, soothes, cheers and lifts them to devotion and thus brings them into better harmony with God's order."[451] Hans Eggebrecht also appeals to the Latin root to explain the "theocentric orientation" of the term.[452] Oskar Söhngen places theological significance also in the word "Gemüt," which he finds to have had a broader meaning at this time, referring not only to the realm of human feelings but to all the powers of the mind and senses. Thus he concludes that "Recreation des Gemütes" entails "a fundamental correction of the whole person."[453]

While Bach might not explicitly disagree with Marti, Eggebrecht and Söhngen, there is no reason to believe that he had given the phrase such profound thought; he had, after all, borrowed it from F. E. Niedt. Nor is there any evidence that people of Bach's day were any more conscious of the etymology of "Recreation" than are we. The seventeenth and early eighteenth century German application of the word is virtually indistinguishable from the twentieth-century English-language application. Recreation is understood to be a non-religious but wholesome activity which fills leisure time in a manner which enhances rather than conflicts with the more serious commitments of work or faith. It is a form of pleasure but not a pursuit of pleasure for its own sake. Thus while it may be said to have spiritual value, it does not make a direct contribution to the spiritual regeneration of the person in the way indicated by Söhngen.

If this definition holds true to some extent for the entire era, what is significant is that the term takes on greater seriousness as the new values of the gallant age begin to emerge. In the editorial marginalia to Dieterich's 1624 organ sermon, the word refers to leisure time activity without a hint of religious purpose[454]; at issue is the Calvinist practice of playing organ music in churches on weekdays to entertain the merchants, and the result, as far as Dieterich is concerned, is to degrade a sacred instrument rather than to refresh thirsty souls.

For Hector Mithobius, music is a wholesome and pleasant activity for one's spare time, but he does not attribute to it any particular religious significance. It was a good family activity for his grandfather and his father, who, together with his father's brothers, formed a well-respected Collegium Musicum. It enabled them to enjoy their leisure hours in an activity by which they also honored God in worship, but Mithobius does not connect the two uses of music in such a manner as to imply that the recreational use honors God.[455]

Not until recreational music became a controversial topic did writers draw such an explicit connection. As we have seen, the theological defenders of opera highlighted its moral purpose in portraying stories of virtue. It also had the spiritual value of providing rest for the soul. But Christopher Rauch goes further to compare opera to other recreational activities such as walking, hunting, playing games and socializing in pubs, which revive "the animal spirits"; like all these, it enables people to return to their daily tasks with renewed energy, but in addition it motivates and teaches. Thus, among the "permissible pleasures" it is the most complete recreation because it refreshes both soul and "animal spirits" and leads ultimately to the glory of God.[456] By saying the "ultimate goal" is the honor of God, Rauch endows leisure with serious purpose but hardly implies anything as fundamental as does Söhngen, who speaks of the original condition of creation as that from which music "re-creates" people.[457]

Johann Beer took the more radical approach of defending recreation as a value unto itself needing no theological justification. For him it belonged to a morally neutral middle ground between pleasure and work. In moderation there should be no moral objection to it.

> Does "se recreare" mean to make a profession of it? Or to amuse oneself? A little bit for the home, then it's over. Once is not always. I am not speaking of a profession but of recreation. There is a time for laughter.[458]

Wolfgang Caspar Printz likewise uses the word to distinguish a professional from a leisure activity. Before he considered pursuing music as his profession, he reports, he was so drawn to the wonders of music "that in those hours which were to be dedicated to my recreation I most eagerly endeavored to investigate its nature and secrets."[459]

Johann Mattheson explicitly applies the word to secular music; yet even secular art, when it provides such innocent pleasure, is a gift of God: "...music also, insofar as it may be called secular, is of all the arts especially given by God to humans for recreation and contains the proper sweetness almost alone by itself."[460] Music is second only to theology (à la Luther) because other studies consist of "nothing but odious pros and cons" whereas music is a "disinterested harmonic science."(26) While more utilitarian skills may be necessary, music is close to theology because it was founded "out of pleasure and only out of pleasure" and is therefore of nobler origin.(31) With what Buttstedt regarded as a trivialization of heavenly harmony, Mattheson described music as "der Engel Zeitvertreib," the pastime of the angels.[461]

Mattheson, then, refused to respond to the pietist and rationalist critique of recreational activities with a justification of music's moral purpose. For him music was valuable precisely because it provided pleasant relief from everything that was merely useful. In contrast also to those cosmological music theorists such as Buttstedt and Werckmeister, who saw music as part of the moral order, Mattheson moved toward a defense of aesthetics as independent from, perhaps even superior to ethics.

We have too few pieces of the Bach puzzle to know whether his theology of music resembled more closely that of Mattheson or that of Werckmeister. Because Mattheson has been associated with the opera and Bach with the church, Mattheson has been considered less serious and less devout than Bach. But the phrase "zulässiger Ergötzung des Gemüths," which Bach adopted in his treatment of thoroughbass (*BD* II, 334), had been associated with the defense of opera and thus places him in the camp of those intent on legitimizing leisure. This evidence, combined with the dedication of "gallantries" in the first part of the *Klavierübung* to music lovers for their "Gemüths Ergoetzung" (*BD* I, 232), should prevent us from searching for theological profundity in Bach's every word or note.

Mattheson was no secularist, however; in his *Der Musicalische Patriot*, he described the religious purpose of all music in a manner which could very well explain Bach's frame of mind when inscribing a secular piece with "SDG":

> No efforts of our composers, singers, and instrumentalists will endure unless, without the least hypocrisy and with proper Davidic seriousness, they have as a goal the honor and praise of God, whether directly or indirectly. Sing and play in operas, instruct and compose as long as you will, finally the church must provide a solid position....So the main point is to form a proper concept of church music and to apply everything that was learned in operas or concerts or in schools and colleges, insofar as it concerns knowledge, toward the praise of the Highest and the edification of the Christian community.[462]

Such openness to worldly activities as ultimately serving a divine cause may be a legitimate interpretation of Luther's doctrine of vocation, but there is no evidence that Mattheson perceived any such connection. Previous writers had been concerned to keep church music sacred, not to sanctify secular music. Mattheson's affirmation of the sacred goal of secular music is most likely a result of his attraction to physico-theology; and given the absence of the sacred-secular unity in the seventeenth century, Bach is more likely to have been influenced by his eighteenth century contemporaries than by a long-lost teaching of Luther.

On another topic in which an unbroken line from Luther to Bach is often drawn, Mattheson again proves to be a much more plausible source. In fact, Mattheson criticizes Luther and the Lutheran tradition for not admitting the ability of music, like that of the preached word, to convey faith through hearing. He suggests that Luther's translation of Romans 10:17 could be improved by returning to the original Greek. He notes that both the Latin (Vulgate) and English (King James) translations, in accordance with the Greek, use the word "hearing" twice, whereas Luther substitutes the word "preaching," which fails to include music's ability to evoke faith through the Word:

Greek: ἄρα ἡ πίστις ἐξ ἀκοῆς, ἡ δὲ ἀκοὴ διὰ ῥήματος Χριστοῦ.

Vulgate: Ergo fides ex auditu, auditus autem per verbum Christi.

King James: So then faith comes by hearing, and hearing by the word of God.

> Luther: So kompt der glaube aus der predigt, Das predigen aber durch das wort Gottes.

The broader meaning of the Greek would have prevented such an overemphasis on the sermon in Lutheran worship, Mattheson argues: "Saving faith comes not from the sermon alone but equally from listening to a beautiful piece of sacred music, which may then be called a true main sermon."[463]

In spite of all that has been said about music as the **viva vox evangelii** in Lutheranism,[464] there is indeed no evidence that anyone prior to Mattheson dared to suggest that music could serve as well as the sermon for proclaiming the Gospel. Söhngen's evidence that Luther regarded music as a means of proclaiming the word rests on two brief passages from Table Talk which are hardly explicit on this topic and on the Schmalkald Articles which specify the various means by which the Gospel is made available: preaching, baptism, the sacrament of the altar, the power of the keys, and "mutuum colloquium et consolatio fratrum."[465] Only by connecting this phrase with the words of Col. 3:16 and Eph. 5:18 is it possible to understand music as included in this mode of proclamation. A recent article by Matthias Viertel points out that Söhngen's translation of Col. 3:16 connects Word and singing in a way that Luther's does not. Placing more importance on the critical comments by Luther which Söhngen attributes to an earlier phase of Luther's development, Viertel calls into question the view of Söhngen and others that Luther assigned music a kerygmatic function.[466]

When the close relationship between music and the Word in the Lutheran tradition is discussed, the focus is generally on the way in which the biblical text is set to music. Thus Heinrich Schütz is praised as a biblical interpreter and J. S. Bach is labelled the Fifth Evangelist. But the passage from the Table Talk on which Söhngen placed such importance—"God has also preached the gospel through music" (*WA TR* 1258)—makes no reference to the text; in fact, the word "gospel" here is being used not in reference to the written word but in opposition to "law". Thus the compositions of Josquin des Pres communicate the gospel because they "flow freely, gently, and cheerfully, are not forced or cramped by rules," (*LW* 54, 130) not because they effectively communicate textual meaning.

Even if the power of music to preach the Word was sometimes implicit in Lutheran thought prior to the eighteenth century, my research leads me to conclude that Johann Mattheson was not the end of a line which placed preacher and cantor on the same level[467] but was the first to make such a claim explicit. The implications of this equalization of status extended not only to the use of the cantata as a form of sermon but also to practical questions of the rights and duties of cantors. We have seen evidence of tension on this question in the writings of Mithobius and Muscovius, who both clearly asserted the authority of the pastor to choose hymns for services. When therefore Bach complained that he was being deprived of the right to choose the hymns before and after the sermon, "which was always left to me and my predecessors to determine" (*BR*, 114), he was entering territory long held in dispute. If indeed it was the "custom and practice" in Leipzig for the cantor to make these decisions, it was because the pastors decided not to assert the authority which the weight of the tradition granted them.

Johann Kuhnau, in his 1688 dissertation on the canon law of church music, had cited several sources affirming the sole right of pastors to authorize musical innovations: "Whence also we may conclude that it is not in the power of the cantor to introduce new sacred hymns."[468] Of course, in the dispute between Bach and preacher Gaudlitz, it was the musician accusing the pastor of innovation; the latter justifiably labelled Bach's charges an "idle pretext" and asked to retain the privilege accorded to his colleagues in the ministry (*BD* I, 56). Gaudlitz' plea to the authorities that his aim is "solely for the glory of God" ("allein zur Ehre Gottes") alerts us to the potential use of this phrase as a reinforcement of one's position as well as an expression of devotion.

Another instance of conflicting claims of prerogative is the famous dispute between Bach and Rector J. A. Ernesti concerning the appointment of choral prefects. Whereas Paul Minear has preferred to see this as a struggle between "two epochs, two cultures, two philosophies of education,"[469] I think it is important to take the power struggle seriously for its own sake. In the very extensive testimony of both Bach and Ernesti, the issues at stake never extend into educational philosophy or biblical interpretation, which Minear and Robert Stevenson have considered the root of the conflict.[470] What is disputed are the actual facts of the episode and the prerogatives of cantor and rector.

Anyone who reads the testimony of both Bach and Ernesti with an open mind will have difficulty agreeing with Karl Geiringer that "clearly the right was on Bach's side."[471] The issue was not so simple as whether Johann Gottlieb Krause was competent to be musical prefect but whether Bach had reversed his opinion on Krause's competency for ulterior motives and had unfairly tested his musical skills. It is clear from the school order then in effect (though as the dispute continued Bach argued that this school order had never been ratified) that the cantor did not have sole authority over the appointment of prefects; yet Bach insisted that "the choice of the **praefecti chororum** from among the school boys belongs to me, without the concurrence of the Rector, and has always been so made not only by me but by my predecessors" (*BR* 153).

The general predisposition of Bach scholars to side with Bach has led to the conclusion that Ernesti was indeed attempting an intrusion on Bach's rights and that Bach was upholding the traditionally accepted privileges of cantors. Viewed from the standpoint of Ernesti, however, it appeared that Bach was wilfully denying the legitimate authority of the rector, which he had recognized as a matter of course until it no longer suited his cause to do so.

An impartial observer of this dispute in the larger historical context would have to recognize that there was no unanimity concerning the cantor-rector relationship. We have observed the animosity which Gottfried Vockerodt aroused when he entered the musical arena. Like Vockerodt, Ernesti has gone down in history as an enemy of music, but this is surely a caricature of Ernesti as much as of Vockerodt. A 1706 treatise by Johann Phil. Bendeler, cantor at Quedlinburg, is devoted entirely to the questions being disputed concerning the role of rector in relation to cantor.[472] As might be expected, the cantor-author denies the rector any authority over musical affairs. The rector may be head of the school, but this does not give him directorship over music, as church music is a function of the church, not of the school. "Is not the cantor as cantor," Bendeler asks, "just as much a servant of the church as the preacher, organist, or sexton?"(4) Bendeler minimizes the role of rector in accepting pupils for the choir, confirming the prefects, and dispensing choir money. As the money is for church music, it should really be dispensed by the cantor, and even though pupils who wish to join the choir must report to the rector, it is the cantor who decides whether or not they are capable. And the rector "cannot appoint any prefect against the will of the cantor, because the cantor has to judge his capability in music and must have someone who is able (*tüchtig*) to take his place in an emergency."(9) Conversely, in response to the question whether a cantor who wishes to dismiss a singer who persistently offends against church music and the choir must submit the case to the rector for investigation, Bendeler denies this "**in totum.**"(19)

Bendeler's work thus gave full support for all of Bach's contentions and grievances in the struggle against Ernesti. The problem for Bach was that the school ordinance drafted in 1723 appears to have been directed explicitly against such claims of cantorial independence. At least three qualifying phrases limit the authority of the cantor in appointing singers and prefects: "with permission of the rector"; "each time, however, to present them to the principal"; "to choose, however, with prior knowledge and approval of the principal." (*BD* I, 84)

It is beyond the scope of this study to provide a thorough investigation into whether Bach was justified in seeing these restrictions as an infringement on the traditional rights of cantors. Even though Bendeler presented an uncompromising defense of a cantor's absolute authority, the very title of his work indicates that these are questions which had been in dispute for some time: *...Thorough Examination of those Disputed Questions...between School Rectors and Cantors.* Books of church law did not generally go into such detail, however. Benedikt Carpzov's *Jurisprudentia Ecclesiastica seu Consistorialiis* included ministers of the church and the school in the same category; both are subject to the magistrates for appointment to office and removal for disciplinary reasons.[473] The hierarchy of authority within this group, and specifically between cantor and rector, is not discussed.

In sum, if Bach conceived of his cantatas as sermons in music, it was part of the emerging trend toward independence of music from religion. This trend was part of a large cultural change affecting all the arts. From the perspective of secularists it was the beginning of the emancipation of art from religion; for historians of worship, it was the beginning of the decline of liturgy. The continuing debate on whether Bach's cantatas are suitable for contemporary worship suggests that they were already part of the move from the church to the concert hall. The fact that the Leipzig main Sunday worship service in Bach's time was long enough to accommodate cantatas does not demonstrate that there was any coherence or unity which kept worshippers in place and involved for the entire three or four hour period. We have seen enough 17th-century criticisms of the habit of arriving just in time for the sermon to suspect that the practice was still evident in Bach's time. At the same time, there were undoubtedly those who came primarily to hear the music. The divisions between aesthetically-oriented and verbally-oriented worshippers did not originate or terminate during this period, but they reached a critical turning point. So long as the critics of art were primarily in another denomination, Lutheran preachers and musicians joined in a common front and strengthened their defense. When critics emerged within their ranks, however, preachers and musicians grew suspicious of one another and the united force disintegrated.

In this context it is an oversimplification to divide Lutheran camps into "Orthodox," "Pietist," and "Rationalist" and to depict the latter two as undermining the first.[474] Researchers are now in general agreement that Bach, in spite of the sentimentality of some of his texts and in spite of his possession of works of Spener, could not have been a Pietist. But if, as seems to be the current consensus, he should be labelled "Orthodox," it ought to be clarified that his was not the Orthodoxy of the 17th century or even of 18th-century theologians. Theologically well-informed as he was, his primary loyalty was to music. Music and theology were inseparable for him, as they were for Kircher, Werckmeister and Buttstedt, whom Werner Braun in his study of Mattheson designates, along with Bach, as "Baroque Rationalists."[475] Even the Enlightenment elements which Bach shared with Mattheson are incorporated into a theological framework. Furthermore, the biblical interpretation which found solid grounding for figural church music in the Hebrew temple, as indicated, for instance, in Bach's marginal comments on I Chronicles 25 and 28, had been a standard Orthodox approach.[476]

That times had changed, however, is evident in the frequency with which Bach employed dance rhythms in his church music. In what Doris Finke-Hecklinger calls a "penetration of worldly-instrumental types of movement" into the church cantata,[477] the lines drawn in the 17th century to separate musical styles were erased. In this respect Bach was much closer to Lübeck cantor Caspar Rüetz writing in 1752 than to any of the 17th-century writers, either theologians or musicians, who had decried courants and other dances in church. Rüetz, showing his gallant colors, defends the social and physical merits of dancing and sees no reason to bar the door between the dance hall and the church:

> As far as the dance floor is concerned, if it is arranged as it should be, it is by no means a dishonorable place. It is the school of elegance, courteousness, and bodily dexterity....But if it should by

> chance happen that just such a rhythm as conforms to this or that style of dance should be heard in a piece of church music, would the place or the worship service be desecrated by that?[478]

Rüetz further denies the equation of martial or theatrical music with worldly or irreligious activities:

> So let us go for a short while to war, to the dance floor and to the stage in order to see what unholy and worldly things are to be found which must be avoided in music for worship. Say there occurred such movements in a church composition as would also be suited for refreshing soldiers on the field or stirring up the fire of a dancer: what dangerous consequences would follow from that? Is it not the same Word of God which edifies the hearts of the children of peace in the holy gathering places and which must also take away the fear of death from heroes before the battle? Is it not the same Sacrament which strengthens us in this life in the church, on sickbed and deathbed, and prepares us for the blessed homeward journey; and which before a battle must arm soldiers against an unhappy eternity in case the outcome is the termination of their lives? If then one and the same Word of God and one and the same Sacrament are used in times both of war and peace, why not one and the same music?[479]

A like statement affirming sacred and secular unity is not to be found prior to the eighteenth century, even though the view has often been attributed to the entire Lutheran tradition before Bach. The Orthodox defense of figural music depended, after all, on being able to communicate the difference between martial and spiritual music through rhythms rather than words.

The 18th-century union of sacred and secular music was a result not of Luther's doctrine of vocation but of musicians' assertiveness over against the dominance of the clergy. Art has a momentum of its own, and churchmen had since the mid-17th century tried to slow and control that momentum within the church. The hostility which emerged between the camps was itself evidence that musicians had begun to identify themselves as artists, not as servants of the church. Even if Großgebauer had been more conciliatory, it is doubtful that the ministers could have regained control. The theological tensions built into the Lutheran view of music pulled the clergy apart instead of enabling them to close ranks against musicians. The latter took advantage of the resulting power vacuum to declare their independence. By no means secularists, musicians increasingly found God through their art as readily as through the church, a phenomenon which ultimately would work to the detriment of the church. In the meantime, the desire of musicians to stay in the forefront of their profession meant that some great music in the latest styles was introduced into the church. However much

Bach's style may have differed from that of other composers, the differences were small compared to the differences between theologians and musicians. The story of Bach as a conservative Lutheran with his finger in the dike to hold back the flood of new musical ideas and styles is as much a legend as that of the little Dutch boy.

NOTES

1. See, for example, Alfred John Pike, *A Theology of Music* (Toledo: Gregorian Institute, 1953); Carl Halter, *God and Man in Music* (St. Louis: Concordia Publishing House, 1963); Erik Routley, *Church Music and Theology* (Philadelphia: Fortress Press, 1965); Calvin M. Johansson, *Music and Ministry: A Biblical Counterpoint* (Peabody, Massachusetts: Hendrickson Publishers, 1984); David B. Pass, *Music and the Church* (Nashville: Broadman Press, 1989).

2. Responding to this lack, Professor Robin Leaver of Westminster Choir College and Drew University, has recently announced a new series of *Studies in Liturgical Musicology*, to be published by Scarecrow Press. See Leaver, "'Then the whole congregation sings': the sung word in Reformation worship," *Drew Gateway* 60 (Fall 1990), pp. 55–73.

3. The 1983 celebration of the 500th anniversary of Luther's birth brought forth a spate of articles on Luther, with music receiving its share of attention. Almost uniformly they praise Luther's musical and poetic skill and the sensitivity of his liturgical and pastoral understanding. See, for example, Gracia Grindal, "Luther and the Arts: A Study in Convention," *Word and World* 3 (1983): 373–81; Jean-Denis Kraege, "Luther: théologien de la musique," *Études théologiques et religieuses* 58 (1983): 449–63; Fritz Wieninger, "Die Musik im pastoralen Konzept Martin Luthers," *Diakoni* 14 (1983): 372–77; Edith Weber, "Martin Luther, poète, musicièn et hymnologue," *Unité Chrétienne* (November, 1983), 100–08. More recently Carl Schalk has published another encomion to Luther in *Luther on Music: Paradigms of Praise* (St. Louis: Concordia Publishing House, 1988).

4. Oskar Söhngen, "Theologische Grundlagen der Kirchenmusik," *Leiturgia: Handbuch des evangelischen Gottesdienstes* IV (Kassel: Johannes Stauda-Verlag, 1961).

5. Oskar Söhngen, *Theologie der Musik* (Kassel: Johannes Stauda-Verlag, 1967), 84, quoting from Dedo Müller, *Musik als Problem lutherischer Gottesdienstgestaltung* (Berlin, 1947), p. 10. Throughout the present work any translation not otherwise indicated is my own.

6. Söhngen, *Theologie der Musik*, p. 84.

7. *Ibid.*, p. 86.

8. *Ibid.*, p. 86.

9. *Ibid.*, p. 91.

10. *Ibid.*, p. 88.

11. *Ibid.*, p. 95.

12. *Ibid.*, p. 97.

13. *Ibid.*, p. 99. The correct year of publication of *Das Schöne Confitemini* is 1530.

14. See Karl Honemeyer, *Luthers Musikanschauung* (Diss. Münster, 1941), p. 23.

15. Söhngen, p. 291.

16. "Each man can in his mirth be free
    Since such a joy no sin can be.
    But God in me more pleasure finds
    Than in all joys of earthly minds." (*LW* 53, 320)

17. Söhngen, p. 108.

18. Relying on Augustine, Cassiodorus, and Jerome, Luther contrasts the harp, which "has its resonance from the lower part," with the psaltery, which "has the same things from the upper part and sounds louder and better than the harp" (*LW* 10, 152). The harp then comes to represent Christ in his human form stretched on the cross; the psaltery is Christ in his divine nature dwelling among the angels. They thus complement each other and in effect contain the entire meaning of Christian theology: "Indeed, whatever there is in the world is for the saints harp and psaltery and all things in Christ" (*LW* 10, 153).

19. Honemeyer, p. 66.

20. *Ibid.*, p. 67. One might ask whether Luther's references to **jubilus** should not be understood primarily on a metaphorical level. Appearing in his early psalm commentaries, they follow his early inclination of preferring the spiritual to the literal interpretation. Söhngen quotes the statement from Luther's Psalm 44 lectures, "For a song and singing spring from the fullness of a rejoicing heart," but does not proceed to the next sentence, "But a spiritual song, or spiritual melody, is the very jubilation of the heart" (*LW* 10, 208).

21. Honemeyer, p. 74.

22. *Ibid.*, pp. 77–8.

23. Without directly attempting to resolve the differences between the two approaches, Patrice Veit, in *Das Kirchenlied in der Reformation Martin Luthers: Eine thematische und semantische Untersuchung* (Stuttgart: Franz Steiner Verlag, 1986), esp. pp. 8–35, has achieved a balance between respecting Luther's original contribution and recognizing the perspectives he shared with predecessors and contemporaries.

24. See, for examples the entries "Cano" and "Musica" in Johannes Botsack, *Moralium Gedanensium* (Frankfurt am Main, 1655).

25. The Augsburg Confession, article XV, from *The Book of Concord*, trans. Theodore G. Tappert (Philadelphia: Fortress Press, 1959), p. 36.

26. Joachim Mehlhausen, "Der Streit um die Adiaphora," *Bekenntnis und Einheit der Kirche: Studien zum Konkordienbuch*, eds. Martin Brecht and Reinhard Schwarz (Stuttgart: Calwer, 1980), p. 106.

27. For a more complete treatment of the differences between Karlstadt and Luther on this issue, see James S. Preus, *Carlstadt's Ordinaciones and Luther's Liberty: A Study of the Wittenberg Movement 1521–22* (Cambridge: Harvard University Press, 1974).

28. Concerning this incident as well as Hoffmann's relations with Karlstadt and with Luther, see Calvin Augustine Pater, *Karlstadt as the Father of the Baptist Movements: The Emergence of Lay Protestantism* (Toronto: University of Toronto Press, 1984), esp. 189–201.

29. "Nihil est adiaphoron in casu scandali et confessionis" from Matthias Flacius Illyricus, *Quod hoc tempore nulla penitus mutatio in religione sit in gratiam impiorum facienda* (n.p., 1549).

30. *The Book of Concord*, p. 492.

31. *Colloquium Mompelgartense. Gespräch in Gegenwart des Durchleuchtigen Hochgebornen Fürsten unnd Herrn, Herrn Friderichen, Graven zu Würtemberg und Mümpelgart* (Tübingen, 1587), pp. 730–732.

32. *Ibid.*, p. 732.

33. *Ibid.*, p. 735.

34. *Ibid.*, p. 750.

35. *Ibid.*, p. 751.

36. *Ibid.*, p. 750.

37. *Erinnerungsschrifft etlicher vom Adel und Städten, An den Durchleuchtigen Hochgebornen Fürsten unnd Herrn, Herrn Johann Georgen, Fürsten zu Anhalt, Graven zu Ascanien, Herrn zu Zerbst und Bernburg* (Amberg, 1597), p. 70. Pages cited correspond to those of the original Zerbst edition as noted in the margins of this second edition with appended reply to the Wittenbergers.

38. *Ibid.*, p. 74.

39. *Ibid.*, p. 75.

40. *Ibid.*, p. 73.

41. *Notwendige Antwort Auff die im Fürstenthumb Anhalt Ohn langsten ausgesprengte hefftige Schrift* (Wittenberg, 1597), reprinted in Georg Dedeken, *Thesauri Consiliorum et Decisionum* I (Hamburg, 1623): 1073–1077. Some of the other titles reveal more of

the mood of the controversy: Georg Mylius, *Carolstadius Redivivus* (Wittenberg, 1597); Abraham Taurerus, *Hochnothwendiger Bericht Wider den newen Bildstürmerischen Carlstadtischen Geist im Fürstenthumb Anhalt* (Mansfeld, 1597); Adamus Cratonus Northusanus, *Examen, Der Anhaltischen genanten, und von Doctor Carlstat entlehnter Schlußsprüche, von abtilgung der Altarn und Bilder, In den reformirten Kirchen Augspurgischer Confession verwandt, mit nicht geringer Unruhe und Wiederwillen der Christlichen Gemeinen, auch vieler Trewhertziger vom Adel und Praedicanten im Lande* (Magdeburg, 1597).

42. Dedeken, pp. 1073–1074. The list of items appeared in Luther's "Vermanung an die Geistlichen versamlet auff dem Reichstag zu Augsburg," *Werke* (Wittenberg, 1572) VIII, fol. 425–426. This list of ceremonial practices of "the hypocritical church" had been preceded by another list of doctrines and practices which Luther considered essential matters for discussion during the assembly.

43. Dedeken, p. 1076.

44. *Ibid.*

45. Philipp Arnoldi, *Caeremoniae Lutheranae, Das ist, Ein christlicher Gründlicher Unterricht von allen fürnembsten Caeremonien so in den Lutherischen Preussischen Kirchen...adhibirt werden...den Calvinischen Ceremonienstürmern entgegengesetzt* (Königsberg, 1616), p. 171.

46. *Ibid.*

47. *Ibid.*, p. 177.

48. Balthasar Meisner, *Collegii Adiaphoristici Calvinianis oppositi* (Wittenberg, 1620), Disputation I (De Libertate Christiana et Adiaphoris in genere), fol. Bii.

49. *Ibid.*, I, fols. Cii–Dii.

50. *Ibid.*, I, Bi.

51. *Ibid.*, Disp. XI (De Festis et Lectionibus Dominicalibus, de Musica Figurali, et Organis), fol. Biv$_b$.

52. *Ibid.*, XI, fol. Ci.

53. *Ibid.*, I, fol. Bi.

54. *Ibid*, XI, fol. Ci.

55. *Ibid.*, XI, fol. Cii.

56. *Ibid.*, I, fol. Bi$_b$.

57. *Ibid.*, XI, fol. Ci$_b$.

Notes 157

58. Fridericus Balduinus, *Didactica Apostolica, hoc est, S. Apostoli Pauli Epistola ad Colossenses Commentarius* (Wittenberg, 1624), p. 211.

59. Hieronymus Theodoricus, *Corona Templi* (Nürnberg, [1621?]), fol. Liii. The sermon was preached at the dedication of the organ in Sommerhausen on July 17, 1621. The only other available biographical evidence regarding Theodoricus is that he preached a funeral sermon on the death of Frederick VII of Limpurg on February 9, 1596, also in Sommerhausen (Karl Schottenloher, ed., *Bibliographie zur Deutschen Geschichte im Zeitalter der Glaubensspaltung 1517–1585*, III [Leipzig: Hiersemann, 1936], p. 254).

60. Johannes Olearius, *Wider den Calvinistischen Grewel der Verwüstung in des Fürstenthumb Anhalts Kirchen* (Halle, 1597), p. 66. As source for the phrase, "Tubas Antichristi," Olearius cites the Antitrinitarian book *De Falsa et vera Dei agnitione*, printed in Karlsburg (Siebenbürgen), Rumania, in 1567. The work is attributed to Georg Blandrata (Biandrata) and others with the slightly different title *De vera et falsa cognitione Dei* by Severin Walther Slueter, *Propylaeum Historiae Christianae* (Frankfurt, 1680), p. 195.

61. Peter Martyr Vermigli, *Loci Communes* (Zürich, 1587), Classis Tertiae, cap. 13, p. 677.

62. Peter Martyr Vermigli, *In Priorem D. Pauli Apostoli ad Corinthios Epistolam Commentarius* (Basel, 1570), p. 199.

63. *Ibid.*

64. Aegidius Hunnius, *Commentarius in Epistolam Beati Pauli Apostoli ad Colossenses*, in *Opera Latina* IV (Frankfurt, 1606), 680.

65. Hunnius, *Commentarius in Epistolam Beati Pauli Apostoli ad Ephesios* in *Opera Latina* IV: 584.

66. Hunnius also discussed music in his commentary on I Corinthians (*Epistolae Divi Apostoli Pauli ad Corinthios Prioris Expositio* [Frankfurt am Main, 1596], p. 549), again without a direct confrontation of Calvinist points.

67. Matthias Hoe, *Commentaria in Beati Apostoli et Evangelistae Johannis Apocalypsim* II (Leipzig, 1611).

68. *Ibid.*, p. 217. The word αμουσοι was frequently used as a term of abuse by Lutherans to refer to Calvinists.

69. *Ibid.*

70. *Ibid.*, p. 214.

71. See Henry A. Bruinsma, "The Organ Controversy in the Netherlands Reformation to 1640," *Journal of the American Musicological Society*, VII (1954): 205–12.

72. Conrad Dieterich, *Ulmische Orgel Predigt* (Ulm, 1624), p. 32.

73. *Ibid.*, p. 30.

74. Johann Scarlach, *Drey Nützliche Unterweisungen* (Wittenberg, 1610), p. 191.

75. Christoph Frick (Friccius), *Musica Christiana* (Leipzig, 1615), p. 53.

76. Martin Rößler, for unstated reasons, doubts that Frick published such a work in 1615 and considers the Gotha copy of the 1631 version (*Music-Büchlein*, 2 parts [Lüneburg, 1631]) the only one in existence. Both versions, however, are to be found in the Herzog August Bibliothek, Wolfenbüttel. Locations of other copies are noted in *Repertoire International des Sources Musicales* B_{VI}^1 (Munich-Duisberg: Henle, 1971), pp. 330–331. Part I of the *Music-Büchlein* is substantially equivalent to the *Musica Christiana*. In spite of a new preface, the old prefatory material is also retained, including a letter of Johann Arndt dated June 7, 1615, which Rößler failed to note. Martin Rößler, *Bibliographie der Deutschen Liedpredigt* (Nieuwkoop: De Graaf, 1976), p. 197, and Rößler, "Die Frühzeit hymnologischer Forschung," *Jahrbuch für Liturgik und Hymnologie* 19 (1975): 126.

77. Frick, *Music-Büchlein* (Pt. II), pp. 229ff.

78. *Ibid.*, p. 232.

79. Söhngen, p. 246. Friedrich Kalb's work first appeared in German as *Die Lehre vom Kultus der lutherischen Kirche zur Zeit der Orthodoxie*, Arbeiten zur Geschichte und Theologie des Lutherthums, Vol. III (Berlin: Lutherisches Verlagshaus, 1959); Eng. trans.: *Theology of Worship in 17th-Century Lutheranism*, tr. Henry P. A. Hamann (St. Louis: Concordia, 1965). As Söhngen recognized in a footnote, Christian Bunners' *Kirchenmusik und Seelenmusik* (Göttingen: Vandenhoeck & Ruprecht, 1966) reveals a more complex picture of Lutheran orthodoxy.

80. "Est enim Musica tam Instrumentalis quam Vocalis, Spiritus Sancti eximium donum, et magnam vim habet in concitandis ac sedandis animorum affectibus. Nequaquam igitur contemnanda aut ex templis eliminanda, sed potius suo loco et debito modo exercenda et magnificanda." Cyriacus Schneegass, *Nova et exquisita Monochordi Dimensio* (Erfurt, 1590), Aii.

81. Martin Luther, "Preface to Georg Rhau's Symphoniae iucundae (1538)," translation from *LW* 53, 323 except for change from "Holy Ghost" to "Holy Spirit." For comparison, Calvin's statement on music shows a similar appreciation of its devotional value but no attribution of the effects to the power of God: "We know by experience that singing has great power and strength for moving and inflaming the hearts of men, for invoking and praising God with a more vehement and ardent zeal." Jean Calvin, "Epistre au Lecteur," *La Forme des Prières et Chantz Ecclesiastiques* (1542), from Pierre Pidoux, ed., *Le Psautier Huguenot* (Basel: Bärenreiter, 1962), II, 17.

82. See Hermann Abert, *Die Musikanschauung des Mittelalters und ihre Grundlagen* (reprint, Tutzing: Hans Schneider, 1964), pp. 94–102.

83. See Walter Blankenburg, "Luther und die Musik," *Kirche und Musik* (Göttingen: Vandenhoeck & Ruprecht, 1979), pp. 19–20.

84. Söhngen, *Theologie der Musik*, p. 88.

Notes 159

85. *Ibid.*, pp. 89–90.

86. See Oliver Strunk, *Sources Readings in Music History: Antiquity and the Middle Ages* (New York: W. W. Norton & Company, 1965), pp. 4–12.

87. Saint Augustine, *Confessions*, trans. R. S. Pine-Coffin (Penguin Books, 1961), pp. 238–39 (Book X, 33).

88. Balduinus, *Didactica Apostolica*, p. 210.

89. Balduinus, *Programa Apostolicum, hoc est, S. Apostoli Pauli Epistola ad Ephesios Commentarius* (Wittenberg, 1623), p. 284, quoting from Augustine, *Confessions*, X, 33.

90. Theodoricus, *Corona Templi*, fol. Li–Lii.

91. Dieterich, *Ulmische Orgel Predigt*, pp. 32–33.

92. Peter Martyr Vermigli, *Loci Communes*, Classis Tertiae, cap. 13, p. 676.

93. *Ibid.*, p. 677.

94. *Ibid.*, p. 676.

95. Peter Martyr Vermigli, *In Priorem D. Pauli Apostoli ad Corinthios Epistolam Commentarius*, p. 198. See also John Patrick Donnelly, S.J., *Calvinism and Scholasticism in Vermigli's Doctrine of Man and Grace* (Leiden: E. J. Brill, 1976), esp. 68–94.

96. See David Löfgren, *Die Theologie der Schöpfung bei Luther* (Göttingen: Vandenhoeck & Ruprecht, 1960), esp. pp. 58–60. See also Paul Althaus, "Der Schöpfungsgedanke bei Luther," *Sitzungsberichte der Bayerischen Akademie der Wissenschaften, Philosophisch-Historische Klasse*, 1959, no. 7.

97. Rudolph Schlick, *Exercitatio qua Musices Origo Prima, Cultus Antiquissimus, Dignitas Maxima, & Emolumenta, quae tam animo quam corpori humano confert summa, breviter ac dilucide exponuntur* (Speyer, 1588), p. 8.

98. Theodoricus, p. Kii$_b$.

99. Arnoldi, *Caeremoniae Lutheranae*, p. 167.

100. *Ibid.*

101. Dieterich, p. 16–17.

102. Wolfgang Silber, *Encomion Musices; Lob der Edlen Kunst der Musicen* (Leipzig, 1622), p. 15.

103. Silber, pp. 14–15.

104. Nicolaus Selneccer, "Auslegung des 73. Psalm Davids," *Der Ander Teil des Psalters vom funffzigsten Psalm an bis zu dem 101.* (Leipzig, 1571), fol. 115.

105. See, for example, Alfred Sendrey and Mildred Norton, *David's Harp: The Story of Music in Biblical Times* (New York: New American Library, 1964), pp. 193–204. Hermann Abert (p. 101) discusses the "apotropaic" use of music to ward off evil, tracing it back to Neoplatonism, which in its later stages gave music a prominent role in interaction with the demonic world.

106. Luther's pithy analysis of the relationship between the preacher and God's work can also illuminate the manner in which the Spirit works through music: "Predige du und laß ihn die Herzen fromm machen" (*WA* 31/1, 436, quoted by Althaus, p. 6). For a thorough exposition of Luther's teaching on the Holy Spirit, see Regin Prenter, *Spiritus Creator*, trans. John M. Jensen (Philadelphia: Muhlenberg Press, 1953).

   To show the similarity between singer and preacher in relation to Word and Spirit does not, I believe, systematically elevate music to the same level as preaching for Luther. See further discussion of this topic below, pp. 146–47.

107. Luther, "Von den letzten Worten Davids," (1543), *WA* 54, 34.

108. Luther, "Preface to Symphoniae iucundae," *LW* 53, 323–4.

109. References from Werner Kümmel, "Melancholie und die Macht der Musik: Die Krankheit König Sauls in der historischen Diskussion," *Medizinhistorisches Journal* 4 (1969): 197.

110. Johannes Brentius, "Homiliae in Cap. XVI, Lib. I Samuelis," *Opera* II (Tübingen, 1576), p. 598. Martin Brecht, in *Die frühe Theologie des Johannes Brenz* (Tübingen: J. C. B. Mohr [Paul Siebeck], 1966) noted that Luther's theology was not the only basis of Brenz' thought: "Die oberdeutschen Theologen haben alle mehr oder weniger die lutherische Konzeption mit ihrem humanistischen Spiritualismus verbunden. Auch Brenz kann diese Herkunft nicht verleugnen" (p. 319).

111. *Ibid.*, p. 599.

112. Dieterich, p. 18. Dieterich follows here the biblical wording except for the expansion of the phrase "spielte David auf der Harfe" into "und David nach seiner Harpfen griffe/ mit derselbigen eins auffmachte."

113. Dieterich, p. 32.

114. Frick, *Music-Büchlein*, pp. 76–77; *Musica Christiana*, p. 68.

115. Frick, *Music-Büchlein*, p. 182, cited from Georg Strigenitz' sermons on the first chapter of Jonah. Strigenitz (1548–1603), a popular Lutheran preacher, published 122 sermons on the book of Jonah in 1593, reprinted in 1595, 1602, and 1619. (*Allgemeine Deutsche Biographie* [Leipzig, 1893], 36: 594–95.)

116. Frick, *Music-Büchlein*, pp. 183–4. (Slightly longer version in *Musica Christiana*, pp. 78–9.)

117. *Ibid.*, p. 184.

| Notes | 161 |

118. *Ibid.*, pp. 37–8. (*Musica Christiana*, p. 41.)

119. *Ibid.*, pp. 36–7. Anecdote credited to Georg Steinhard. (*Musica Christiana*, p. 41.)

120. Josua Stegmann, *Icon Christognosia* (Marburg, 1630).

121. Oskar Söhngen, "Music and Theology: A Systematic Approach," in Joyce Irwin, ed. *Sacred Sound: Music in Religious Thought and Practice* (Chico, California: Scholars Press, 1983), p. 13.

122. *Theologie der Musik*, p. 257.

123. For example, Christoph Wolff, in *Der stile antico in der Musik Johann Sebastian Bachs: Studien zu Bachs Spätwerk* (Wiesbaden: Franz Steiner, 1968), p. 9, remarks that there was in Lutheran circles of the pre-Bach era no attempt to glorify the old style of vocal polyphony, as had happened in the Catholic Counter-Reformation, and thus no contrast between secular and sacred music. Günther Stiller, after blaming Pietism for the "disintegration of the church music tradition," exalts Lutheran theology for not having undertaken a distinction between the sacred and the secular (*Johann Sebastian Bach and Liturgical Life in Leipzig* [St. Louis: Concordia Publishing House, 1984], p. 149.)

124. *WA* 24, 417 ("…ein fromer Christ müge der welt yhr recht auch lassen").

125. *WA* 24, 418. ("Gott lesset es geschehen der hochzeit zu ehren, das sie also gepreiset werde. Darumb mus man der welt yhr recht lassen, ausgenomen den uberflus.")

126. *WA* 24, 419. ("Darumb weil tantzen auch der welt brauch ist, des jungen volcks, das zur ehe greifft, so es auch züchtig on schandbare weise, worten odder geperde nur zur freude geschicht, ists nicht zu verdammen.")

127. *WA TR* 2/2 no. 1434. ("Wenn die jungfrauen und jungen gesellen krentz aneinander absingen und das erlich mitt gesang und geperden zu gehet, so ist es **officium humanitatis** das mir wol gefelt.")

128. *WA TR* 5, no. 5603. ("Wie geht es zu, das wir in **carnalibus** so manch fein **poema** und so manch schön **carmen** haben, und in **spiritualibus** haben wir so faul, kalt ding?")

129. *WA* 17/2, 121 ("welltlichen, fleyschlichen und unhubschen gesenge").

130. *WA TR* 2/2, no. 1258. ("Was lex ist, gett nicht von stad; was evangelium ist, das gett von stadt. Sic Deus praedicavit evangelium etiam per musicam, ut videtur in Iosquin, des alles composition frolich, willig, milde herausfleust, ist nitt zwungen und gnedigt per regulas, sicut des fincken gesang.")

131. Stiller, *op. cit.*, p. 143.

132. *Colloquium Mompelgartense*, p. 734.

133. *Die evangelischen Kirchenordnungen des XVI. Jahrhunderts*, ed. Emil Sehling (Leipzig, 1902–13; reprint, Aalen: Scientia Verlag, 1970), II, 168.

134. Church order for the duchy of Lauenburg, printed in Lübeck in 1585 and 1651, from Sehling, V, 422. The word used here, "sortiziren," is equivalent to the Latin "sortisatio," defined in *NG* 17, 540, as "a word for improvised counterpoint, and especially for florid melodies added to a **cantus prius factus**, used in Germany from c1500 to the middle of the 17th century."

135. Dedeken, 1076.

136. Dieterich, *Orgel Predigt*, p. 33. A similar argument appears in Arnoldi, *Caeremoniae Lutheranae*, pp. 177–78.

137. Dieterich, p. 42.

138. Dieterich, p. 44.

139. See Dieter Krickeberg, *Das Protestantische Kantorat im 17. Jahrhundert* (Berlin: Verlag Merseburger, 1965) for a study of the office of cantor, including education and social status with comparison to those of organists.

140. Silber, p. 16. Music theorists also found fault with the Italian style but were more inclined to object to lack of skill in its implementation than to abandonment of accepted stylistic principles. Daniel Friderici omitted instruction in the Italian style from his *Musica Figuralis* (Rostock, 1614) because it was too difficult for young boys and because "in der that und warheit viel davon vor Phantasey und grossen Mißbrauch des **colorirens** mag gehalten werden, wormit der Gesang dermassen deformiret und vertunckelt wird, daß er kaum mag erkennet werden, Und auch denen, so der Kunst Wissenschaft tragen, nicht erfrewlich, sondern vielmehr verdrießlich, und fast lächerlich vor kompt." (Ernst Langelütje, ed., *Die Musica figuralis des Magister Daniel Friderici: Eine Singefibel des 17. Jahrhunderts als musikgeschichtlicher Beitrag* [Berlin, 1901], p. 127.)

141. Moevius Volschov, *Aureum Pietatis Saeculum* (Greiffswald, 1645), 337.

142. Volschov, p. 338.

143. Gratian, *Decretum*, Dist. 92, cap. 1. This medieval canon law corpus was printed numerous times from the late fifteenth through the early seventeenth century.

144. David Lobechius, *Disputationes Theologicae XXX. Articulorum Augustanae Confessionis* (Rostock, 1599), p. 399.

145. Matthias Hoe, *Commentariorum in...Apocalypsim*, p. 218.

146. Fridericus Balduinus, *Didactica Apostolica*, p. 184.

147. Balthasar Meisner, *Collegii Adiaphoristici*, Cii.

148. The lengthiest lists of such sources appear in Christoph Frick, *Music-Büchlein*, pp. 44–53, and Josua Stegmann, *Icon Christognosia*, pp. 401–404.

149. See, for instance, Peter Martyr Vermigli's commentary on I Corinthians 14:7–9 and Wilhelm Zepperus' *De politia ecclesiastica* (Herborn, 1595), pp. 105–107.

150. Söhngen, p. 257.

151. Arnoldi, p. 174.

152. Nicolaus Selneccer, *Der Ander Teil des Psalters...*, pp. 114–5 (commentary on Psalm 73). On tenor masses and imitation or "parody" masses in the late fifteenth and early sixteenth centuries, see Lewis Lockwood, art. "Mass II, 6–7" in *NG* 11, 784-788.

153. Because church historians have long divided history into Reformation/Orthodoxy and Pietism/Enlightenment, the circle of devotional writers with mystical leanings who emerged at the turn of the seventeenth century tends to be regarded as a preview of an age yet to come, in other words as pre-Pietist. F. Ernest Stoeffler, in *The Rise of Evangelical Pietism* uses the title "Preparing the Way" to introduce some of the writers, of whom Johann Arndt is the best known, and makes connections throughout the chapter with Pietists of several decades later. Other scholars of Pietism have criticized Stoeffler's stretching of the Pietist era, but the result is that this devotional movement gets mentioned only in passing. Among church historians, Winfried Zeller is a lonely example of one who studied this "neue Frömmigkeit" for its intrinsic interest rather than as a stepping stone. Cf. Winfried Zeller, *Der Protestantismus des 17. Jahrhunderts* (Bremen: Carl Schünemann Verlag, 1962), pp. xxiii–xxx.

154. The translations offered in this chapter are intended to render the meaning of the text faithfully, not to communicate the power of the poetry.

> Pluck the strings on the cithara
> And let the sweet music
> > Resound with great joy:
>
> That I may with dear Jesus,
> My lovely bridegroom,
> > Be together in constant love.
>
> Sing/ Jump/
> Rejoice/ Exult
> Thank the Lord,
> Great is the King of Glory.

Philipp Nicolai, *Freudenspiegel des ewigen Lebens* (1599), reprinted with foreword by Reinhard Mumm (Soest: Westfälische Verlagsbuchhandlung Mocker & Jahn, 1963), p. 411.

155. *Ibid.*, p. 413.

> Glory be sung to you
> With tongues of men and angels,
> > With harps and beautiful cymbals:
>
> Of twelve pearls are the gates
> At your place/ we are consorts
> > Of the angels high around your throne.

> No eye has ever perceived,
> No ear has ever heard
> > Such joy.
> Of this we are glad/ yo/ yo
> Forever in sweet jubilation.

156. *Ibid.*, p. 72.

157. Reinhold Hammerstein, *Die Musik der Engel* (Bern: Francke Verlag, 1962), pp. 254–257.

158. Johann Walther, "Lob und Preis der löblichen Kunst Musica," (Wittenberg, 1538), Ciii–Civ.

> Music remains with God eternally;
> it drives out all the other arts.
> In heaven after the Day of Judgment
> it will finally be in proper balance.
> Now we have only the husks,
> there the kernel will be opened up.
> There all will be cantors;
> they will need no other skills.
> . . . . . .
> They all sing a new little song
> of God's love and great faithfulness.
> Such singing will never pass away,
> as it says in the Apocalypse.
> God help us all thereto
> that we with one mind in God's presence
> and like all the elect
> sing with joy in God's kingdom.
> Laud, honor, wisdom and great thanks,
> Praise and power be given from the beginning
> forever and eternally.
> So let us also now begin
> and praise God the Lord
> and his name with great resounding.
> Amen, Amen, may it be true;
> God bestow his grace on us thereto.

159. Georg Frölich, "Vom preiss, lob, und nutzbarkeit der Musica," from Johann Kugelmann, *Etliche Psalmen und geistliche Lieder* (Augsburg, 1540), fol. bb$_{ii}$.

160. Ingeborg Röbbelen, *Theologie und Frömmigkeit im deutschen evangelisch-lutherischen Gesangbuch des 17. und frühen 18. Jahrhunderts* (Göttingen: Vandenhoeck & Ruprecht, 1957), p. 77.

161. Harold B. Segel, *The Baroque Poem: A Comparative Survey* (New York: E. P. Dutton & Co., 1974), p. 30.

162. John Rupert Martin, *Baroque* (London: Allen Lane, 1977), p. 119.

163. Irmgard Otto, *Deutsche Musikanschauung im 17. Jahrhundert* (Diss: Berlin, 1937), p. 9.

164. Claude Palisca, for example, urges music historians not to pursue abstractions but to describe the technical features of music from this period: "The similarity of appearances should not, however, be attributed to a 'spirit of the time'—a Baroque 'Zeitgeist'—but rather to the common underlying conditions that sometimes express themselves in uncanny resemblances" (*NG* 2:176).

165. Hermann Zenck, "Grundformen deutscher Musikanschauung," *Jahrbuch der Akademie der Wissenschaften in Göttingen* (1941–42), pp. 15–40, esp. 33–36.

166. Rolf Dammann, *Der Musikbegriff im deutschen Barock* (Cologne: Arno Volk Verlag, 1967), p. 8. Dammann provides extensive documentation from original sources of the Baroque concepts of musical order, musical rhetoric, the affections, natural philosophy and mythology. For further discussion of the notion of the world as a stage, see Peter Skrine, *The Baroque* (London: Methuen, 1978): "The microcosm that is man, from the moment of his conception caught up in his role and act,...is seen by the German poet as a reflection here below of activities on an altogether vaster and more sublime plane" (p. 9).

167. Johann Matthaeus Meyfart, *Das Himlische Jerusalem, Oder Das Ewige Leben der Churkinder Gottes Auff Historische weiß beschriben* (Coburg, 1627), fol. Aiv$_b$.

168. *Ibid.*, Av$_b$. While composers used rhetorical devices in music to express the sense of the text, Meyfart regarded effective speech as a form of music: "An artistic speech is a secret harmony or music" (*Teutsche Rhetorica* [Coburg, 1634] 2:12). For a discussion of Meyfart's significance in applying rhetorical traditions toward the creation of German rhythmic prose, see the commentary by Erich Trunz in Johann Matthäus Meyfart, *Tuba Novissima: Das Ist Von den vier letzten Dingen des Menschen*, Deutsche Neudrucke, Reihe: Barock, 26 (Tübingen: Max Niemeyer, 1980).

169. *Ibid.*, p. 445f.

170. *Ibid.*, pp. 449–50.

171. Valerius Herberger, *Hertz Postilla* (Leipzig, 1613), p. 481. Frick, *Music-Büchlein*, p. 346–47. For a sketch of Herberger and his contribution to German hymnody, see Wilhelm Lueken, *Lebensbilder der Liederdichter und Melodisten* in *Handbuch zum Evangelischen Kirchengesangbuch*, vol. II, pt. I (Göttingen: Vandenhoeck & Ruprecht, 1957), pp. 125–130.

172. Johann Arndt, *Vier Bücher Vom Wahren Christenthumb* (Lüneburg, 1670), p. 562 (Book 2, ch. 43).

173. *Ibid.*, p. 837 (Book 4, ch. 4).

174. *Ibid.*, p. 546 (Book 2, ch. 41).

175. *Ibid.*, 547.

176. Johann Arndt, letter to Christopher Frick (Friccius) in the latter's *Musica Christiana*, p. 4.

177. *Vom Wahren Christenthumb*, p. 681 (Book 2, ch. 58).

178. Frick, *Musica Christiana*, p. 56; *Music-Büchlein*, p. 58–59.

179. Valerius Herberger, *Paradisz-Blümlein/ Aus dem Lustgarten der 150. Psalmen* (Leipzig, 1670), p. 71–72. Frick, *Music-Büchlein*, p. 35.

180. Herberger, *Hertz Postilla*, p. 481.

181. *Ibid.*, pp. 480–81.

182. Frick, *Musica Christiana*, p. 56; *Music-Büchlein*, p. 58.

183. Herberger, *Paradisz-Blümlein*, p. 72.

184. Frick, *Musica Christiana*, p. 57; *Music-Büchlein*, p. 60.

185. Frick, *Music-Büchlein*, p. 232.

186. Gioseffo Zarlino, *Istitutioni Harmoniche* (Venice, rev. ed. 1573), p. 9.

187. Rudolph Schlick, *Exercitatio qua Musices Origo Prima*, pp. 8–11, as translated in Benito V. Rivera, *German Music Theory in the Early 17th Century* (Ann Arbor: UMI Research Press, 1974), pp. 139–40.

188. Cyriacus Schneegass, *Isagoges Musicae Libri Duo* (n.p., 1591), Av_b.

189. Joannis Lippius, *Synopsis Musicae Novae* (Strassburg, 1612), p. ii.

190. See Dammann, *Der Musikbegriff*, ch. 1 and illustrations between pages 504 and 505; also Walter Blankenburg, "Der Harmonie-Begriff in der lutherisch-barocken Musikanschauung," *Kirche und Musik* (Göttingen: Vandenhoeck & Ruprecht, 1979), pp. 205–217.

191. See Michael Dickreiter, *Der Musiktheoretiker Johannes Kepler* (Bern: Francke Verlag, 1973), and Daniel P. Walker, "Keplers Himmelsmusik," *Hören, Messen und Rechnen in der frühen Neuzeit*, Geschichte der Musiktheorie, vol. 6 (Darmstadt: Wissenschaftliche Buchgesellschaft, 1987), pp. 83–107.

192. Preface to Johann Valentin Andreae, *Christianopolis 1619*, edited and introduced by Richard van Dülmen (Stuttgart: Calwer Verlag, 1972), p. 14.

193. *Ibid.*, p. 149.

194. *Ibid.*, p. 151.

195. See Lueken, *Lebensbilder...*, pp. 181ff.

196. In view of the fact that Frick and Stegmann do not cite each other, one might tend to presume that Frick's German work derived from Stegmann's Latin writings. The 1615 date of Frick's first book and internal evidence lead me to the opposite conclusion, however. A comparison of their treatments of the fifth use of music, that of calming the emotions, reveals the similarity of Frick's 1615 version and Stegmann's work. Two anecdotes appear in each of these which are lacking in Frick's 1631 version. One is the story of the trumpeters, which appears in a different context in Frick's later work. The other is the story of the angels' revelation of the words

    Holy God   }
    Holy Strong God   }   have mercy on us
    Holy Immortal God   }

    during an earthquake in the reign of Theodosius. When these words were sung, the earthquake ceased. (Frick [1615], 80–81; Stegmann, 412.) One piece of evidence which might weaken this hypothesis is that in the list of music's seven effects, the third is missing from Frick's 1615 work, whereas the 1631 work coincides exactly with Stegmann's. This, however, seems to raise the possibility of yet another source used by both Frick and Stegmann.

197. Josua Stegmann, *Icon Christognosia*, p. 343.

198. *Ibid.*, p. 345. Stegmann refers here to some of the leading composers of the previous century. Aside from Josquin des Pres (1440–1521), who belonged to the High Renaissance, this group represents a transitional period between late Renaissance and Baroque. Jacobus Gallus or Handl (1550–1591), Luca Marenzio (1553 or 1554–1599), and Orlando di Lasso (1532–1594) all worked in Catholic territories. The Praetorius referred to here is presumably Michael (1571 or 1572–1621) but could also be Hieronymus (1560–1629), both of whom were Lutheran. I have not been able to identify Maxentius.

199. Johann Gerhard, *Postilla Salomonaea, Das ist, Erklärung etlicher Sprüche auß dem Hohenlied Salomonis* (Jena, 1631; revised ed., Jena, 1652), II, 118–135.

200. Zarlino, p. 9.

201. The negative picture of Dannhauer painted by August Tholuck, *Das akademische Leben des siebzehnten Jahrhunderts* (Halle, 1853/54) imposed categories from the pietistic period on the thought of Dannhauer and thereby set the tone for later characterizations. F. Bosse's treatment of Dannhauer in *Realencyklopädie für protestantische Theologie und Kirche* (Leipzig, 1898) was a reaction against Tholuck rather than a fresh start. Johannes Wallmann's valuable discussion of Dannhauer is nevertheless also intended as an examination of early influences on Spener (*Philipp Jakob Spener und die Anfänge des Pietismus* [Tübingen, 1970], pp. 96–123).

202. Johann Conrad Dannhauer, *Hodomoria Spiritus Calviniani* (Strasbourg, 1654), pp. 1239–40.

203. *Ibid.*, p. 1242.

204. At issue was the authenticity of the work known as *Responsiones ad Orthodoxos*. Abraham Scultetus advanced several reasons for considering it inauthentic (*Medulla theologiae patrum* [Amberg, 1598], pp. 29–30). Andreas Rivet drew explicitly on Scultetus' research for his similar conclusion in *Critici Sacri Libri IV* (Geneva, 1626), pp. 183–4. Prior to Rivet's publication, Robert Cooke, also cited by Dannhauer, had circulated such doubts within England (*Censura quorundam scriptorum* [London, 1623], pp. 64–65).

205. Joseph Scaliger, *De emendatione Temporum* (rev. ed., Geneva, 1629), p. 684.

206. Hugo Grotius, *Annotata ad Vetus Testamentum*, I (Paris, 1644), pp. 220–1, 226.

207. J. C. Dannhauer, *Catechismusmilch, oder Der Erklärung deß Christlichen Catechismi, Erster Theil* (Strasbourg, 1642), pp. 521–2.

208. *Catechismusmilch...Achter Theil* (Strasbourg, 1666), p. 544.

209. Ambrosius Lobwasser's German translation of the Huguenot Psalter of Marot and Beza, published in 1573, had become extremely popular in both Reformed and Lutheran circles and thus was often a subject of attack by Lutheran theologians critical of the doctrinal implications. Here, for instance, Dannhauer objects that the Christological element of the Psalms is lost by Lobwasser.

210. Wallmann, p. 101, provides reference to K. H. Möckel, *Die Eigenart des Straßburger orthodoxen Luthertums in seiner Ethik* (Diss. Greifswald, 1952), p. 128.

211. André Rivet, *Commentarii in Librum secundum Mosis qui Exodus apud Graecos inscribitur* (Leiden, 1634), p. 364.

212. *Catechismusmilch...Sechster Theil* (Strasbourg, 1657), p. 405.

213. This quotation was used by Augustine in *The City of God* (Bk. 2, ch. 21) but was not one of the commonplaces in the music-historical tradition among the Lutheran theologians up to this time.

214. *Catechismusmilch...Ander Theil* (Strasbourg, 1658), p. 37.

215. One of Dannhauer's statements against those who credited Arndt with undue authority, from *Catechismusmilch* I, 410, was quoted by Wallmann, pp. 118–9, fn. 133. (Wallmann's page number refers to the second edition of *Catechismusmilch*.) Another passage is to be found on I, 431:

> Folgen nun mehr die Untugenden/ so in anhörung Göttlichen Worts begangen werden/ under denselben steht vornen an/ und führt gleichsam das Regiment/ 1. neglectus, die versaumnuss und verachtung der anhörung Göttlichen Wortes/ der jenigen die Gottes Wort nicht hören/ verlassen die offentlichen versamlungen/ sitzen daheim warten auff treum und entzuckungen: andere lassen sich bedunken/ es seye eben so viel/

wann sie daheim ein Postill (ausser dem nothfall/ der alzeit excipirt) oder Johann Arnds Christenthumb oder sonst ein Bett- und Andachtsbuch lesen/ oder hören lesen/ und dasselbe mit verunehrung dess offentlichen Predigambts.

216. *Catechismusmilch...Dritter Theil* (Strasbourg, 1661), p. 386.

217. Wallmann, p. 107.

218. Book II, third sermon on the general command of love of neighbor.

219. Book VI, 34th sermon on the church or fifth sermon on the unity of the Christian churches and the communion of saints.

220. VI, 413. See also II, 38.

221. Music as praise of God is the focus of Christian Bunners' discussion of Dannhauer in *Kirchenmusik und Seelenmusik*, pp. 15–23.

222. "...dann wer die gabe zu singen nicht hat/ der ist so wol entschuldigt/ als ein stummer der Gottes Werck nit außsprechen kan/ als ein Tauber der Gottes Wort nit hören kan" (I, 521).

223. On the university of Rostock, see Otto Krabbe, *Die Universität Rostock im 15. und 16. Jahrhundert* (Rostock and Schwerin, 1854) and *Geschichte der Universität Rostock 1419–1969* (Berlin: VEB Deutscher Verlag der Wissenschaften, n.d.).

224. Philipp Julius Rehtmeyer, *Das Leben Des seligen Herrn Joachimi Lütkemans*, prefixed to J. Lütkemann, *Der Vorschmack Göttlicher Güte* (Braunschweig, 1720), p. 9.

225. Joachim Lütkemann, *Apostolische Auffmunterung zum lebendigen Glauben* (Hannover and Wolfenbüttel, 1706), p. 256.

226. *Ibid.*, p. 256f.

227. *Ibid.*, p. 258.

228. *Ibid.*

229. Lütkemann, *Der Vorschmack Göttlicher Güte*, p. 215.

230. *Apostolische Auffmunterung*, p. 257.

231. *Ibid.*, p. 1021.

232. *Ibid.*

233. *Ibid.*, p. 1022.

234. *Ibid.*, p. 1021f.

235. Lütkemann, *Harpffe Von Zehen Seyten/ Das ist: Gründliche Erklärung Zehen Psalmen Davids* (Wolfenbüttel, 1658), p. 557f. Published posthumously.

236. On allegorical interpretations of musical instruments in patristic and medieval thought, see Abert, *Die Musikanschauung des Mittelalters*, pp. 210–223, and T. Gérold, *Les péres de l'Église et la musique* (Paris, 1931), pp. 123–34.

237. This interpretation is found in each of the theologians' comments on Psalm 150:7. Origen, *Patrologia Graeca*, ed. Migne, vol. 12; Athanasius, *PG*, vol. 27; Augustine, *Patrologia Latina*, vol. 40. Cf. also chapter 1, fn. 18 on Luther's application of the analogy.

238. Lütkemann, *Harpffe*, p. 416.

239. The *RSV*, by contrast, places the maidens between the singers and the minstrels: "the singers in front, the minstrels last, between them maidens playing timbrels." The German tradition of translating this verse is maintained in Artur Weiser's *The Psalms: A Commentary*, trans. H. Hartwell (Philadelphia: Westminster Press, 1962): "The singers walked in front, the players of stringed music followed surrounded by maidens beating the timbrels."

240. Athanasius, *PG* 27, col. 299; Augustine, *Enarrationes in Psalmos*, (Turnholt, 1956), vol. 39 of *Corpus Christianorum, Series Latina*, p. 893.

241. Lütkemann, *Harpffe*, p. 417.

242. *Ibid.*, p. 416.

243. *Ibid.*, p. 418.

244. *Ibid.*, p. 545.

245. *Ibid.*, pp. 562–63.

246. *Ibid.*, p. 558.

247. *Ibid.*, p. 547.

248. Heinrich Müller, *Geistliche Seelenmusik/ Bestehend In zehen betrachtungen/ und vier hundert auserlesenen/ Geist- und Krafft-reichen/ so wol alten/ als neuen Gesängen* (Rostock, 1659), pp. 202–3. Numbers in text in the remainder of this chapter refer to pages in this book.

249. As with Lütkemann, those who do not have a gift for singing can still fulfill the most important function of song: "hastu die Gabe der Stimme nicht/ das du mit deiner Zungen nicht lieblich singen kanst/ oder empfindest mehr/ als der Mund kan aussprechen/ so singe desto lieblicher und kräfftiger in deinem Geist oder Hertzen" (147).

250. *Ibid.*, preface.

251. Johannes Tarnovius, *In Prophetam Amos Commentarius* (Rostock, 1628), p. 158. Tarnov's exegetical approach in general was more historical and practical than dogmatic, leading him to criticize exegeses of Chemnitz, Hunnius, and even Luther. See *Allgemeine Deutsche Biographie*, vol. 37, p. 397.

252. John Calvin, *Commentaries on the Twelve Minor Prophets*, tr. John Owen (Edinburgh, 1846), II, 310.

253. Tarnovius, p. 158.

254. Bunners, p. 120.

255. In the nineteenth century, also, Müller's orthodoxy was staunchly defended by his biographer Otto Krabbe in *Heinrich Müller und seine Zeit* (Rostock, 1866).

256. Krabbe, p. 190.

257. Bunners, *Kirchenmusik und Seelenmusik*, p. 98.

258. Johann Quistorp, *Pia Desideria*, p. 24.

259. *Ibid.*, p. 27.

260. *Ibid.*, p. 25.

261. Röbbelen, *Theologie und Frömmigkeit...*, p. 18.

262. Theophilus Großgebauer, *Drey Geistreiche Schrifften/ 1. Wächterstimme Aus dem verwüsteten Zion...* (Frankfurt and Leipzig, 1710), p. 189. Numbers in text in the remainder of this chapter refer to pages in this book.

263. The citation is a German translation of a passage from Julius Caesar Scaliger, *Exotericarum Exercitationum Liber XV De Subtilitate* (Frankfurt, 1592), p. 902.

264. Großgebauer's portrayal of the use of music in wartime marks a departure from the customary depiction of soldiers motivated to bravery in battle. Großgebauer tended to pacifism, arguing elsewhere against those court preachers who defended war through scripture (*Preservatif Wieder die Pest der heutigen Atheisten* [Rostock, n.d.], pp. 20ff.) Here he follows up the usual formulation of "cheering up faint-hearted soldiers" to describe them as becoming "brutish and barbarian" and advancing "like cattle into the clutches of death and the jaws of hell" (*Wächterstimme*, p. 193).

265. Großgebauer cites Eusebius' *Life of Constantine* here, though Eusebius himself does not specifically mention Constantine's musical leadership.

266. *Revidirte Kirchenordnung: Wie es mit christlicher Lehre/ reichung der Sacrament/ Ordination der Diener des Evangelii/ ordentlichen Ceremonien in der Kirchen/ Visitation/ Consistorio und Schulen: Im Hertzogthumb Meckelnburg/...gehalten wirdt* (Rostock, 1602), fol. 154_b.

267. See Hans Jürgen Daebeler, *Musiker und Musikpflege in Rostock von der Stadtgründung bis 1700* (Rostock phil. diss., 1966), pp. 82ff.

268. Krickeberg, *Das Protestantische Kantorat*, p. 150.

269. Daebeler, pp. 151–52.

270. Theophilus Großgebauer, *XXVI Geistreiche und erbauliche Predigten über die Epistel Pauli an die Ephesier* (Frankfurt and Leipzig, 1689), pp. 745–46.

271. On the effect of Anglican devotional literature on the German reform movements, see Hans Leube, *Die Reformideen in der deutschen lutherischen Kirche zur Zeit der Orthodoxie* (Leipzig, 1924), pp. 162–180.

272. Karl Holl, "Die Bedeutung der großen Kriege für das religiöse und kirchliche Leben innerhalb des deutschen Protestantismus," *Gesammelte Aufsätze zur Kirchengeschichte III* (Tübingen: J. C. B. Mohr [Paul Siebeck], 1928), p. 337.

273. Wallmann, *Philipp Jakob Spener*, p. 157.

274. Großgebauer, *Preservatif Wieder die Pest*, pp. 9–15.

275. Such is the criticism of Daebeler, p. 180.

276. Bunners, *Kirchenmusik und Seelenmusik*, p. 25.

277. The frontispiece of Mithobius's book displays this perspective vividly: the musicians on the church balcony are not too distant from the angels in heaven and the patriarchs in the middle but the congregation below seems far removed and insignificant.

278. Hector Mithobius, *Psalmodia Christiana...Das ist, Gründliche Gewissens-Belehrung/ Was von der Christen Musica, so wol Vocali als Instrumentali zu halten?* (Jena, 1665), p. 180. Because Mithobius' book is now exceedingly rare (I used the copy in the British Library) and and because it is the most extensive (though not necessarily the most influential) work on music written by a Lutheran preacher of this period, I will quote generously from it in this chapter, giving page numbers in parentheses in the text.

279. This selection from the preface to Hilary's psalm commentary is found in James McKinnon, ed., *Music in Early Christian Literature* (Cambridge: Cambridge University Press, 1987), p. 124. Quoted by Mithobius on p. 184.

280. P. 162. Other comparable lists vary somewhat in content and number of reasons; Mithobius' list resembles those of Christoph Frick (*Music-Büchlein*, 54–107) and Johannes Botsack (*Moralium Gedanensium*, 136–37).

281. Bernhard Waldschmidt, *Pythonissa Endorea, das ist: acht u. zwantzig Hexen- und Gespenst- Predigten* (Frankfurt, 1660), p. 618.

282. Dannhauer, *Catechismusmilch* I, 525.

283. Clearly Bunners (pp. 76–81) is correct in emphasizing Mithobius' receptivity to Italian music as well as his opposition to an uncritical use of new styles in the church. Mithobius is pleased to report that his grandfather sent his sons to Italy to study music with famous teachers (45). What Bunners does not stress is that Mithobius draws a line not between Italian and German styles but between sacred and secular:

> Und nach [Luther] ermahnen unsere **Theologi** mit grossem Ernst und Eyffer/ daß man ja die Music in der Kirchen/ mit heiliger Andacht/ Erbarkeit/ Gravität/ Gottesfurcht/ zierlicher Bescheidenheit/ und Christlichem Wolstande führen/ und sich für aller Welt-Manier/ Leichtfertigkeit/ üppiger Neuerung/ Fleisches-Kützel und ärgerlichen Wollust/ auf das allerfleissigste hüten und fürsehen solle; damit ein Unterscheid sey unter dem Gottes-hause/ und einer offentlichen Zeche/ Comoedien- und Spiel-Hause oder Tantzplatz. (272)

284. As a piece of evidence in the ongoing attempt to ascertain when organ accompaniment of hymns began, this appears to indicate that Mithobius knew of the practice but that it was not yet accepted in the churches with which he was familiar. He may have learned of it from Heinrich Scheidemann, whose dedicatory recital in Otterndorf he described, and whom he called his "brother-in-law," as Scheidemann was married to the daughter of Mithobius' grandmother's brother. See Kerala J. Snyder, *Dieterich Buxtehude: Organist in Lübeck* (New York: Schirmer Books, 1987), pp. 98–99.

285. See Friedrich Blume, *Protestant Church Music: A History*, (New York: W. W. Norton, 1974), pp. 226, 231, on the popularity of Hammerschmidt in his own day.

286. On Maximilian's patronage of music, see Louise Cuyler, *The Emperor Maximilian I and Music* (London: Oxford U. Press, 1973). A general biography of Manuel I is Elaine Sanceau's *The Reign of the Fortunate King, 1495-1521* ([Hamden, CT]: Archon Books, 1969).

287. Although Praetorius served the Elector only briefly, Schütz spent most of his career at the Dresden court. Mithobius' reference is Hoe's *Commentaria in...Apocalypsim*, pp. 216, 219, 516. For a brief selection from Hoe describing Schütz's music, see Carol MacClintock, ed., *Readings in the History of Music in Performance* (Bloomington: Indiana University Press, 1979), pp. 137–39.

288. Großgebauer, *Preservatif Wieder die Pest der heutigen Atheisten*, pp. 21–22.

289. See further my article "German Pietists and Church Music in the Baroque Age," *Church History* (March, 1985), 29–40.

290. See the collection of articles in Martin Greschat, ed., *Zur Neueren Pietismusforschung* (Darmstadt: Wissenschaftliche Buchgesellschaft, 1977), especially those of Johannes Wallmann ("Pietismus und Orthodoxie," pp. 53–81) and Michel Godfroid ("Gab es den deutschen Pietismus?" pp. 91–110). For a survey of research on Pietism, see Martin Schmidt, "Epochen der Pietismusforschung," in J. van den Berg and J. P. van Dooren, eds., *Pietismus und Reveil* (Leiden: E. J. Brill, 1978), pp. 22–79.

291. Martin Geck, *Die Vokalmusik Dietrich Buxtehudes und der frühe Pietismus*, Kieler Schriften zur Musikwissenschaft, vol. 15 (Kassel: Bärenreiter Verlag, 1965), p. 115.

292. See Snyder, *Dieterich Buxtehude*, pp. 148–52.

293. Geck, *Buxtehude*, pp. 109–115.

294. Geck, p. 111.

295. Geck, p. 112. A similar position has recently been taken by Donald Nevile, "Pietism and Liturgical Worship: An Evaluation," *Consensus* 16/2 (1990), p. 104: "In this brief study we have tried to show that the perceived conflict between "Orthodox" Lutheranism and the Pietist tradition in the realm of public worship is not as profound as often imagined, at least in the case of Pietism's original and most highly-respected leaders. Their purpose was to reform the church spiritually, and this appears to have involved no fundamental challenge to the historic form of Lutheran liturgical worship."

296. Christian Kortholt, *Offentlicher Gottesdienst der alten und heutigen Christen/ Absonderlich soviel die Sontags-Feir betrifft* (Frankfurt/Main, 1672), p. 57.

297. Kortholt, p. 52.

298. Kortholt, p. 53.

299. Kortholt, p. 57.

300. Kortholt, pp. 47–48.

301. Kortholt, p. 53.

302. Christian Gerber, *Die Unerkannten Wolthaten Gottes* (Dresden, 1704), fol. B7.

303. Samuel Schelwig, *Cynosura Conscientiae oder Leit-Stern des Gewissens* (Frankfurt and Leipzig, 1692), p. 177.

304. Cf. Friedrich Blume, *Protestant Church Music: A History*, p. 260: "The hymnbooks of the late 17th century, however, provide significant testimony to the effect of anithistorical and rationalistic Pietism on even the most loyal adherents to Lutheran orthodoxy. The more Pietistic a hymnbook was, the more its traditional stock of hymns was crushed, modernized, and rationalized, and the more traditional hymns were discarded."

305. "Da die Menschen juckende Ohren haben/ nach allerhand Neuerungen; Da das alte gute verhaßet/ u. das neue böse nur allzusehr geliebet wird. Wie mancher irriger Teuffel gehet mit Samuelis Mantel bedecket/ und bringet unter dem schein großer Heiligkeit/ ein unheiliges u. ungöttliches Leben u. Lehre unter die Menschen." Johann Lassenius, *Lob-singende Andacht...Alte und Neue Lieder...für die Teutsche Gemeine zu St. Petri in Copenhagen* (Copenhagen, 1686), fol. A3$_b$.

306.	Lassenius, fols. A4–5. Lassenius may have had in mind the widely criticised 1680 hymnbook revision of Christian von Stöcken, general superintendent in Rendsburg. On von Stöcken and other revisers, see Paul Graff, *Geschichte der Auflösung der alten gottesdienstlichen Formen in der evangelischen Kirche Deutschlands* I (Göttingen: Vandenhoeck & Ruprecht, 1937), p. 251.
307.	Philipp Jakob Spener, *Theologische Bedencken* (Halle, 1700–1709), IV, ch. 7, art. 2, sect. 40 (p. 322). Other references cited in Geck, "Ph. J. Spener und die Kirchenmusik," *Musik und Kirche* 31 (1961), 102–3.
308.	Ernst Salomon Cyprian, *De Propagatione Haeresium per Cantilenas Oder Vom Fortpflanzung derer Secten durch die Lieder* (Jena, 1715), fols. C–C2.
309.	Johann Brunnemann, *De jure ecclesiastico tractus posthumus in usum ecclesiarum evangel. & consistoriorum concinnatus* (Wittenberg, 1721), p. 181.
310.	Benedict Carpzov, *Jurisprudentia Ecclesiastica seu Consistoriales* (Leipzig, 1649), pp. 4, 90–99, 223, 394–96.
311.	Johann Muscovius, *Bestraffter Mißbrauch der Kirchen-Music und Kirchhöfe aus Gottes Wort zur Warnung und Besserung vorgestellet* ([Lauban], 1694), p. 87. Muscovius, pastor in Lauban, is little known beyond his interchange with his music director Christian Schiff, whose two works, *Lob der in Gottes Wort wolbegründeten vocal- und instrumental Kirchen-Music* and *Vom rechten Gebrauch u. Mißbrauch der Kirchenmusik*, I have not been able to locate. Muscovius' theological position and his reference to Spener (p. 74) warrant designating him a Pietist.
312.	*Theologische Bedencken* I, Ch. 2, Art. 3, Sect. 11 (pp. 656–62).
313.	*Theologische Bedencken* I, Ch. 2, Art. 4, Sect. 31 (pp. 109a–113a).
314.	For a general history of Protestant church law in Germany, see Emil Sehling, *Geschichte der protestantischen Kirchenverfassung* (Leipzig: B. G. Teubner, 1907).
315.	On the efforts of Duke August of Braunschweig-Lüneburg to shape religious life in his territory, see Dieter Breuer, "Absolutistische Staatsreform und neue Frömmigkeitsformen," in Breuer, ed., *Frömmigkeit in der Frühen Neuzeit: Studien zur religiösen Literatur des 17. Jahrhunderts*, Chloe: Beihefte zum Daphnis, vol. II (Amsterdam: Rodopi, 1984), pp. 21–25. On church-state relations in three lands affected by Pietism, see Mary Fulbrook, *Piety and Politics: Religion and the Rise of Absolutism in England, Württemberg and Prussia* (Cambridge: Cambridge University Press, 1983).
316.	Schelwig, pp. 178–79.
317.	Johann Ernst Schulenberg, *Schrifftmäßiger Unterricht Vom Rechten Gebrauch und Fanatischen Mißbrauch der Christlichen Freyheit in äußerlichen Kirchen Ceremonien und Ordnungen* (Quedlinburg, 1711), pp. 366–67.
318.	Schulenberg, pp. 378–79.

319. Christian Thomasius, *De jure Principis circa Adiaphora* (Halle, 1695), p. 40.

320. See, for example, Paul Gottfried Praetorius, *Vernünfftiger Gottesdienst im Singen* (Danzig, [1689]).

321. Gisbert Voetius, *Politicae Ecclesiasticae* I (Amsterdam, 1663), Pt. I, Lib. II, Tract. II, Cap. III (pp. 544–598). Undoubtedly the most thorough compilation available of arguments for and against organs, Voetius' work was useful even for those who did not agree with his Calvinist position.

322. Johann Samuel Stryk, *Commentatio de iure sabbathi* (Jena, 1756), 211–15 (first published as *De jure Sabbathi* by the Halle orphanage press in 1702). Because of Stryk's willingness to abandon even good practices if they were associated with superstition, Graff (p. 76) sees in this work the beginnings of the Enlightenment. I have classified him with Pietists on the basis of Johann Friedrich Mayer's *Kurtzer Bericht von Pietisten* (Leipzig, 1706). Admittedly, however, the response to Mayer by the theological faculty of the university of Halle absolved the director of the orphanage of any responsibility for Stryk's opinions. (*Der Theologischen Facultät auf der Universität zu Halle Verantwortung gegen D. Joh. Friedrich Mayers...sogenannten kurtzen Bericht von Pietisten* [Halle, 1707], p. 138).

323. Spener, *Concilia et Iudica theologica latina* (Frankfurt/Main, 1709), I, 397.

324. Marcus Steffens, *Geistliche Gedanken* (Oldenburg, 1687), p. 53. Significantly, Steffens, who in this work on church music tried to ward off charges of Calvinism, switched to the Reformed church in 1690.

325. *Ibid.*, p. 47.

326. *The Book of Concord*, p. 33.

327. "The Sacraments: Baptism and the Lord's Supper," in George W. Forell and James F. McCue, *Confessing One Faith: A Joint Commentary on the Augsburg Confession by Lutheran and Catholic Theologians* (Minneapolis: Augsburg Publishing House, 1982), p. 218.

328. Gottfried Arnold, *Unparteiische Kirchen- und Ketzerhistorie* (Frankfurt/Main, 1729), p. 586 (T. II, B. XVI, C. XI, par. 31.) For an account of the sources of income for the cantor of the Freiberg cathedral, see Krickeberg, *Das Protestantische Kantorat*, p. 62–75.

329. *Ibid.*, p. 587.

330. Arnold's work, in spite of the word "unparteiisch," revealed his sympathies to lie with the heretics. The Donatists, among others, were shown to have been unfairly treated by the orthodox clergy (pp. 215–224, T. I, B. IV, C. VIII, par. 34–52).

331. "Wir meynen, wenn wir aus dem Fleische so prächtig gesummt, gebrummt, geschryen, gepfiffen, gedrommelt, gepaucket, gefiedelt, äußerlich musiciret, auch die Predigten also angehöret haben, und darbey dennoch in allen Greueln, derer man gewohnt, sicher fort-

Notes 177

leben, daß damit Gott gedienet u. versöhnet werde." Muscovius, *Bestraffter Mißbrauch*, p. 39.

332. *Ibid.*, p. 90.

333. *Ibid.*, p. 23.

334. *Ibid.*, p. 16.

335. *Ibid.*, p. 36.

336. Christian Gerber, *Unerkannte Sünden der Welt* (Dresden and Leipzig, 1705–19), I, 1061–2.

337. Christian Gerber, *Der Andere Theil der Historie derer Wiedergebohrnen in Sachsen* (Dresden, 1726), pp. 520–21.

338. Georg Motz, *Verteidigte Kirchenmusik* (n.p., 1703), p. 37.

339. *Ibid.*, p. 239.

340. *Ibid.*, pp. 33–35.

341. *Ibid.*, p. 37.

342. *Ibid.*, p. 39.

343. *Ibid.*, pp. 191–199.

344. *Ibid.*, p. 53.

345. Gerber, *Unerkannte Sünden*, p. 1065.

346. *Ibid.*, p. 41.

347. *Ibid.*, p. 39.

348. *Ibid.*, p. 148.

349. Steffens, *Geistliche Gedancken*, p. 53, and Gerber, *Unerkannte Sünden*, p. 1073.

350. Motz, p. 240.

351. Andreas Werckmeister, *Musicalische Paradoxal-Discourse* (Quedlinburg, 1707), pp. 36–37.

352. *Ibid.*, p. 36.

353. *Ibid.*, p. 35.

354. Andreas Werckmeister, *Der Edlen Music-Kunst Würde, Gebrauch und Mißbrauch* (Frankfurt, 1691), pp. 13–15.

355. *Ibid.*, p. 15. On the changing relationship between talent and virtue in German thought, see Anthony La Vopa, *Grace, Talent, and Merit: Poor students, clerical careers, and professional ideology in eighteenth-century Germany* (Cambridge: Cambridge University Press, 1988.)

356. Werckmeister, *Paradoxal-Discourse*, p. 7.

357. Gottfried Vockerodt, *Mißbrauch der freyen Künste, insonderheit Der Music* (Frankfurt, 1697), p. 29–30.

358. Werckmeister, *Paradoxal-Discourse*, p. 35.

359. Vockerodt, p. 29.

360. Werckmeister, *Paradoxal-Discourse*, p. 26.

361. *Ibid.*, pp. 31-32.

362. For recent, English-language treatments of the topic, see Gloria Flaherty, *Opera in the Development of German Critical Thought* (Princeton, 1978) and W. Gordon Marigold, "Opera, Politics and Religion in Hamburg, 1678–1715," *Lutheran Quarterly* III/1 (Spring, 1989), pp. 65–90.

363. *Vier Bedencken Fürnehmen Theologischen und Juristischen Facultäten, wie auch Herrn Doct. Johann Friederich Mayers, P.P. und Königl. Schwedischen Ober-Kirchenraths Was doch von denen so genandten Operen zu halten* (Frankfurt/Main, 1693 [written in 1687]). Portions of this document are included in Heinz Becker, ed. with Wolfgang Osthoff, Herbert Schneider and Hellmuth Christian Wolff, *Quellentexte zur Konzeption der europäischen Oper im 17. Jahrhundert* (Kassel: Bärenreiter, 1981), pp. 179–182.

364. Albrecht Christian Rotth, *Höchstnöthiger Unterricht von so genanten Mittel-Dingen* (Leipzig, [1698]), p. 45.

365. *Ibid.*, p. 43.

366. *Ibid.*, p. 77.

367. *Ibid.*, p. 87.

368. On the Pietist theory of education, particularly that of Francke, see Gerhard Schmalenberg, *Pietismus-Schule-Religionsunterricht: Die Christliche Unterweisung im Spiegel der vom Pietismus bestimmten Schulordnungen des 18. Jahrhunderts* (Bern: Herbert Lang, 1974).

369. In Bach's conflict with J. A. Ernesti, the rector is usually regarded as a spokesman for Rationalism, but in their approach to education Pietism and Rationalism reveal their affinities over against Orthodoxy. For an analysis of the dispute, see Paul S. Minear, "J. S. Bach and J. A. Ernesti: A Case Study in Exegetical and Theological Conflict," in John Deschner and others, *Our Common History as Christians: Essays in Honor of Albert C. Outler* (New York: Oxford University Press, 1975), pp. 131–55; and Jaroslav Pelikan, *Bach Among the Theologians* (Philadelphia: Fortress Press, 1986), pp. 34–39.

370. Scharlau, *Athanasius Kircher als Musikschriftsteller*, p. 339.

371. Johann Beer, *Ursus murmurat* (Weimar, 1697), pp. 9, 13. The most prominent Dutch Precisionist was Gisbertus Voetius, whose discussion of organs in church was familiar to German Pietists. Vockerodt brushed aside the charge of Precisionism in this case by noting that the ancient biographies of the emperors sufficed for conveying awareness of vice and shame (Vockerodt, *Mißbrauch der freyen Künste*, p. 102). Yet Beer is justified in drawing this connection, and Vockerodt does cite Voetius at several points. One of the goals of precision, according to Voetius, is "reformation of life and manners, private and public, down to the smallest claim of the flesh, the least breath of popular corruption, and the glory of the world, even scandal and the appearance of evil in matters that are adiaphoristic, especially those that seem to suggest evil....This means especially that one considers spiritually, and stays away from, those activities which common and easygoing Christians do not consider wrong....Such activities include gambling, wagers on future events,...and, in connection with the seventh commandment, dramas, dancing, vain adornment of the hair, luxury in dress, and the like." (From G. Voetius, "Concerning 'Precision'," in John W. Beardslee III, ed. and trans., *Reformed Dogmatics: J. Wollebius, G. Voetius, F. Turretin*, [New York: Oxford University Press, 1965], p. 323.)

372. *Ursus murmurat*, p. 14.

373. *Ibid.*, pp. 17-18.

374. *Ibid.*, p. 21.

375. *Ibid.*, p. 35.

376. Gottfried Vockerodt, *Mißbrauch der freyen Künste insonderheit der Music/ nebenst abgenöthigter Erörterung der Frage: Was nach D. Luthers und anderer Evangelischen Theologorum und Politicorum Meinung von Opern und Comödien zu halten sey?* (Frankfurt, 1697), p. 13.

377. *Ibid.*, pp. 14-5.

378. *Ibid.*, p. 20.

379. *Ibid.*, p. 22.

380. Beer, *Ursus Vulpinatur, List wieder List, oder Musicalische Fuchs-Jagd* (Weißenfels, 1697), p. 28. Beer's titles play not only on his name, which was sometimes spelled Bähr, as in the German word for the animal, but also on his love for the hunt. His journal records numerous hunting escapades, one of which, unfortunately, resulted in his death by accidental gunshot. See *Johann Beer: sein Leben, von ihm selbst erzählt*, ed. Adolf Schmiedecke (Göttingen: Vandenhoeck & Ruprecht, 1965), esp. pp. 62, 76, 93.

381. *Ibid.*, p. 46.

382. *Ibid.*, p. 47.

383. Vockerodt, *Mißbrauch der freyen Künste*, p. 28.

384. *Ibid.*, p. 21.

385. *Ibid.*, p. 43.

386. *Ursus Murmurat*, p. 20.

387. *Ursus Vulpinatur*, p. 54.

388. Vockerodt, *Wiederholetes Zeugnüs der Warheit*, p. 141.

389. *Ibid.*

390. Supplement ("Zugabe") to *Wiederholetes Zeugnüs*, p. 21.

391. Vockerodt, *Erleuterte Auffdeckung des Betrugs u. Ärgernisses*, pp. 89-104.

392. *Ibid.*, p. 144.

393. *Ibid.*, p. 199.

394. *Ulpus Vulpinatur*, p. 70.

395. *Mißbrauch der freyen Künste*, p. 75.

396. *Ibid.*

397. See Johann Beer, *Musicalische Discurse* (Nürnberg, 1719; reprint, Leipzig: VEB Deutscher Verlag für Musik, 1982), ch. 28 ("Ob die Musici Theoretici oder Practici praevaliren"), esp. pp. 99–103.

398. Heinz Krause, *Johann Beer, 1655-1700: Zur Musikauffassung im 17. Jahrhundert* (Saalfeld/Ostpr.: Günthers Buchdruckerei, 1935), p. 74.

399. Beer's manuscript on composition, *Schola-Phonologica sive Tractatus Doctrinalis de Compositione Harmonia*, present in the Leipzig Musikbibliothek in a copy from another hand, begins with praise of harmony as that in and through which everything exists (fol. 2) in a manner characteristic of musical theorists since Zarlino.

400. Quoted in Philipp Spitta, *Johann Sebastian Bach*, trans. Clara Bell (London: Novello, Ewer & Co., 1884), I, 473.

401. Stiller, *Johann Sebastian Bach and Liturgical Life in Leipzig*, p. 143. Internal quotes from P. Brausch, *Die Kantate: Ein Beitrag zur Geschichte der deutschen Dichtungsgattung* (Diss. Heidelberg, 1921), pp. 51ff., 64.

402. Alfred Dürr, "Johann Sebastian Bachs Kirchenmusik in seiner Zeit und Heute," *Musik und Kirche* 27 (1957): 68. Henry Raynor, while recognizing Pietists' opposition to the new form, sees it nevertheless as fulfilling the Pietist demand for personal expression: "It was of course anathema to the Pietists, who saw in it the sacrilege of taking into the

church the most worldly of all musical forms, but at the same time it suggested to composers that the untrammelled expression of their own religious perceptions and beliefs was a valid religious activity." (Henry Laynor, *A Social History of Music from the Middle Ages to Beethoven* [New York: Taplinger Publishing, 1978], pp. 208–9.) The use of "expression of individual feeling" as an identifying characteristic of Pietism has caused considerable confusion in understanding their musical attitudes. See my "German Pietists and Church Music in the Baroque Age," *Church History* 54/1 (1985): 29–40.

403. Basil Smallman, *The Background of Passion Music: J. S. Bach and his Predecessors* (New York: Dover Publications, 1970), pp. 119–20.

404. Quoted in Spitta, I, 478.

405. Gottfried Ephraim Scheibel, *Zufällige Gedancken von der Kirchen-Music Wie Sie heutiges Tages beschaffen ist* (Frankfurt and Leipzig, 1721), p. 39. Little is known of Scheibel (1696–1759) apart from the entry in Zedler's *Universallexikon* of 1742 which reported that Scheibel was at that time teaching at Elizabeth Gymnasium in his home town of Breslau. The works listed as in print, in press, or in preparation suggest a primary interest in religious poetry set to music and some interest in translating plays of Voltaire and Racine. Because of his references to Leipzig, we may surmise that he studied there; J. G. Walther's *Musikalisches Lexikon* (1732) describes him as "Candidatus Ministerii."

406. Johann Kuhnau, *Der Musicalische Quack-Salber* (Dresden, 1700), p. 527.

407. Johann Heinrich Buttstedt, *Ut, Mi, Sol, Re, Fa, La, Tota Musica et Harmonia Aeterna* (Erfurt, 1716), p. 6.

408. Friedrich Erhardt Niedt, *Musicalische Handleitung*, Pt. III, published posthumously with preface by Johann Mattheson (Hamburg, 1717).

409. Wolff, *Der Stile Antico*, p. 9.

410. Ulrich Meyer, *J. S. Bachs Musik als theonome Kunst* (Diss. Mainz, 1976), pp. 22–24.

411. Kerala Snyder, art. "Christoph Bernhard," *NG* 2:625. For the text of Bernhard's work in English translation, see W. Hilse, trans. and ed., "The Treatises of Christoph Bernhard," *Music Forum* 3 (1973), pp. 1–196, esp. 35.

412. *Ibid.*, p. 24.

413. Cf. Wolff, p. 9: "Die kirchliche Kunst hielt sich grundsätzlich offen für die Bewahrung traditioneller Elemente wie für die Aufnahme von Neuerungen jeder Art, ohne daß daraus ein theologischer Prinzipienstreit entstanden wäre. Von daher gesehen gab es auch keinen Gegensatz von weltlicher und geistlicher Musik."

414. Andreas Marti, *"...die Lehre des Lebens zu hören". Eine Analyse der drei Kantaten zum 17. Sonntag nach Trinitatis von Johann Sebastian Bach unter musikalisch-rhetorischen und theologischen Geschichtspunkten.* (Bern: Peter Lang, 1981), p. 169.

415. Christhard Mahrenholz, "Johann Sebastian Bach und der Gottesdienst seiner Zeit," *Musik und Kirche* 20 (1950): 156.

416. Gottfried Tilgner, preface to Erdmann Neumeister, *Fünffache Kirchen-Andachten bestehend in theils eintzeln, theils niemahls gedruckten Arien, Cantaten und Oden* (Leipzig, 1717).

417. On Kircher's theory of affections, see Scharlau, *Athanasius Kircher*, pp. 213–233.

418. Scheibel uses here the same term, "wohlbestellte," which Bach uses in his 1730 draft to the Leipzig city council. The fact that Scheibel uses it also in reference to secular music ("Kan eine wohlbestellte weltliche Musik uns über eitlen und vielmahl sündlichen Dingen frölich oder traurig machen/ wie gutt wär es/ wenn dieses in der Kirchen geschähe") makes it unlikely that weighty ecclesiological connotations should be read into Bach's usage of the term. Mahrenholz, for instance, regards it as evidence of Bach's insistence on the liturgical traditions of Orthodoxy: "Aber nur die viel verlästerte Orthodoxie hält als solcher Auffassung von der regulierten, d.h. der in eine feste kirchliche und obrigkeitliche Ordnung gestellten ('wohlbestallten') und von allen anerkannten und geförderten Kirchenmusik fest." (Mahrenholz, *op. cit.*, p. 156.)

419. No composer is listed for this opera or for "Artaxeris" (spelled "Artaxerxes") in Franz Steiger, *Opernlexikon* (Tutzing: Hans Schneider, 1975). The date given for "Jupiter und Semele" is 1718, for "Artaxerxes" 1717.

420. This presumably refers to Johann Gottfried Vogler, successor to Melchior Hofmann at the New Church in Leipzig and director of the Collegium Musicum. Telemann spoke highly of him as composer and violinist, but he was released from office in 1720 after he attempted to escape from paying his financial debts. Robert Eitner, *Biographisch-Bibliographisches Quellen Lexikon* (Leipzig, 1903; reprint Graz, 1959), 9:132.

421. Michael Tilmouth writes in the article "Parody (i)" in *NG* 14:238f.: "Although the use of borrowed material persisted through the Baroque period, to employ the term 'parody' in connection with it is in many ways unfortunate since the particular techniques of 16th-century parody are often not in evidence."

422. Scheibel, *Die Geschichte der Kirchen-Music alter und neuer Zeiten* (Breslau, 1738), p. 3. This most likely refers to Mattheson, whose encouragement of Scheibel was reported in Zedler's *Universallexikon*.

423. Art. "Joachim Meyer," in Ernst Ludwig Gerber, *Neues Historisch-Biographisches Lexikon der Tonkünstler (1812–1814)*, Pt. 3 (reprint, Graz: Akademische Druck u. Verlagsanstalt, 1966).

424. Joachim Meyer, *Unvorgreiffliche Gedanken über die Neulich eingerissene Theatralische Kirchen-Music* ([Lemgo], 1726), p. 58.

425. Johann Mattheson, *Der neue Göttingische Aber Viel schlechter, als Die alten Lacedamonischen, urtheilenden Ephorus* (Hamburg, 1727), p. 37.

426. Tilgner, preface to Neumeister, p. vi.

427. Joachim Meyer, *Der anmassliche Hamburgische Criticus sine crisi* (Lemgo, 1728), p. 143.

428. *Ibid.*, p. 122.

429. *Ibid.*, p. 78.

430. Mattheson, *Der neue Göttingische...*, p. 6.

431. *Ibid.*, p. 91.

432. For an extensive analysis of Mattheson's place within the intellectual movements of the eighteenth century, see Werner Braun, *Johann Mattheson und die Aufklärung* (Diss. Halle, 1951). Mattheson's position in the history of aesthetic theory is well described by Bellamy Hosler, *Changing Aesthetic Views of Instrumental Music in 18th-Century Germany* (Ann Arbor: UMI Research Press, 1981), pp. 69–86.

433. Martin Heinrich Fuhrmann, *Gerechte Wag-Schal* (Altona, 1728), p. 19.

434. *Der abgewürdigte Wagemeister, oder der fälschlich genannten gerechten Wagschale eines verkapten, aber wohl bekannten Innocentii Frankenburgs auf dem Parnaß erkannte Ungerechtigkeit und Betrug* (1729), listed by Gerber, *Neues Historisch-Biographisches Lexikon der Tonkünstler (1812–1814)*.

435. Spitta, I, 479.

436. Martin Dibelius, "Individualismus und Gemeindebewußtsein in Joh. Seb. Bachs Passionen," *Archiv für Reformationsgeschichte* 41 (1948): 140.

437. Walter Blankenburg, "Bachs kirchengeschichtlicher Standort und dessen Bedeutung für das gegenwärtige Bachverständnis," *Archiv für Musikwissenschaft* X (1953): 315.

438. See Schmalenberg, *Pietismus-Schule-Religionsunterricht*, p. 46: "Da Francke zudem von seiner Anthropologie her auch die natürlichen Affekte des Menschen für sündig hielt, vermag der Mensch seiner Überzeugung nach in keiner Weise an diesem Prozeß mit den eigenen Affekten mitzuwirken. Nicht nur im Akt der Rechtfertigung, sondern auch in dem der Buße ist der Mensch somit ganz und gar der Empfangende."

439. From Spener, "Meditation on the Suffering of Christ," in Peter C. Erb, ed. *Pietists: Selected Writings* (New York: Paulist Press, 1983), p. 78.

440. Christian Gerber, *Historie der Kirchen-Ceremonien in Sachsen* (Dresden and Leipzig, 1732), p. 288.

441. A recent attempt to harmonize the two positions has been made by Hans Heinrich Eggebrecht, "Thomaskantor Bach," *Musik und Kirche* 61 (1991): 63–72.

442. Walter Blankenburg, "Die Bachforschung seit etwa 1965 (III)," *Acta Musicologica* 55 (1983): 52.

443. Beer, *Ursus Vulpinatur*, pp. 46–47.

444. See, for example, the novel concerning the pope who wished to canonize Bach: Johannes Rüber, *Die Heiligsprechung des Johann Sebastian Bach: Eine Papst-Legende* (Schwieberdingen: Verlag Günter Rüber, 1973). Admittedly, the basis for canonization in the story is not his personal saintliness but the miraculous power of his music.

445. Wolfgang Caspar Printz, for example, ends his *Historische Beschreibung der Edelen Sing- und Kling-Kunst* (Dresden, 1690) with the words SOLI DEO GLORIA. For further examples, see Robin A. Leaver, *J. S. Bach and Scripture: Glosses from the Calov Bible Commentary* (St. Louis: Concordia Publishing House, 1985), p. 105. My colleague Joseph Swain informs me that Haydn used similar inscriptions for his string quartets.

446. Blankenburg, "Bachforschung," p. 44.

447. Buttstedt, p. 175.

448. For a further exploration of this theme, see Blankenburg, "Johann Sebastian Bach und die Aufklärung," *Bach-Gedenkschrift 1950*, pp. 25–34 and "Bachforschung," pp. 44–52.

449. Cf. Stiller, p. 190: "But if the question about Johann Sebastian Bach's real ambition is asked, on which tasks and offices in the course of his life he focused his attention particularly, certainly among the various services and duties he undertook in his lifetime his total love for the Lutheran Church and for a liturgical office in this church becomes evident again and again."

450. In this I am in agreement with Eggebrecht, "Thomaskantor Bach," p. 65: "Zunächst sei klargestellt: 'Endzweck' bezieht sich auf den Mühlhausener Bestallungsauftrag, auf nichts sonst."

For the text of Bach's letter, see *Bach-Dokumente* Vol 1: *Schriftstücke von der Hand Johann Sebastian Bachs* (Leipzig: VEB Deutscher Verlag für Musik, 1963), pp. 19–20; English translation in Hans T. David and Arthur Mendel, eds., *The Bach Reader* (New York: W. W. Norton & Company, 1966), pp. 60–61. Hereinafter abbreviated as *BD* and *BR*.

451. Marti, "*die Lehre des Lebens zu hören...*", p. 173.

452. "Lateinisch recreatio heißt Wiederherstellung—ab aegritudine, von Erkrankung, Unpäßlichkeit, Gram und Kummer: Recreation des Gemüts ist die Erholung, Erfrischung, Erquickung der Seele gegenüber der Betrübnis, der Verworrenheit, Traurigkeit und Beladenheit" (Eggebrecht, 71).

453. English version as quoted in Stiller, p. 209. The German original in Söhngen, p. 273, reads: "*Recreation des Gemütes*, damit ist also zutiefst ein Zurechtbringen des ganzen Menschen gemeint, zu dem dieser selber freudig Ja sagt." For those of us working in English, the word "Gemüt" poses translation difficulties precisely because it seems more multifaceted than "spirit" or "heart".

454. "Brauchen sie zur täglichen *recreation* für die lang weil." Dieterich, p. 29.

Notes 185

455. Mithobius, p. 46.

456. Christophorus Rauch, *Theatrophania, Entgegen gesetzt Der so genanten Schrifft Theatromania* (Hannover, 1682), pp. 47–8.

457. Söhngen, p. 273.

458. Beer, *Ursus vulpinatur*, p. 56: "Heisset dann se recreare eine Profession machen? Oder sich ergötzen? Ein bißlein vors Hauß/ damit ists aus. Semel non est semper. Ich rede von keiner Profession, sondern Recreation. Lachen hat seine Zeit."

459. Printz, *Historische Beschreibung*, preface.

460. Johann Mattheson, *Das Neu-Eröffnete Orchestre, Oder Universelle und gründliche Anleitung/ Wie ein Galant Homme einen vollkommnen Begriff von der Hoheit und Würde der edlen MUSIC erlangen...möge* (Hamburg, 1713), p. 25.

461. Mattheson, *Das Neu-Eröffnete Orchestre*, p. 32; Buttstedt, p. 5.

462. Mattheson, *Der Musikalische Patriot* (Hamburg, 1728), p. 9. For more on Mattheson and church music, see Arno Forchert, "Mattheson und die Kirchenmusik," in Friedhelm Krummacher and Heinrich W. Schwab, *Gattung und Werk in der Musikgeschichte Norddeutschlands und Skandinaviens*, Kieler Schriften zur Musikwissenschaft, XXVI (Kassel: Bärenreiter Verlag, 1982), pp. 114–122.

463. Mattheson, *Das Forschende Orchestre, oder desselben Dritte Eröffnung* (Hamburg, 1721), pp. 132–3 and footnote pp. 134–5.

464. Most influential is the interpretation of Söhngen, pp. 92, 97, 217, 228. But see also Günther Stiller, "Glaube und Frömmigkeit des Luthertums im Leben und Werk Johann Sebastian Bachs," *Ökumenische Rundschau* 31/1 (Jan. 1986): 65: "Im gottesdienstlichen Amt und Auftrag aber stand Bach noch immer *gleichberechtigt* neben den Theologen, was in Luthers Indienststellung der Musik für die so bezeichnete 'klingende Predigt' begründet ist."

465. *Die Bekenntnisschriften der evangelisch-lutherischen Kirche* (Göttingen: Vandenhoeck & Ruprecht, 3rd ed., 1956), p. 449.

466. Matthias Silesius Viertel, "Kirchenmusik zwischen Kerygma und Charisma," *Jahrbuch für Liturgik und Hymnologie* 29 (1985): 111–123.

467. Cf. Söhngen, p. 333: "...Johann Mattheson kann noch im Jahre 1725 in seiner *Critica Musica* Prediger und Kantor auf eine Ebene stellen."

468. Kuhnau, *Jura circa Musicos Ecclesiasticos* (Leipzig, 1688), p. 22.

469. Minear, p. 134.

470. Robert Stevenson, "Bach's Quarrel with the Rector of St. Thomas School," *Anglican Theological Review* 33 (1951): 219–230.

471. Karl Geiringer, *Johann Sebastian Bach: The Culmination of an Era* (New York: Oxford University Press, 1966), p. 83. The documents are found in translation in *BR* 137–149, 152–158 and in the original German in *BD* 82–91, 95–106.

472. Joh. Phil. Bendeler, *Directorium Musicum, Oder Gründliche Erörterung Derjenigen Streit-Fragen/ Welche bißhero hin und wieder zwischen denen Schul-Rectoribus und Cantoribus über dem Directorio Musico moviret worden* ([Quedlinburg], 1706).

473. Benedikt Carpzov, *Jurisprudentia Ecclesiastica seu Consistorialiis* (Leipzig, 1649), p. 90 (Lib. I Def. 75); pp. 222–23 (Lib. III, Def. CXX).

474. This view has been advanced most straightforwardly by leading American Lutheran musicologist Carl Schalk. In a musician's reference work edited by Schalk and Carl Halter, *A Handbook of Church Music* (St. Louis: Concordia Publishing House, 1978), p. 71, Schalk asserts: "Both Pietism and Rationalism stood in stark contrast to Bach's piety, which, rooted in confessional orthodoxy, sought to praise God with the best craftmanship that his talent and skill would allow." The same claim of an unbroken tradition from Luther to Bach appears in his more recent publication on Luther, *Luther on Music—Paradigms of Praise*, p. 49: "This attitude [solidarity and continuity with the church Catholic] was to continue to inform the worship and musical practices of Lutheranism until the later individualistic, privatistic, and personalistic practices of both Pietism and rationalism were to invade and wreak havoc with both its liturgy and its music."

475. Werner Braun, *Johann Mattheson und die Aufklärung* (Diss. Halle, 1951), p. 84.

476. Concerning Bach's comments, see Leaver, *J. S. Bach and Scripture*, esp. pp. 93–96.

477. Doris Finke-Hecklinger, *Tanzcharaktere in Johann Sebastian Bachs Vokalmusik* (Trossingen: Hohner Verlag, 1970), p. 10.

478. Caspar Rüetz, *Widerlegte Vorurteile von der Beschaffenheit der heutigen Kirchenmusic und von der Lebens-Art einiger Musicorum* (Lübeck, 1752), pp. 34–35.

479. Rüetz, pp. 33–34.

BIBLIOGRAPHY

ABBREVIATIONS

LW: Martin Luther. *Works*. American edition. Edited by Jaroslav Pelikan and Hartmut Lehmann. St. Louis: Concordia Publishing House; Philadelphia: Fortress Press, 1955–. 56 vols.

NG: *The New Grove Dictionary of Music and Musicians*. Edited by Stanley Sadie. 20 vols. London: Macmillan Publishers, 1980.

WA: *D. Martin Luthers Werke*. Kritische Gesamtausgabe. Weimar, H. Böhlau, 1883–.

WA TR: *D. Martin Luthers Werke*. Tischreden. Weimar, 1912–21.

PRIMARY SOURCES CONSULTED

Andreae, Johann Valentin. *Christianopolis 1619*. Edited and introduced by Richard van Dülmen. Stuttgart: Calwer Verlag, 1972.

Arndt, Johann. *Vier Bücher Vom Wahren Christenthumb*. Lüneburg, 1670.

Arnold, Gottfried. *Unparteiische Kirchen- und Ketzerhistorie*. Frankfurt, 1729.

Arnoldi, Philipp. *Caeremoniae Lutheranae, Das ist, Ein christlicher Gründlicher Unterricht von allen fürnembsten Caeremonien so in den Lutherischen Preussischen Kirchen...adhibirt werden...den Calvinischen Ceremonienstürmern entgegengesetzt*. Königsberg, 1616.

Balduinus, Fridericus. *Didactica Apostolica, hoc est, S. Apostoli Pauli Epistola ad Colossenses Commentarius*. Wittenberg, 1624.

———. *Programma Apostolicum, hoc est, S. Apostoli Pauli Epistola ad Ephesios Commentarius.* Wittenberg, 1623.

Beer, Johann. *Bellum musicum oder Musikalischer Krieg.* Weimar, 1701.

———. *Musicalische Discurse.* Nürnberg, 1719. Reprint, Leipzig: VEB Deutscher Verlag für Musik, 1982.

———. *Sein Leben, von ihm selbst erzählt.* Edited by Adolf Schmiedecke. Göttingen: Vandenhoeck & Ruprecht, 1965.

———. *Schola-Phonologica sive Tractatus Doctrinalis de Compositione Harmonia.* N.d., n.p. Handwritten manuscript in the Leipzig Musikbibliothek.

———. *Ursus murmurat.* Weimar, 1697.

———. *Ursus Vulpinatur, List wieder List, oder Musicalische Fuchs-Jagd.* Weißenfels, 1697.

Bendeler, Joh. Phil. *Directorium Musicum, Oder Gründliche Erörterung Derjenigen Streit-- Fragen/ Welche bißhero hin und wieder zwischen denen Schul-Rectoribus und Cantoribus über dem Directorio Musico moviret worden.* [Quedlinburg], 1706.

Beza, Theodore. *Ad Acta Colloqui Montisbelgardensis.* Geneva, 1588.

Botsack, Johannes. *Moralium Gedanensium.* Frankfurt am Main, 1655.

Brentius (Brentz), Johannes. *Opera.* Vol. II. Tübingen, 1576.

———. *De Poenitentia.* Schwäbisch Hall, 1545.

———. *In Prophetam Amos Expositio.* Haganau, 1533.

Brunnemann, Johann. *De jure ecclesiastico tractus posthumus in usum ecclesiarum evangel. & consistoriorum concinnatus.* Wittenberg, 1721.

Bytemeister, Henricus Jo. *Commentarius Historicus de Vita. Scriptis et Meritis Supremorum Praesulum In Ducatu Lunaeburgensi.* Helmstedt, 1728.

Buttstedt, Johann Heinrich. *Ut, Mi, Sol, Re, Fa, La, Tota Musica et Harmonia Aeterna.* Erfurt, 1716.

Calvin, John. *Commentaries on the Twelve Minor Prophets.* Translated by John Owen. Edinburgh, 1846.

———. *La Forme des Prieres et Chantz Ecclesiastiques* (1542). In *Le Psautier Huguenot*, ed. by Pierre Pidoux. Basel: Bärenreiter, 1962.

Calvisius, Seth, *Exercitatio Musica Tertia.* Leipzig, 1611.

———. *Melopoeia Sive Melodiae Condendae Ratio quam vulgo Musicam Poeticam vocant.* [Erfurt], 1592.

Calvör, Caspar. *De Musica ac sigillatim de Ecclesiastica eoque spectantibus Organis.* Leipzig, 1702.

Carpzov, Benedikt. *Jurisprudentia Ecclesiastica seu Consistorialiis.* Leipzig, 1649.

Carpzov, Johann Benedict. *Isagoge in Libros Ecclesiarum Lutheranarum Symbolicos.* Leipzig, 1675.

Colloquium Mompelgartense. Gespräch in Gegenwart des Durchleuchtigen Hochgebornen Fürsten unnd Herrn, Herrn Friderichen, Graven zu Würtemberg und Mümpelgart. Tübingen, 1587.

Cooke, Robert. *Censura quorundam scriptorum.* London, 1623.

Cyprian, Ernst Salomon. *De Propagatione Haeresium per Cantilenas Oder Vom Fortpflanzung derer Secten durch die Lieder.* Jena, 1715.

Dannhauer, Johann Conrad. *Catechismusmilch, oder Der Erklärung deß Christlichen Catechismi.* 9 vols. Strasbourg, 1642-72.

———. *Hodomoria Spiritus Calviniani.* Strasbourg, 1654.

Dedeken, Georg. *Thesauri Consiliorum et Decisionum.* Vol. I. Hamburg, 1623.

Dieterich, Conrad. *Ulmische Orgel Predigt.* Ulm, 1624.

Durellus, Johannes. *Historia Rituum Sanctae Ecclesiae Anglicanae.* London, 1672.

Erinnerungsschrifft etlicher vom Adel und Städten, An den Durchleuchtigen Hochgebornen Fürsten unnd Herrn, Herrn Johann Georgen, Fürsten zu Anhalt, Graven zu Ascanien, Herrn zu Zerbst und Bernburg. Amberg, 1597.

Flacius Illyricus, Matthias. *Ein buch von waren und falschen Mitteldingen.* Magdeburg, 1550.

———. *Quod hoc tempore nulla penitus mutatio in religione sit in gratiam impiorum facienda.* N.p., 1549.

Francke, August Hermann. *Einrichtung des Paedagogii zu Glaucha an Halle.* Halle, 1699.

———. *Der Jungfrauen-Stand Der Kinder Gottes Aus der Offenbahrung Joh. XIV, 4-5.* Halle, 1702.

———. *Sonn- Fest- und Apostel- Tags- Predigten.* 7th ed. Halle, 1734.

Friccius (Frick), Christophorus. *Musica Christiana.* Leipzig, 1615.

———. *Music-Büchlein, Oder Nützlicher Bericht von dem Uhrsprunge, Gebrauche und Erhaltung Christlicher Music.* 2 parts. Lüneburg, 1631. Reprint Kassel: Bärenreiter, 1976.

Friderici, Daniel. *Musica Figuralis.* Rostock, 1614.

Frölich, Georg. "Vom preiss, lob, und nutzbarkeit der Musica." In *Etliche Psalmen und geistliche Lieder.* Edited by Johann Kugelmann. Augsburg, 1540.

Fuhrmann, Martin Heinrich. *Gerechte Wag-Schal.* Altona, 1728.

———. *Musikalische Strigel.* [Leipzig, 17--].

———. *Musikalischer Trichter.* [Berlin], 1706.

———. *Das in unsern Opern-Theatris und Comödien-Bühnen Siechende Christenthum und Siegende Heidenthum.* [Berlin, 1728].

Gerber, Christian. *Der Andere Theil der Historie derer Wiedergebohrnen in Sachsen.* Dresden, 1726.

———. *Historie der Kirchen-Ceremonien in Sachsen.* Dresden and Leipzig, 1732.

———. *Unerkannte Sünden der Welt.* 3 vols. Dresden and Leipzig, 1705–19.

———. *Die Unerkannten Wolthaten Gottes.* Dresden, 1704.

Gerhard, Johann. *Postilla Salomonaea, Das ist, Erklärung etlicher Sprüche auß dem Hohenlied Salomonis.* Jena, 1631; revised ed., Jena, 1652.

Großgebauer, Theophilus. *Drey Geistreiche Schrifften/ 1. Wächterstimme Aus dem verwüsteten Zion/ 2. Praeservativ wider die Pest der heutigen Atheisten/ 3. Alte Religion.* Frankfurt and Leipzig, 1710.

———. *XXVI Geistreiche und erbauliche Predigten über die Epistel Pauli an die Ephesier.* Frankfurt and Leipzig, 1689.

———. *Preservatif Wieder die Pest der heutigen Atheisten.* Rostock, n.d.

Grotius, Hugo. *Annotata ad Vetus Testamentum.* Paris, 1644.

Hafenreffer, Matthias. *Templum Ezechielis Sive in IX. Postrema Prophetae Capita Commentarius.* Tübingen, 1613.

Hartmann, Joh. Ludovico. *Denck- und Danck Säule.* Rottenburg, [1673].

Herberger, Valerius. *Hertz Postilla.* Leipzig, 1613.

———. *Paradisz-Blümlein/ Aus dem Lustgarten der 150. Psalmen.* Leipzig, 1670.

Hoe, Matthias. *Commentariorum in Beati Apostoli et Evangelistae Johannis Apocalypsin* Vol. 2 vols. Leipzig, 1610–11.

Hunnius, Aegidius. *Epistolae Divi Apostoli Pauli ad Corinthios Prioris Expositio*. Frankfurt am Main, 1596.

———. *Opera Latina*. Vol. IV. Frankfurt, 1606.

Kirchenordnung Herrn Frantzen, Hertzogen zu Sachsen, Engern und Westphalen. 2nd ed. Lübeck, 1651.

Kircher, Athanasius. *Musurgia Universalis*. Rome, 1650. Reprint, Hildesheim: G. Olms, 1970.

Kortholt, Christian. *Offentlicher Gottesdienst der alten und heutigen Christen/ Absonderlich soviel die Sontags-Feir betrifft*. Frankfurt, 1672.

Kuhnau, Johann. *Jura circa Musicos Ecclesiasticos*. Leipzig, 1688.

———. *Der Musicalische Quack-Salber*. Dresden, 1700. In Deutsche Literaturdenkmale des 18. und 19. Jahrhunderts. Neue Folge 33/38. Edited by Kurt Benndorf. Berlin, 1900.

Lassenius, Johann. *Lob-singende Andacht...Alte und Neue Lieder...für die Teutsche Gemeine zu St. Petri in Copenhagen*. Copenhagen, 1686.

Lippius, Joannis. *Disputatio Musica Prima*. Wittenberg, 1609.

———. *Disputatio Musica Tertia*. Wittenberg, 1610.

———. *Synopsis Musicae Novae*. Strassburg, 1612.

Lobechius, David. *Disputationes Theologicae XXX. Articulorum Augustanae Confessionis*. Rostock, 1599.

Lorber, Johann Kristof. *Lob der edlen Musik*. Weimar, 1696.

———. *Verteidigung der edlen Musik wieder einen angemaßten Musik-Verächter außgefertiget*. Weimar, 1697.

Lütkemann, Joachim. *Apostolische Auffmunterung zum lebendigen Glauben*. Hannover and Wolfenbüttel, 1706.

———. *Harpffe Von Zehen Seyten/ Das ist: Gründliche Erklärung Zehen Psalmen Davids*. Wolfenbüttel, 1658.

———. *Der Vorschmack Göttlicher Güte*. Braunschweig, 1720.

Mattheson, Johann. *Behauptung der Himmlischen Musik aus den Gründen der Vernunft, Kirchen-Lehre und Heiliger Schrift*. Hamburg, 1747.

―――. *Das Forschende Orchestre, oder desselben Dritte Eröffnung*. Hamburg, 1721.

―――. *Grundlage einer Ehren-Pforte*. 1740. Edited by Max Schneider. Berlin, 1910.

―――. *Das Neu-Eröffnete Orchestre, Oder Universelle und gründliche Anleitung/ Wie ein Galant Homme einen vollkommnen Begriff von der Hoheit und Würde der edlen Music erlangen...möge*. Hamburg, 1713.

―――. *Der neue Göttingische Aber Viel schlechter, als Die alten Lacedamonischen, urtheilenden Ephorus*. Hamburg, 1727.

―――. *Der Musikalische Patriot*. Hamburg, 1728.

Mayer, Johann Friedrich. *Kurtzer Bericht von Pietisten*. Leipzig, 1606.

―――. *Museum ministri ecclesiae*. N.p., 1693.

Meibom, Marcus. *Antiquae Musicae Auctores Septem*. 2 vols. Amsterdam, 1652.

Meisner, Balthasar. *Collegii Adiaphoristici Calvinianis oppositi*. Wittenberg, 1620.

Mengering, Arnold. *Informatorium conscientiae evangelicum*. Jena, 1661.

Meyer, Joachim. *Der anmassliche Hamburgische Criticus sine crisi*. Lemgo, 1728.

―――. *Unvorgreiffliche Gedanken über die Neulich eingerissene Theatralische Kirchen-Music*. [Lemgo], 1726.

Meyfart, Johann Matthäus. *Das Himlische Jerusalem, Oder Das Ewige Leben der Churkinder Gottes Auff Historische weiß beschriben*. Coburg, 1627.

―――. *Teutsche Rhetorica*. Coburg, 1634.

―――. *Tuba Novissima: Das Ist Von den vier letzten Dingen des Menschen*. Deutsche Neudrucke, Reihe: Barock, 26. Tübingen: Max Niemeyer, 1980.

Mirus, Adam Erdmann. *Kurtze Fragen aus der Musica Sacra*. Görlitz, 1707.

Mithobius, Hector. *Psalmodia Christiana... Das ist, Gründliche Gewissens-Belehrung/ Was von der Christen Musica, so wol Vocali als Instrumentali zu halten?* Jena, 1665.

Motz, Georg. *Die Vertheidigte Kirchen-Music*. N.p. 1703.

Müller, Heinrich. *Geistliche Seelenmusik/ Bestehend In zehen betrachtungen/ und vier hundert auserlesenen/ Geist- und Krafft-reichen/ so wol alten/ als neuen Gesängen*. Rostock, 1659.

―――. *Geistliche Erquickstunden oder Dreyhundert Hauß- und Tisch- Andachten*. Frankfurt, 1700.

Muscovius, Johann. *Bestraffter Mißbrauch der Kirchen-Music und Kirchhöfe aus Gottes Wort zur Warnung und Besserung vorgestellet*. [Lauban], 1694.

Mylius, Georg. *Carolstadius Redivivus*. Wittenberg, 1597.

Neumeister, Erdmann. *Fünffache Kirchen-Andachten bestehend in theils eintzeln, theils niemahls gedruckten Arien, Cantaten und Oden*. Leipzig, 1717.

Nicolai, Philipp. *Freudenspiegel des ewigen Lebens* (1599). Reprinted with foreword by Reinhard Mumm. Soest: Westfälische Verlagsbuchhandlung Mocker & Jahn, 1963.

Niedt, Friedrich Erhardt. *Musicalische Handleitung*. Pt. I. Hamburg, 1710. Pt. III. Published posthumously with preface by Johann Mattheson. Hamburg, 1717.

Northusanus, Adamus Cratonus. *Examen, Der Anhaltischen genanten, und von Doctor Carlstat entlehnter Schlußsprüche, von abtilgung der Altarn und Bilder, In den reformirten Kirchen Augspurgischer Confession verwandt, mit nicht geringer Unruhe und Wiederwillen der Christlichen Gemeinen, auch vieler Trewhertziger vom Adel und Praedicanten im Lande*. Magdeburg, 1597.

Notwendige Antwort Auff die im Fürstenthumb Anhalt Ohn langsten ausgesprengte hefftige Schrift. Wittenberg, 1597.

Olearius, Johannes. *Wider den Calvinistischen Grewel der Verwüstung in des Fürstenthumb Anhalts Kirchen*. Halle, 1597.

Pareus, David. *In Divinam ad Corinthios priorem S. Pauli apostoli epistolam Commentarius*. Frankfurt, 1619.

Praetorius, Michael. *Syntagma musicum*. Wittenberg, 1614–15. Reprint: Kassel, 1959.

Praetorius, Paul Gottfried. *Vernünfftiger Gottesdienst im Singen*. Danzig, [1689].

Printz, Wolfgang Caspar. *Historische Beschreibung der Edelen Sing- und Kling-Kunst*. Dresden, 1690.

Quistorp, Johann. *Pia desideria*. Rostock, 1663.

Rauch, Christophorus. *Theatrophania, Entgegen gesetzt Der so genanten Schrifft Theatromania*. Hannover, 1682.

Revidirte Kirchenordnung: Wie es mit christlicher Lehre/ reichung der Sacrament/ Ordination der Diener des Evangelii/ ordentlichen Ceremonien inder Kirchen/ Visitation/ Consistorio und Schulen: Im Hertzogthumb Meckelnburg/...gehalten wirdt. Rostock, 1602.

Rivet, Andreas. *Commentarii in Librum secundum Mosis qui Exodus apud Graecos inscribitur*. Leiden, 1634.

———. *Critici Sacri Libri IV*. Geneva, 1626.

Rotth (Rothe), Albrecht Christian. *Höchstnöthiger Unterricht von so genanten Mittel-Dingen*. Leipzig, [1698?].

———. *Wiederholter und ferner ausgeführter Unterricht von Mittel-Dingen*. Leipzig, [1698?].

Rüetz, Caspar. *Widerlegte Vorurteile von der Beschaffenheit der heutigen Kirchenmusic und von der Lebens-Art einiger Musicorum*. Lübeck, 1752.

Scaliger, Joseph. *De emendatione Temporum*. Rev. ed. Geneva, 1629.

Scaliger, Julius Caesar. *Exotericarum Exercitationum Liber XV De Subtilitate*. Frankfurt, 1592.

Scarlach, Johann. *Drey Nützliche Unterweisungen*. Wittenberg, 1610.

Schamelius, J. Martinus. *Vindiciae Cantionum S. Ecclesiae Evangelicae, das ist, Theologische Rettung und Beantwortung....* Leipzig, 1719.

Scheibel, Gottfried Ephraim. *Die Geschichte der Kirchen-Music alter und neuer Zeiten* Breßlau, 1738.

———. *Zufällige Gedancken von der Kirchen-Music Wie Sie heutiges Tages beschaffen ist*. Frankfurt and Leipzig, 1721.

Schelwig, Samuel. *Cynosura Conscientiae oder Leit-Stern des Gewissens*. Frankfurt and Leipzig, 1692.

———. *Synopsis Controversiarum sub Pietatis Praetextu Motarum*. 3rd ed. Wittenberg, 1705.

Schlick, Rudolph. *Exercitatio qua Musices Origo Prima, Cultus Antiquissimus, Dignitas Maxima, & Emolumenta, quae tam animo quam corpori humano confert summa, breviter ac dilucide exponuntur*. Speyer, 1588.

Schneegass, Cyriacus. *Isagoges Musicae Libri Duo*. N.p., 1591.

———. *Nova et exquisita Monochordi Dimensio*. Erfurt, 1590.

Schulenberg, Johann Ernst. *Schrifftmäßiger Unterricht Vom Rechten Gebrauch und Fanatischen Mißbrauch der Christlichen Freyheit in äußerlichen Kirchen Ceremonien und Ordnungen*. Quedlinburg, 1711.

Scultetus, Abraham. *Medulla theologiae patrum*. Amberg, 1598.

Seidel, Christoph Matthaeus. *Christliches und erbauliches Gespräch Von Zechen/ Schelgen/ Spielen und Tantzen....Daß dergleichen Fleischliche Wollüste nicht zugelassene Mittel-Dinge/ sondern allerdings verdammliche Sünden seyn*. Halle, 1698.

Selneccer, Nicolaus. *Der gantze Psalter Davids ausgelegt*. Leipzig, 1571.

Silber, Wolfgang. *Encomion Musices: Lob der Edlen Kunst der Musicen*. Leipzig, 1622.

Slueter, Severin Walther. *Propylaeum Historiae Christianae*. Frankfurt, 1680.

Spener, Philipp Jakob. *Concilia et Iudica theologica latina*. Frankfurt/Main, 1709.

———. *Theologische Bedencken*. 4 vols. Halle, 1712–1715.

Steffens, Marcus. *Geistliche Gedanken*. Oldenburg, 1687.

Stegmann, Josua. *Icon Christognosia*. Marburg, 1630.

Stryk, Johann Samuel. *Commentatio de iure sabbathi*. Jena, 1756.

Tarnovius (Tarnow), Johannes. *In Prophetam Amos Commentarius*. Rostock, 1628.

Taurerus, Abraham. *Hochnothwendiger Bericht Wider den newen Bildstürmerischen Carlstadtischen Geist im Fürstenthumb Anhalt*. Mansfeld, 1597.

Theodoricus, Hieronymus. *Corona Templi, das ist Zwo Predigten von der schönen Kirchen Cron oder Heiligen Kirchengeschmuck*. Nürnberg, [1621?].

Der Theologischen Facultät auf der Universität zu Halle Verantwortung gegen D. Joh. Friedrich Mayers...sogenannten kurtzen Bericht von Pietisten. Halle, 1707.

Thomasius, Christian. *De jure Principis circa Adiaphora*. Halle, 1695.

Vermigli, Peter Martyr. *Loci Communes*. Zürich, 1587.

———. *In Priorem D. Pauli Apostoli ad Corinthios Epistolam Commentarius*. Basel, 1570.

Vier Bedencken/ Fürnehmen Theologischen/ und Juristischen Facultäten,/ wie auch/ Herrn Doct. Johann Friederich/ Mayers, P.P. und Königl. Schwedischen Ober-Kirchenraths/ Was doch von denen so genannten/ Operen zu halten. Frankfurt/Main, 1693.

Vockerodt, Gottfried. *Erleuterte Auffdeckung des Betrugs und Ärgernisses So mit denen vorgegebenen Mitteldingen und vergönneten Lust In der Christenheit angerichtet worden*. Halle, 1699.

———. *Der Fürsten-Schule zu Gotha Hohe Förderer und Gönner...werden zu Denen öffentlichen Reden welche von Falscher Artzeney unrichtiger Gemüther gehalten werden sollen...eingeladen*. Gotha, 1696.

———. *Mißbrauch der freyen Künste insonderheit der Music*. Frankfurt, 1697.

———. *Wiederholetes Zeugnüs der Warheit gegen die verderbte Music und Schauspiele/ Opern/ Comödien und dergleichen Eitelkeiten Welche die heutige Welt vor unschuldige Mitteldinge will gehalten wissen*. Frankfurt and Leipzig, 1698.

Voetius, Gisbert. *Politicae Ecclesiasticae* Vol. I. Amsterdam, 1663.

Volschov, Moevius. *Aureum Pietatis Saeculum.* Greiffswald, 1645.

Waldschmidt, Bernhard. *Pythonissa Endorea, das ist: acht u. zwantzig Hexen- und Gespenst-Predigten.* Frankfurt, 1660.

Walther, Johann. *Lob und Preis der löblichen Kunst Musica.* Wittenberg, 1538. Reprint, Kassel: Bärenreiter Verlag, 1938.

Werckmeister, Andreas. *Der Edlen Music-Kunst, Würde, Gebrauch und Mißbrauch.* Frankfurt and Leipzig, 1691.

———. *Musicalische Paradoxal-discourse.* Quedlinburg, 1707.

Zarlino, Gioseffo. *Istitutioni Harmoniche.* Rev. ed. Venice, 1573.

Zepperus, Wilhelm. *De politia ecclesiastica sive Forma, Ac Ratio Administrandi, et Gubernandi.* Herborn, 1595.

SELECTED SECONDARY SOURCES

Abert, Hermann. *Die Musikanschauung des Mittelalters und ihre Grundlagen.* Halle, 1905. Reprint. Tutzing: Hans Schneider, 1964.

Althaus, Paul. "Der Schöpfungsgedanke bei Luther," *Sitzungsberichte der Bayerischen Akademie der Wissenschaften, Philosophisch-Historische Klasse,* 1959, no.7.

Bach-Dokumente. Vol 1: *Schriftstücke von der Hand Johann Sebastian Bachs.* Leipzig: VEB Deutscher Verlag für Musik, 1963.

Beardslee, John W. III, ed. and trans. *Reformed Dogmatics: J. Wollebius, G. Voetius, F. Turretin.* New York: Oxford University Press, 1965.

Beck, Dorothea. *Krise und Verfall der protestantischen Kirchenmusik im 18. Jahrhundert.* Inaug.-Diss. Halle-Wittenberg, 1951.

Becker, Heinz, ed., with Wolfgang Osthoff, Herbert Schneider and Hellmuth Christian Wolff. *Quellentexte zur Konzeption der europäischen Oper im 17. Jahrhundert.* Kassel: Bärenreiter, 1981.

Bibliography

Die Bekenntnisschriften der evangelisch-lutherischen Kirche. 3rd ed. Göttingen: Vandenhoeck & Ruprecht, 1956.

Blankenburg, Walter. *Kirche und Musik.* Göttingen: Vandenhoeck & Ruprecht, 1979.

———. "Bachs kirchengeschichtlicher Standort und dessen Bedeutung für das gegenwärtige Bachverständnis." *Archiv für Musikwissenschaft* X (1953): 311-22.

———. "Die Bachforschung seit etwa 1965 (III)." *Acta Musicologica* 55 (1983): 1-58.

———. "Johann Sebastian Bach und die Aufklärung." In *Bach-Gedenkschrift 1950*, edited by K. Matthaei, pp. 25-34. Freiburg im Breisgau: Atlantis Verlag, 1950.

Blume, Friedrich. *Protestant Church Music: A History.* New York: W. W. Norton, 1974.

Braun, Werner. *Johann Mattheson und die Aufklärung.* Diss. Halle, 1951.

Brecht, Martin. *Die frühe Theologie des Johannes Brenz.* Tübingen: J. C. B. Mohr [Paul Siebeck], 1966.

Breuer, Dieter. *Frömmigkeit in der Frühen Neuzeit: Studien zur religiösen Literatur des 17. Jahrhunderts.* Chloe: Beihefte zum Daphnis, Vol. II. Amsterdam: Rodopi, 1984.

Bruinsma, Henry A. "The Organ Controversy in the Netherlands Reformation to 1640." *Journal of the American Musicological Society* VII (1954): 205-12.

Bunners, Christian. *Kirchenmusik und Seelenmusik.* Göttingen: Vandenhoeck & Ruprecht, 1966.

Daebeler, Hans Jürgen. *Musiker und Musikpflege in Rostock von der Stadtgründung bis 1700.* Diss. Rostock, 1966.

Dammann, Rolf. *Der Musikbegriff im deutschen Barock.* Cologne: Arno Volk Verlag, 1967.

David, Hans T. and Arthur Mendel, eds. *The Bach Reader.* New York: W. W. Norton & Company, 1966.

Dibelius, Martin. "Individualismus und Gemeindebewußtsein in Joh. Seb. Bachs Passionen." *Archiv für Reformationsgeschichte* 41 (1948): 132-154.

Dickreiter, Michael. *Der Musiktheoretiker Johannes Kepler.* Bern: Francke Verlag, 1973.

Donnelly, John Patrick S.J., *Calvinism and Scholasticism in Vermigli's Doctrine of Man and Grace.* Leiden: E. J. Brill, 1976.

Dürr, Alfred. "Johann Sebastian Bachs Kirchenmusik in seiner Zeit und Heute." *Musik und Kirche* 27 (1957): 65-74.

Eggebrecht, Hans Heinrich. "Thomaskantor Bach." *Musik und Kirche* 61 (1991): 63-72.

Eitner, Robert. *Biographisch-Bibliographisches Quellen Lexikon* Leipzig, 1903. Reprint. Graz, 1959.

Finke-Hecklinger, Doris. *Tanzcharaktere in Johann Sebastian Bachs Vokalmusik.* Trossingen: Hohner Verlag, 1970.

Flaherty, Gloria. *Opera in the Development of German Critical Thought.* Princeton, 1978.

Forchert, Arno. "Mattheson und die Kirchenmusik." In *Gattung und Werk in der Musikgeschichte Norddeutschlands und Skandinaviens*, edited by Friedhelm Krummacher and Heinrich W. Schwab, pp. 114–122. Kieler Schriften zur Musikwissenschaft, XXVI. Kassel: Bärenreiter Verlag, 1982.

Fulbrook, Mary. *Piety and Politics: Religion and the Rise of Absolutism in England, Württemberg and Prussia.* Cambridge: Cambridge University Press, 1983.

Geck, Martin. *Die Vokalmusik Dietrich Buxtehudes und der frühe Pietismus.* Kieler Schriften zur Musikwissenschaft, vol. 15. Kassel: Bärenreiter Verlag, 1965.

———. "Ph. J. Spener und die Kirchenmusik." *Musik und Kirche* 31 (1961): 97–106, 172–184.

Geiringer, Karl. *Johann Sebastian Bach: The Culmination of an Era.* New York: Oxford University Press, 1966.

Gerber, Ernst Ludwig. *Neues Historisch-Biographisches Lexikon der Tonkünstler (1812-1814).* Pt. 3. Reprint, Graz: Akademische Druck u. Verlagsanstalt, 1966.

Gérold, Theodor. *Les péres de l'Église et la musique.* Paris: Hirsch, 1931.

Graff, Paul. *Geschichte der Auflösung der alten gottesdienstlichen Formen in der evangelischen Kirche Deutschlands.* Vol. I. Göttingen: Vandenhoeck & Ruprecht, 1937.

Greschat, Martin, ed., *Zur Neueren Pietismusforschung.* Darmstadt: Wissenschaftliche Buchgesellschaft, 1977.

Grindal, Gracia. "Luther and the Arts: A Study in Convention." *Word and World* 3 (1983): 373-81.

Hammerstein, Reinhold. *Die Musik der Engel.* Bern: Francke Verlag, 1962.

Hilse, W., trans. and ed. "The Treatises of Christoph Bernhard." *Music Forum* 3 (1973): 1–196.

Holl, Karl. "Die Bedeutung der großen Kriege für das religiöse und kirchliche Leben innerhalb des deutschen Protestantismus." In *Gesammelte Aufsätze zur Kirchengeschichte,* vol. 3, pp. 302–384. Tübingen: J. C. B. Mohr (Paul Siebeck), 1928.

Honemeyer, Karl. *Luthers Musikanschauung.* Diss. Münster, 1941.

———. *Thomas Müntzer und Martin Luther: Ihr Ringen um die Musik des Gottesdienstes.* Berlin: Verlag Merseburger, 1974.

Hosler, Bellamy. *Changing Aesthetic Views of Instrumental Music in 18th-Century Germany.* Ann Arbor: UMI Research Press, 1981.

Irwin, Joyce. "German Pietists and Church Music in the Baroque Age." *Church History* 54/1 (1985): 29-40.

Kalb, Friedrich. *Die Lehre vom Kultus der lutherischen Kirche zur Zeit der Orthodoxie.* Arbeiten zur Geschichte und Theologie des Lutherthums, Vol. III. Berlin: Lutherisches Verlagshaus, 1959. Eng. trans.: *Theology of Worship in 17th-Century Lutheranism.* Trans. by Henry P. A. Hamann. St. Louis: Concordia, 1965.

Krabbe, Otto. *Heinrich Müller und seine Zeit.* Rostock, 1866.

———. *Geschichte der Universität Rostock 1419-1969.* Berlin: VEB Deutscher Verlag der Wissenschaften, n.d.

———. *Die Universität Rostock im 15. und 16. Jahrhundert.* Rostock and Schwerin, 1854.

Kraege, Jean-Denis. "Luther théologien de la musique." *Études théologiques et religieuses* 58 (1983): 449-63.

Krause, Heinz. *Johann Beer, 1655-1700: Zur Musikauffassung im 17. Jahrhundert.* Saalfeld/Ostpr.: Günthers Buchdruckerei, 1935.

Krickeberg, Dieter. *Das Protestantische Kantorat im 17. Jahrhundert.* Berlin: Verlag Merseburger, 1965.

Kümmel, Werner. "Melancholie und die Macht der Musik: Die Krankheit König Sauls in der historischen Diskussion." *Medizinhistorisches Journal* 4 (1969): 189–209.

Kurzschenkel, Winfried. *Die theologische Bestimmung der Musik.* Trier 1971.

Langelütje, Ernst, ed. *Die Musica figuralis des Magister Daniel Friderici: Eine Singefibel des 17. Jahrhunderts als musikgeschichtlicher Beitrag.* Berlin, 1901.

La Vopa, Anthony. *Grace, Talent, and Merit: Poor students, clerical careers, and professional ideology in eighteenth-century Germany.* Cambridge: Cambridge University Press, 1988.

Laynor, Henry. *A Social History of Music from the Middle Ages to Beethoven.* New York: Taplinger Publishing, 1978.

Leaver, Robin A. *J. S. Bach and Scripture: Glosses from the Calov Bible Commentary.* St. Louis: Concordia Publishing House, 1985.

Leube, Hans. *Die Reformideen in der deutschen lutherischen Kirche zur Zeit der Orthodoxie.* Leipzig, 1924.

Löfgren, David. *Die Theologie der Schöpfung bei Luther*. Göttingen: Vandenhoeck & Ruprecht, 1960.

Lueken, Wilhelm. *Lebensbilder der Liederdichter und Melodisten.* In *Handbuch zum Evangelischen Kirchengesangbuch.* Vol. II, pt. I. Göttingen: Vandenhoeck & Ruprecht, 1957.

MacClintock, Carol, ed. *Readings in the History of Music in Performance.* Bloomington: Indiana University Press, 1979.

McKinnon, James, ed. *Music in early Christian literature.* Cambridge: Cambridge University Press, 1987.

Mahrenholz, Christhard. "Johann Sebastian Bach und der Gottesdienst seiner Zeit." *Musik und Kirche* 20 (1950): 145–58.

Marigold, W. Gordon. "Opera, Politics and Religion in Hamburg, 1678–1715." *Lutheran Quarterly* III/1 (1989): 65–90.

Marti, Andreas. *"...die Lehre des Lebens zu hören". Eine Analyse der drei Kantaten zum 17. Sonntag nach Trinitatis von Johann Sebastian Bach unter musikalisch-rhetorischen und theologischen Geschichtspunkten.* Bern: Peter Lang, 1981.

Martin, John Rupert. *Baroque.* London: Allen Lane, 1977.

Mehlhausen, Joachim. "Der Streit um die Adiaphora." *Bekenntnis und Einheit der Kirche: Studien zum Konkordienbuch.* Edited by Martin Brecht and Reinhard Schwarz. Stuttgart: Calwer, 1980.

Meyer, Ulrich. *J. S. Bachs Musik als theonome Kunst.* Diss. Mainz, 1976.

Minear, Paul S. "J. S. Bach and J. A. Ernesti: A Case Study in Exegetical and Theological Conflict." In *Our Common History as Christians: Essays in Honor of Albert C. Outler*, by John Deschner and others. New York: Oxford University Press, 1975.

Müller, Dedo. *Musik als Problem lutherischer Gottesdienstgestaltung.* Berlin, 1947.

Otto, Irmgard. *Deutsche Musikanschauung im 17. Jahrhundert.* Diss: Berlin, 1937.

Pater, Calvin Augustine. *Karlstadt as the Father of the Baptist Movements: The Emergence of Lay Protestantism.* Toronto: University of Toronto Press, 1984.

Pelikan, Jaroslav. *Bach Among the Theologians.* Philadelphia: Fortress Press, 1986.

Prenter, Regin. *Spiritus Creator.* Trans. by John M. Jensen. Philadelphia: Muhlenberg Press, 1953.

Preus, James S. *Carlstadt's Ordinaciones and Luther's Liberty: A Study of the Wittenberg Movement 1521-22.* Cambridge: Harvard University Press, 1974.

Rivera, Benito V. *German Music Theory in the Early 17th Century.* Ann Arbor: UMI Research Press, 1974.

Röbbelen, Ingeborg. *Theologie und Frömmigkeit im deutschen evangelisch-lutherischen Gesangbuch des 17. und frühen 18. Jahrhunderts.* Göttingen: Vandenhoeck & Ruprecht, 1957.

Rößler, Martin. *Bibliographie der Deutschen Liedpredigt.* Nieuwkoop: De Graaf, 1976.

———. "Die Frühzeit hymnologischer Forschung." *Jahrbuch für Liturgik und Hymnologie* 19 (1975): 126.

Rüber, Johannes. *Die Heiligsprechung des Johann Sebastian Bach: Eine Papst-Legende.* Schwieberdingen: Verlag Günter Rüber, 1973.

Schalk, Carl, and Carl Halter. *A Handbook of Church Music.* St. Louis: Concordia Publishing House, 1978.

Schalk, Carl. *Luther on Music: Paradigms of Praise.* St. Louis: Concordia Publishing House, 1988.

Schmalenberg, Gerhard. *Pietismus-Schule-Religionsunterricht: Die Christliche Unterweisung im Spiegel der vom Pietismus bestimmten Schulordnungen des 18. Jahrhunderts.* Bern: Herbert Lang, 1974.

Schmidt, Martin. "Epochen der Pietismusforschung." In *Pietismus und Reveil*, edited by J.van den Berg and J. P.van Dooren. Leiden: E. J. Brill, 1978.

Segel, Harold B. *The Baroque Poem: A Comparative Survey.* New York: E. P. Dutton & Co., 1974.

Sehling, Emil. *Geschichte der protestantischen Kirchenverfassung.* Leipzig: B. G. Teubner, 1907.

———, ed. *Die evangelischen Kirchenordnungen des XVI. Jahrhunderts.* Leipzig, 1902-13. Reprint, Aalen: Scientia Verlag, 1970.

Sendrey, Alfred and Mildred Norton. *David's Harp: The Story of Music in Biblical Times.* New York: New American Library, 1964.

Skrine, Peter. *The Baroque.* London: Methuen, 1978.

Smallman, Basil. *The Background of Passion Music: J. S. Bach and his Predecessors.* New York: Dover Publications, 1970.

Snyder, Kerala J. *Dieterich Buxtehude: Organist in Lübeck.* New York: Schirmer Books, 1987.

Söhngen, Oskar. "Music and Theology: A Systematic Approach." In *Sacred Sound: Music in Religious Thought and Practice*, edited by Joyce Irwin. Chico, California: Scholars Press, 1983.

———. *Theologie der Musik*. Kassel: Johannes Stauda-Verlag, 1967.

———. "Theologische Grundlagen der Kirchenmusik." *Leiturgia: Handbuch des evangelischen Gottesdienstes*. Vol. IV. Kassel: Johannes Stauda-Verlag, 1961.

Spitta, Philipp. *Johann Sebastian Bach*. Trans. by Clara Bell. London: Novello, Ewer & Co., 1884.

Steiger, Franz. *Opernlexikon*. Tutzing: Hans Schneider, 1975.

Stevenson, Robert. "Bach's Quarrel with the Rector of St. Thomas School." *Anglican Theological Review* 33 (1951): 219–230.

Stiller, Günther. "Glaube und Frömmigkeit des Luthertums im Leben und Werk Johann Sebastian Bachs." *Ökumenische Rundschau* 31/1 (1986): 53–70.

———. *Johann Sebastian Bach and Liturgical Life in Leipzig*. Trans. by Herbert Bouman et alia. St. Louis: Concordia Pubishing House, 1984.

Stoeffler, F. Ernest. *The Rise of Evangelical Pietism*. Leiden: E. J. Brill, 1965.

Strunk, Oliver. *Sources Readings in Music History: Antiquity and the Middle Ages*. New York: W. W. Norton & Company, 1965.

Tholuck, August. *Das akademische Leben des siebzehnten Jahrhunderts*. Halle, 1853/54.

Viertel, Matthias Silesius "Kirchenmusik zwischen Kerygma und Charisma." *Jahrbuch für Liturgik und Hymnologie* 29 (1985): 111-123.

Walker, Daniel P. "Keplers Himmelsmusik." In *Hören, Messen und Rechnen in der frühen Neuzeit*. Geschichte der Musiktheorie, vol. 6. Darmstadt: Wissenschaftliche Buchgesellschaft, 1987.

Wallmann, Johannes. *Philipp Jakob Spener und die Anfänge des Pietismus*. Tübingen: J. C. B. Mohr (Paul Siebeck), 1970.

Weber, Edith. "Martin Luther, poète, musicièn et hymnologue." *Unité Chrétienne* November, 1983: 100-08.

Wieninger, Fritz. "Die Musik im pastoralen Konzept Martin Luthers." *Diakoni* 14 (1983): 372-77.

Wolff, Christoph. *Der Stile Antico in der Musik Johann Sebastian Bachs*. Wiesbaden: Franz Steiner Verlag, 1968.

Zeller, Winfried. *Der Protestantismus des 17. Jahrhunderts*. Bremen: Carl Schünemann Verlag, 1962.

Zenck, Hermann. "Grundformen deutscher Musikanschauung." *Jahrbuch der Akademie der Wissenschaften in Göttingen* 1941-42: 15-40.

INDEX

Abert, Hermann 6, 24n, 30n, 70n
adiaphora 11–22, 59f., 65f. 88, 91f., 107, 117–126
affections 4, 23, 24, 26, 31, 33, 47, 112, 130–132, 134, 139, 142
Alsted, Johann Heinrich 62
Ames, William 62
Amos, Book of 41, 74f., 84, 110
Andreae, Jakob 14, 15, 19, 37
Andreae, Johann Valentin 46, 53
Anhalt 15-17, 19, 21, 38
Antitrinitarians 19
Aristotelianism 28, 120, 124, 125
Aristotle 38, 51, 63, 96, 111
Arndt, Johann 21, 43, 46, 48–50, 53, 54, 64, 65, 69, 109
Arnold, Gottfried 110, 111
Arnoldi, Philipp 17, 28, 29, 38n, 41
Athanasius 27, 68, 70, 71, 80, 120, 131, 143
Augsburg Confession 11, 18, 109, 110
Augustine 4–6, 12, 18, 24–27, 61, 64, 66, 70, 71, 75, 80, 83, 130, 137
Bach, Johann Sebastian ix–xi, 35, 77, 118, 127–129, 131, 133, 134, 141–152
Balduinus, Fridericus 19, 26, 27, 40, 96
Bayly, Lewis 87
Beer, Johann 114, 119–126, 142, 145
Bendeler, Johann Philipp 149
Bernard of Clairvaux 41, 96
Bernhard, Christoph 129
Beza, Theodore 14, 15, 17, 19–21, 37, 59–61
Blankenburg, Walter ix, 24n, 53n, 139, 142, 143n
Braun, Werner 137, 150

Brenz, Johannes 30, 31
Brunnemann, Johann 105, 107
Bucer, Martin 62
Bugenhagen, Johannes 30
Bunners, Christian 22n, 66n, 77, 79, 89, 96n
Buttstedt, Johann Heinrich 120, 128, 138, 143, 145, 150
Calvin, John ix, 4, 12, 24, 35, 37, 41, 45, 60, 74
Calvinism 11, 28, 35, 41, 59, 77, 102, 108n, 125
Calvinists 13, 15, 17–21, 23, 24, 26, 28, 37, 38, 41, 61, 67, 88, 90, 102, 124, 125
cantatas x, 135, 136, 138, 149, 150
cantors 39, 80, 86, 95, 98, 103, 105, 110–112, 128, 134, 141, 147–150
Carpzov, Benedict 104, 149
Catholicism 11, 41, 47, 77
Chronicles, First Book of 62, 95, 97, 150
Chrysostom, John 24, 41, 102
church orders 38, 86
Chytraeus, David 67
Cicero 38, 64
Clement of Alexandria 96
Colossians, Letter to the 15, 17, 21, 26, 36, 40, 41, 60, 69, 91, 147
Communion, Holy 28, 65, 81, 85, 87, 97, 98, 131
Constantine 83, 107
Conzen, Adam 61
Corinthians, First Letter to the 16, 83, 85, 91, 102, 118, 123
Council of Carthage 41
Council of Laodicea 83

Cyprian 104
Dammann, Rolf 47, 53n
dance 36, 38, 42, 96, 120, 121, 123, 124, 135, 136, 150, 151
Dannhauer, Johann Conrad 59–69, 95
Dibelius, Martin 138–139
Dieterich, Conrad 20, 21, 27, 29, 31, 38f, 92, 94–96, 101, 144
Donatism 109–113
Dürr, Alfred 127
Eggebrecht, Hans 141n, 143, 144
Elisha 13, 24, 40
Ephesians, Letter to the 17, 21, 27, 40, 41, 69, 83, 90, 94, 147
Erasmus, Desiderius 80
Ernesti, Johann August 118, 148, 149
Finke-Hecklinger, Doris 150
Flacius Illyricus, Matthias 12, 18
Fludd, Robert 115, 143
Formula of Concord x, 12, 21, 91, 118
Francke, August Hermann 118, 139n
Frick, Christoph 21, 22, 31–33, 41, 48–54, 63, 66, 91, 95
Friderici, Daniel 39n, 86
Frölich, Georg 45
Fuhrmann, Martin Heinrich 138
Geck, Martin 101, 102, 104, 108
Gerber, Christian 103, 111–113, 134, 138–139
Gerhard, Johann 54, 118
Gerhardt, Paul 104
Gratian 40, 41
Großgebauer, Theophilus 67, 79–89, 92–98, 105, 107, 151
Grotius, Hugo 60
Hammerschmidt, Andreas 96f.
Hammerstein, Reinhold 45
Hasse, Nicolaus 86
Herberger, Valerius 46, 48–51, 65
Hilary of Poitiers 91
Hoe, Matthias 20, 40, 97
Holl, Karl 87
Honemeyer, Karl 2, 5–7
Hunnius, Aegidius 20, 74, 96
instrumental music 15–17, 19, 21, 24, 27–29, 31, 45, 61, 64, 87, 91, 93, 96, 106–108, 120, 135, 137
Italian style 37, 39, 61, 84, 87, 96, 129

Jerome 6, 40, 41, 90, 96
Josquin des Pres 37, 54, 147
Jubal 28
jubilus 4, 6
Justin Martyr 60, 83
Kalb, Friedrich 22
Karlstadt, Andreas 3, 12, 16, 21
Kepler, Johannes 53, 115
Kircher, Athanasius 120, 130, 131, 143, 150
Kortholt, Christian 102–103
Krabbe, Otto 67n, 77n, 79
Krause, Heinz 126
Kuhnau, Johann 128, 148
Lassenius, Johannes 104
Latin singing 15, 17, 20, 38, 53, 80, 84, 93, 102, 106, 110, 146
Leipzig Interim 12, 18
Lippius, Joannes 51–53
Lobechius, David 40
Lobwasser, Ambrosius 61
Locke, John 137
Lorber, Johann Kristof 119
Luther, Martin ix–xi, 1–7, 11–13, 15–17, 22–26, 28, 30–32, 35–37, 41, 43, 60, 61, 70, 74, 77, 96, 97, 103, 104, 109, 110, 112, 113, 116, 125, 127, 128, 130, 141, 145–147, 150, 151
Lütkemann, Joachim 67–74, 76, 79, 81
Mahrenholz, Christhard ix, 129, 131
Marti, Andreas 129, 143, 144
Martin, John Rupert 46f.
Mattheson, Johann 120, 128–130, 134–138, 145–147, 150
Meibom, Marcus 130
Meisner, Balthasar 18, 19, 40, 124
Melanchthon, Philip 11, 109, 110
Mersenne, Marin 120
Meyer, Ulrich 129
Meyer, Joachim 134–138
Meyfart, Johann Mattheus 46–48
Minear, Paul 118n, 148
Mithobius, Hector 89–98, 103, 105, 106, 144, 147
Möckel, K. H. 62
modes, Greek 24, 25, 29, 90, 93, 96, 135
Montbéliard 13–15, 19, 20, 37, 59
Motz, Georg 103, 112–114, 143

Index

Müller, Dedo 3
Müller, Heinrich 67, 72-77, 79, 81, 82, 109
Müntzer, Thomas 2
Muscovius, Johann 105, 106, 110, 111, 147
Neoplatonism 6, 30
Neumeister, Erdmann 127–128, 130, 134, 136
Nicolai, Philipp 43f., 46–49, 63, 65
Niedt, Friedrich Erhart 128, 129, 144
operas 117–119, 123, 126, 127, 128, 131–134, 135, 138, 139, 144, 145, 146
opus operatum 61, 109–110
organists 16, 37–39, 80, 84, 86, 87, 94–96, 105, 113, 149
organs 5, 12–16, 18–21, 31, 37, 38, 41, 59, 60, 66, 74, 83, 88, 92, 106–108, 113, 120
Origen 70
Otto, Irmgard 47, 67, 77, 79
papacy 14, 19, 20, 41, 80, 83–84, 106, 125
Pareus, David 59
parody 41, 130, 132–133
Plato 24, 38, 60, 96, 111
Printz, Wolfgang Caspar 142, 145
Puritans 87
Quakers 106
Quistorp, Johann 79–80, 94
Rauch, Christopher 144
Reformed 14, 15, 17, 19, 23, 27, 28, 37, 59–62, 79, 87, 107, 108, 120, 125, 131, 143
Reiser, Anton 117
Rivera, Benito 51f.
Rivet, André 59, 60, 62
Rogge, Heinrich 86
Romans, Letter to the 107, 121, 146
Rotth, Albrecht Christian 118, 119, 124
Rue, Pierre de la 37
Rüetz, Caspar 150, 151
Samuel, First Book of 13, 24, 30, 31, 60, 113
Saul, King 13, 18, 24, 30, 31, 40, 93, 113
Scaliger, Joseph 60, 81, 82
Scaliger, Julius Caesar 81–82
Scarlach, Johannes 21
Scharlau, Ulf 120, 131
Scheibel, Gottfr. Ephr. 128, 130–134, 143
Schelwig, Samuel 103, 106

Schlick, Rudolph 28, 52
Schneegass, Cyriacus 23, 52
Schulenburg, Johann Ernst 106
Schütz, Heinrich x, 97, 147
Segel, Harold B. 46
Selneccer, Nicolaus 29, 30, 41
Senfl, Ludwig 37
Silber, Wolfgang 29, 39
Snyder, Kerala 96, 102, 129
Söhngen, Oskar ix, 2–7, 22, 24, 35, 41, 144, 145, 147
Sonthom, Immanuel 87
Spener, Philipp Jakob 59, 87, 100, 101, 104–106, 108, 139, 150
Spitta, Philipp 127n, 128n, 138–139
Steffani, Agostino 143
Steffens, Marcus 108, 113
Stegmann, Josua 33, 41, 53, 54, 96
Stiller, Günther 35n, 37, 127, 143n, 144n, 147
Stryk, Samuel 107
Tarnov, Johann 67, 74
Telemann, Georg Philipp 132–134
Theodoricus, Hieronymus 19, 27, 28
Thomasius, Christian 107
Tilgner, Gottfried 130, 136
Timotheus Milesius 38
Tinctoris, Johannes 6, 24
Trinity 13, 49–52, 63, 143
Trithemius 6
Vermigli, Peter Martyr 17, 19, 27, 28, 41
Viertel, Matthias 147
Vitalian, Pope 106
Vockerodt, Gottfried 114, 115, 118–126, 134, 148, 149
Voetius, Gisbert 107, 120, 125
Volschov, Moevius 39
Wallmann, Johannes 59, 62, 64, 87, 101n
Walther, Johann 19, 45, 46, 128
Walther, Johann Gottfried 130
Weller, Hieronymus 30
Wentzel, Johann Christoph 119, 125
Werckmeister, Andreas 113–116, 120, 143, 145, 150
Wolff, Christoph 35n, 129
Zarlino, Gioseffo 51, 54, 126
Zenck, Hermann 47
Zwingli, Ulrich 3, 130
Zwinglians 21, 88

www.ingramcontent.com/pod-product-compliance
Lightning Source LLC
Chambersburg PA
CBHW062128160426
43191CB00013B/2231